# The Predicament of Blackness

# The Predicament of Blackness

Postcolonial Ghana and
the Politics of Race

JEMIMA PIERRE

The University of Chicago Press
Chicago and London

PUBLICATION OF THIS BOOK HAS BEEN AIDED BY A
GRANT FROM THE BERINGTON FUND.

**Jemima Pierre** teaches in the Program in African American and Diaspora
Studies at Vanderbilt University.

The University of Chicago Press, Chicago 60637
The University of Chicago Press, Ltd., London
© 2013 by The University of Chicago
All rights reserved. Published 2013.
Printed in the United States of America
22 21 20 19 18 17 16 15 14 13     1 2 3 4 5

ISBN-13: 978-0-226-92302-4 (cloth)
ISBN-10: 0-226-92302-9 (cloth)
ISBN-13: 978-0-226-92303-1 (paper)
ISBN-10: 0-226-92303-7 (paper)
ISBN-13: 978-0-226-92304-8 (e-book)
ISBN-10: 0-226-92304-5 (e-book)

Library of Congress Cataloging-in-Publication Data
Pierre, Jemima.
 The predicament of blackness: postcolonial Ghana and the politics of race / Jemima
Pierre.
      pages; cm
Includes bibliographical references and index.
 ISBN-13: 978-0-226-92302-4 (cloth: alkaline paper)
 ISBN-10: 0-226-92302-9 (cloth: alkaline paper)
 ISBN-13: 978-0-226-92303-1 (paperback: alkaline paper)
 ISBN-10: 0-226-92303-7 (paperback: alkaline paper)
 [etc.]
 1. Blacks—Race identity—Ghana. 2. Race awareness— Ghana. 3. Ghana—Race rela-
tions. 4. Heritage tourism—Ghana. 5. African diaspora. I. Title.
 DT510.42.P54 2013
 305.8009667—dc23                    2012012027

♾ This paper meets the requirements of ANSI/NISO Z39.48-1992
(Permanence of Paper).

*For Toussaint,*
*and in memory of Marjorie "Cherry" Pengelly*

It is necessary, therefore, in planning our movements, in guiding our future development, that at times we rise above the pressing, but smaller questions of separate schools and cars, wage discrimination and lynch law, to survey the whole question of race in human philosophy and higher ideals which may form our guiding lines and boundaries in the practical difficulties of every day. . . . The question, then, which we must seriously consider is this: What is the real meaning of Race; what has, in the past, been the law of race development, and what lessons has the past history of race development to teach the rising Negro people?

W. E. B. DUBOIS, "The Conservation of Races"

So then was W. E. B. Dubois some malevolent wizard cursing humankind into stupidity and intolerance when he said that the problem of the 20th century was going to be that of race? Or was he just an honest prophet? One thing is certain. Seventy years after he spoke and with only a few years of the century left, the issue of race is still allowed to assume all forms, subsume all controversies and consume every little bit of human energy, vision and imagination. The 21st century is almost upon us, and we are still imprisoned in the colours of our skins. How absolutely awful! How humanly pathetic!

AMA ATA AIDOO, *The Girl Who Can and Other Stories*

# CONTENTS

"Race in Ghana? But that's an American problem." It was early summer 2000, and I was sitting with Abe, my Ghanaian friend, in his office at the University of Ghana, Legon. It was my first trip back to the country in four years, and I was explaining my research agenda to Abe. I had described it as an investigation of the workings of race in Ghana. His reaction was not altogether surprising. Indeed, it was the most common rejoinder to my interest in Ghana's racialized cultural and political dynamics and their relations to global structures of power. Everyone—Ghanaian and non-Ghanaian, academics and laypersons—would invariably demand not only lengthy and specific explanations of how Ghana is within reach of global race and racialization processes, but also a defense of the validity of this type of analysis. Eventually, I came to loathe disclosing my research project.

I realized that this reaction was based on some common assumptions about the nature of race in general. For instance, there is often the view that issues of race create considerable concerns only in some Western and multiracial societies with particular histories of overt racial conflict. Clear examples are the United States and South Africa. The idea, therefore, that race-inflected practices significantly shape social relations in a postcolonial and nominally racially homogeneous society such as Ghana—a society with no established legacy of de jure apartheid—seems both anachronistic and absurd. In truth, this reflects the reality that race is often *not* treated as global in scope and content. My point is not that race is not considered to have global resonance; rather, I am suggesting that its various articulations are usually treated as exported products of the contemporary West (and the United States in particular). It is no surprise, then, that the idea of examining contemporary processes of racialization in a place like Ghana would raise more than a few eyebrows.

Confronting race in Ghana over the years both confirmed and normalized for me this society's banality—and universality. Ghana is not unique. How could it be? As Edward Said (1993), among others, reminded us, a major achievement of European imperialism was to bring the world closer together. As a postcolony, Ghana's contemporary realities are connected to an interlinked set of practices, experiences, and belief systems—a specific predicament of the long history of European empire making. A modern, postcolonial space is invariably a racialized one; it is a space where racial and cultural logics continue to be constituted and reconstituted in the images, institutions, and relationships of the structuring colonial moment. It is a space, in other words, still haunted and constrained by what Brackette Williams terms the "ghost of Anglo-European hegemony" (1989). Indeed, the form and culture of domination established under this hegemony continue their structural imposition on Ghanaian identity formation even within efforts to reframe the contemporary national sociopolitical and economic order (Williams 1989, 223–25). This is a living and breathing "ghost," I would further argue, and race is in the blood and bones of its origin and its enduring legacy. In this sense, one can only be surprised by (or resistant to) the idea of race in Ghana if one does not acknowledge the contemporary legacy and impact of European empire making and "racecraft," the design and enactment, practice, and politics of race making.[1]

And yet. There is something about the popular and academic treatment of Africa (and, in this case, Ghana, as Africa's metonymic stand-in) that often demands that the land, its peoples, and its sociopolitical phenomena be conceived outside of modern global racialized processes. For it is only with this sadly common perception of Africa that some can ignore or be disappointed by Accra's cosmopolitanism or "Westernness." Accra, with a population of almost two million people, is a bustling, modern, cosmopolitan metropolis with skyscrapers, freeways, shopping malls, and nightclubs. It is, of course, absurd to have to describe the city's modernity, but our images of Africa, both scholarly and popular, are still of the village or rural areas. But I contend that the particular traditional construction of Africa is at least partly responsible for the continent's ironic exclusion from contemporary analyses of race and racialization processes. I say "ironic" because Africa could not represent a more racialized location—and yet the continent and its peoples are left out of our current discussions and theorizations of race. In other words, while Africa—as trope and geopolitical space—is clearly understood as *the* site of racial otherness, it is this very assumption (and all that it entails) that obstructs sustained analyses of race and its continuous and active processes on the continent. Africa stands in for race but yet, paradoxically, race does not exist in Africa. To me, this situation depends on ideological and intellectual precepts that take Africa's racialized difference as a priori and therefore make any articulation or interrogation of its racialized realities appear redundant.

The research in this book emerged out of my frustration, as an anthropology graduate student in the late 1990s, with the field of African diaspora studies. Coming on the heels of the rise of the Afrocentric movement, new directions in African diaspora scholarship attempted to both provide a counterpoint to Afrocentrism's conception of Africa and to destabilize conventional understandings of the origins and contents of the cultural practices of transnational Black communities.[2] Scholars articulating this new shift in prominent strands of diaspora studies were particularly steadfast in what would become the field's characteristic stance against "essentialisms." Immersed as I was in African diaspora research and theory, I set my goal as the effort to contribute to the theorization of the African diaspora by interrogating the experiences and racial identity politics of postcolonial Africans living in North America. Where did these experiences—of the relatively recent *voluntary* (as opposed to enslaved) population from continental Africa—fit in our conceptualization of the African diaspora? Since many discussions of diasporic identity began with the baseline establishment of the African continent as the site of origin or homeland for the Black communities resulting from the European trade in Africans, I wondered about the place of *modern* Africa in theorizations of the African diaspora. For example, could postcolonial African immigrants be considered part of the African diaspora community as currently conceived? In effect, the effort to theorize diaspora through the experiences of Black African immigrants led me down a path that was distinctly at odds with many of the theoretical and epistemological assumptions underpinning the available models for thinking about diasporic identity formation. Specifically, I found that the African diaspora was conceived in a way whereby the identities and experiences of what Laura Chrisman (1997) calls "new-world, slavery-descended" Black people were, by default, seen to contain and represent all modern Black experience. In other words, forced migration and slavery in current studies of transnational Blackness seem to be not only separated from the brutal history of European colonialism on the African continent, but such recognized "new-world" experiences are also consistently accorded primacy in discussions of modern Black identity. Within this formulation of the African diaspora, then, there was no theoretical space allotted for understanding continental African racialized experiences of slavery, colonialism, and continued racialization in the postcolony. Nor was there space for interrogating Africans' subsequent racialization through both postcolonial voluntary immigration to Euro-capitalist centers and, importantly, the mutual construction of global Black identities on both sides of the Atlantic. Hence, discussions of the "Black experience" often did not include contemporary Black *African* experience, even as it is clear that continental Africans have always been and continue to be racialized as "Black" in a global racial order that denigrates Blackness and exploits and dehumanizes Black people. Moreover, there was no actual engagement with the continent beyond either its dismissal (for the sake of "anti-essentialism") in configurations of diasporic identity, or the obligatory establishment of Africa as "baseline" (Matory 1999) for the diaspora.

Here, diaspora scholars are not alone. With extremely few exceptions—especially outside of southern Africa—scholars of continental Africa generally do not engage the complex ways that race continues to be significant among such communities at this postcolonial moment.[3] If we take anthropology specifically, we find that the discipline's dubious role in "racing" and "exoticizing" Africa rarely translates into theoretical discussions of *racialized* African sociocultural structures of meaning. A quick scan of recent ethnographic studies of various African societies will quickly reveal that, in the wealth of preferred Africanist topics of engagement—globalization, nationalism, ethnicity, ritual and folklore, the (failed) state—race and processes of racialization largely do not figure into the analyses. A search for references on race in Africa sends the researcher almost exclusively to southern Africa and sometimes colonial eastern Africa—areas with white settler populations. Africa is written out of the contemporary *racial* legacies of the transatlantic slave trade, European colonization, and racialized forms of capital, as well as its continued dialogic (Yelvington 2001) relationship to the diaspora.

Thus in my attempt to grapple with events and relationships that clearly reflect processes of racialization over the nearly two decades I have been traveling to Ghana, I was confronted with an astonishing irony: where African diaspora studies generally concerns itself with articulations of race and Blackness but not directly with Africa, so African studies generally concerns itself with Africa but not directly with race and Blackness. Confronting and understanding this irony became a major objective of this project. And more questions than answers emerged for me. For example, how could any postcolonial society not be structured by its legacy of race and racialization—especially when colonialism was, in the most ideological, political, and practical way, racialized rule? How do we, in fact, analyze the persistence of white privilege in postcolonial spaces, or such common practices as skin bleaching or the rigid pigmentocracies that continue exist in postcolonial societies (Charles 2003; Hall 2005)? Naturally, such local practices have to be considered within a global framework and the historical context of empire. I have been attempting, therefore, to provoke a rethinking of the contours of Black identity formation by calling for the mutual interrogation of the practices and experiences of modern continental African and diaspora communities. The first step is to recast Africa within a modern frame so that we may see the experiences and practices of its populations as part of the broad—indeed, global—ideological, cultural, and political-economic terrain established and continually updated by the racial legacies of European hegemony and white supremacy.

The Predicament of Blackness is an ethnography of racialization that insists on shifting the ways we think about Africa and the history of modern identity. I focus specifically on how Ghanaian engagement with discourses, politics, and practices of race and racial difference and privilege occurs within a broader set of processes whereby local relationships expose a very recent history of imperial domination and current global configurations of power and identity. While fully sensitive to the consequence and particularity of historical experience, I take as a point of departure the interdependence of cultural, political, and economic terrains in a modern world constructed in and through the key distinctions around race and the apparatuses of global white supremacy (Mills 1998). Hierarchical racial distinction is a historical and all too common human experience, and, more importantly, processes of racialization *link all modern experience*. Studying racial formation in a place like Ghana—a postcolonial nation that is not the United States or southern Africa—entails demonstration of the ways that local discourses and practices that index race and raced relations resonate and are in dialogue, both with the global political economy and transnational/diasporic identity politics and formations. From the long history of Pan-Africanism and Black racial consciousness to, paradoxically, the significance and status of whiteness and skin-bleaching practices that reflect light-skin color valorization, I have found myself, over the years, in a Ghana that is both intimately familiar and jarringly different. It is a real and modern Ghana. But it is also an unknown Ghana because there has not been the available language or theoretical framework to explore the interrelatedness of such seemingly unrelated events and processes. The goal of this book is to provide a framework for conceptualizing these experiences and practices that together represent the material, cultural, and political realities of this modern moment in continental Africa and beyond—the history and processes of racialization.

So, yes, race in Ghana. And this book demonstrates how and why.

ACKNOWLEDGMENTS

Writing this book would not have been possible without the sacrifices, struggles, and love of my family. I would like to thank my husband and my son, Peter James Hudson and Toussaint Pierre-Vargas (to whom this book is dedicated); my parents, Reverend Delanot and Mrs. Lisette Pierre; my siblings, Moselye, Milca, Marc, and Felton; my numerous aunts and uncles, especially Gertrude St. Louis, Mozeleine and Pierre Williamson, Ernest Celestin, and Jean David Pierre; my "other mother," Marjorie "Cherry" Pengelly (to whose memory this book is also dedicated); my "other brothers," Daryk Pengelly and Richard Pengelly; my in-laws, Michael Hudson, Anna Hudson, Wayne Chase, and Newell Hudson; and the Vargas family—Helion, Anna, Zaira, and Monica—for their unconditional love and support of Toussaint.

Francis Nii Amoo Dodoo introduced me to the study of Africa and the African diaspora and fought hard for me to get a chance to travel to Ghana as an undergraduate student. Thank you, Francis, for teaching by example and by passion. A few close friends have sustained me with love and understanding over the years through research, writing, and the reality of life's ups and downs. They are Ana Aparicio, Jossianna Arroyo, Vladimir Laborde, Jean Longchamps Jr., Candice Lowe, Katherine Oji, Phillis Rambsy, Carlos Ramos, Tonjia Smith, and Rheeda Walker. Bayo Holsey offered me a warm friendship, lots of fun and adventure in Ghana and the United States, as well as critical feedback on the manuscript. This is a much better book because she carefully read it in its entirety and offered incisive criticism. And Tanya Golash-Boza, my friend and comrade, offered insights on the manuscript at a most crucial moment. In the process of making my way through this work, I have also been inspired by the work and vision of journalists and activists Kevin Alexander Gray and Glen Ford (of the *Black Agenda*

*Report*). I appreciate your radical humanism and admire your untiring efforts at making a better world.

In Ghana, the support of Edwin Provencal has been invaluable. From the very beginning of my graduate research, he opened many doors for me, invited me into his circle of friends, introduced me to his family, and showed me many sides of Ghana. Kafui Dey, the friend that I've known longest in Ghana, has been a consistent advocate. Naa Baake Aboagye-Atta offered her friendship and opened her home to me at crucial moments. Thanks to Richard Adzei and Jennifer Pierre for epitomizing the cosmopolitan and diasporic Ghana that I know and love. I am lucky to have had the chance to become friends with the late Alero Olympio, a gentle and generous soul. And a most profound thanks to Sena Daniel Ahiabor, Cynthia Dapaah, and Isaac Aidoo, who helped make possible most of the survey and interview parts of the research for this book.

The research and writing could not have been completed without the help of archives and libraries and without the generosity of several foundations, centers, institutes, and universities. Much appreciation to the staff at the British National Archives (formerly PRO); the Ghana National Archives; the Balme Library at the University of Ghana, Legon; the Institute of African Studies at the University of Ghana, Legon; and the Melville J. Herskovits Library of African Studies at Northwestern University. Thanks to the National Science Foundation, the Social Science Research Council, the Woodrow Wilson Foundation, the Rockefeller Foundation, the Smithsonian Institution, University of Virginia's Carter G. Woodson Institute for the Study of African-American and African Studies, University of Maryland's Driskell Center for the Study of the African Diaspora, the University of Texas College of Liberal Arts, Vanderbilt University's College of Arts and Sciences, and the Robert Penn Warren Center for the Humanities. The fellows at the Carter G. Woodson Institute—Charles Bwenge, Adrian T. Gaskins, Joseph Hellweg, Frederick Knight, Meta Jones, Hanan Sabea, Jesse Weaver Shipley, Olúfémi Táíwò (Malam), and Brian Wagner—helped give birth to this project. Thank you especially to Malam for being such a wonderful mentor.

I am also grateful for the opportunity to have participated in a number of workshops and symposiums where I gained much insight from the exchange of ideas that allowed this project to blossom. Thank you Tina Campt and Deborah Thomas for organizing the Diasporic Hegemonies Symposium that brought together such wonderful and generous scholars to debate and discuss the idea of diaspora. From this rich experience, I found ready interlocutors who carefully engaged with my work. I am particularly grateful for Harvey Neptune and Jacqueline Nassy Brown, the first people to have seen—and to have provided comments on—the messier parts of the manuscript. And thanks to Minkah Makalani and Mia Bay for inviting me to participate in the Diaspora and the Difference Race Makes Workshop at Rutgers University in 2007. Minkah deserves recognition for including me in this important discussion, as does Abena Busia, who brought me into the fold. Thanks also to the University of Illinois at Chicago's Department of African American Studies for inviting me to the 2008 symposium, The Dilemma of Blackness: Challenges and Continuities for the Twenty-First Century.

David Brent deserves special thanks for maintaining faith in my project over the years, his efforts on behalf of the manuscript, and for shepherding the book to fruition. Thanks also to his assistant, Priya Nelson, for patiently handling my many questions, and to Kate Frentzel for her diligent copy-editing. The anonymous reader gave extremely constructive feedback and helped improve the project. Petal Samuel, my indefatigable research assistant, came to this project toward its end but fully embraced the Herculean task of making the manuscript presentable—and all with an easy smile. Thank you!

I thank my former colleagues at the University of Texas at Austin—especially Jafari Sinclair Allen, Kevin Foster, Maria Franklin, Charles Hale, Danny Mendez, Sam Wilson, and my student and friend Naomi Reed. Most of my research travel would not have been possible without the administrative help of Jenni Jones and Adriana Dingman at Austin. My new friends and colleagues at Vanderbilt University have been wonderful—especially those who overwhelmed my family with their friendship and generosity during a most difficult summer of 2011: Mona Frederick, Ifeoma Nwankwo, Samira Sheikh, Richard and Cheryl Blackett, Celso and Jessica Castilho, Sherry Baird and Jim Epstein, Elizabeth Lunbeck and Gary Gerstle, Allison Schachter and Ben Tran, and Eddy Wright-Rios and Gini Pupo-Walker.

And finally, back to Toussaint and Peter. To Toussaint: I am honored to be your mommy! You have taught me unconditional love and to smile despite myself, regardless of our circumstances. You are a kind and beautiful soul, and I am so excited to watch you grow and mature. And Peter: I continue to be awed by your searing and voracious intellect, your broad generosity, your kindness, and your endless sense of humor. Thank you for helping my ideas make sense and for pushing me to be a better scholar and teacher. Thank you for coming into my life at the most perfect time, for trusting me with your heart, and for accepting mine. And thank you for helping to create our safe space. What a world we are making!

INTRODUCTION

*The Predicament of Blackness: Postcolonial Ghana and the Politics of Race*
presents an ethnography of racial formation in urban Ghana in order to
make a much broader claim about the importance of race as a multifaceted global process and about Africa as a modern space. The book has two
interlinked central arguments. First, drawing on the manifold processes of
racialization in Ghana, I make the case both for recognizing postcolonial
African societies as structured through and by global White supremacy (Mills
1998) and for addressing such societies within current discussions of race
and Blackness. Indeed, Ghana's historical position in the European trade
in Africans, its experience of racial colonialism, its continued prominent
role in African diaspora politics, as well as its own active processes of what
I'm calling "racecraft" clearly reflect how its local realities are structured by
global *racial* configurations of identity, culture, economics, and politics.
To speak of racialization in urban Ghana—and in relation to postcolonial
Africa in general—is to also contend with the various transnational political
and cultural significations associated with constructions of "Blackness." And
this recognition necessarily forces concrete engagement with the processes of
African diasporic identity formation. Consequently (and this is the second
part of my argument), racialization processes in postcolonial Africa are such
that they render analogous the experiences and relationships of continental
Africans and those of African descent in the diaspora. Contemporary African
societies, in other words, are so thoroughly structured by processes of racialization that they deserve to be treated as historically coeval (Fabian 1983)
with Black communities in the diaspora rather than either as historically,
politically, and culturally distinct or as representative of a past cultural survival into the present (Matory 2005).

The arguments in *The Predicament of Blackness* center on interventions in anthropology around the relationships of Africa, race, and modernity. In the first instance, the focus is on racial formation in postcolonial Africa—specifically, the existence and persistence of race making where the predicaments of "Blackness" depend on modern racializing processes that include the interaction with "Whiteness," among other identities and communities. This is a theoretical and epistemological intervention. But it is also one that bucks against established disciplinary orthodoxy to ask: What is the status of race in Africanist anthropology? And what is the status of Africa in African diaspora studies? The recent postcolonial frameworks through which many African societies are conceptualized within African studies often do not account for the continued existence of racially structured unequal (national and global) relationships and practices. On the other hand, African diaspora studies, which clearly recognizes that the social and political constructs of race significantly inform various forms of identification in Black communities, often does not engage contemporary Africa as an active site of racialized identity formation. In addressing these trends, *The Predicament of Blackness* foregrounds the practices of race that, southern Africa aside, have received less attention in historiographic and ethnographic studies of Africa.[1] The book provides an original approach to the study of postcolonial Africa, one that links the continent's current condition and predicament to a set of global cultural and political configurations that include race as a key aspect of identity and community formation, as well as to histories of other similarly structured communities outside of the continent. My ultimate hope is to demonstrate the potential for a global theory of racial formation that has broad implications, in this age of extensive transnational interactions, for exploring and rethinking identities and communities as well as for challenging ongoing structures of race and power.

## Why Racialization?

This book is not a detailed analysis of the concept of race. It is an exploration of the various sites through which racial meanings are crafted, where racialization is deployed and articulated. My examination takes the constitution of race and racial categories—as well as the historically overdetermined assumptions about them—as given, and it explores the various ways they are continuously reformulated through ongoing processes of interpellation and self-making (Althusser 1971). I must stress here that I see the significance of establishing the *fact* of the occurrence of racialization in purportedly unusual or unsuspecting places. As such, the analysis in this book forces the appreciation of the *long duree* of European empire making, whereby conquest, the commerce in Africans, slavery (both in Africa and the "New World"), and the colonization of the Western hemisphere, the African continent, and Asia are all seen as an interlocking set of practices that have cemented the commonality of our modern experience. What is significant here is the *racial* dimension of this international system of power and the attendant global White supremacy through which it is enacted and experienced.

The need to establish the importance of European empire making in making race global—and, importantly, local—was again recently made apparent to me in the discussions surrounding Barack Obama's visit to Ghana in June 2009. In the incessant media coverage of the event, in Ghana and abroad, there seemed to be a thematic unity in the framing of the first Black U.S. president's visit to Africa that epitomizes how the continent is placed within conventional narratives of slavery and race. Specifically, there was a clear "systematic isolation" (Chrisman 2003, 30) of exploring Ghana's relationship to the transatlantic slave trade and slavery, as well as to processes of racialization. A revealing example of this was an article about the event written for the *Christian Science Monitor* by a U.S. history professor teaching in Ghana for the summer. His commentary on Obama's visit was titled "Ghana's Hype over Obama: Beyond Race," and it included a subtitle and description that read, in part, "Ghanaians take a special pride in the fact that neither they nor Obama are descended from slaves" (Zimmerman 2009). Ghanaians, the author insisted, do not have to confront the same baggage of race during a visit from Obama. Rather, he writes, "unlike blacks in the United States, most Ghanaians here don't have ancestors who suffered the horrors and indignities of slavery. So, they're less touchy than we are about race." What's more, he continues, when race does come up in Ghana—when, for example, people shout out "Obruni"[2] as he, a White man, walks through the streets of Accra—"it's all in good fun." This kind of analysis is based on commonplace conventions of Ghanaian–African diaspora historiography. Its logic is as follows: slavery is not the property of Ghanaians; it is (solely) that of African Americans; it is because African Americans experienced slavery that they tend to be obsessed with issues of race; Ghanaians are not "descendants of slaves," nor do they have ancestors who suffered its horrors and indignities, and therefore race is a nonissue for them; and thus, even when Ghanaians make references that seem racial, such references are not really racial, they are "in good fun." In this formulation, racial thinking is associated with the history of slavery, and slavery and race are designated issues of concern only for diaspora Blacks. The other subtext of this understanding is the silence on colonialism—both its direct connection to the slave trade *and* its racial legacy. I contend, however, that it is only an epistemic blindness—a blindness that is *trained*—that can explain the persistent scholarly separation of slavery from colonialism, and of these two historical experiences from the historical development of racial capitalism (Robinson 1983).

I frame the discussion of Ghana's racial formation within the context of global White supremacy[3] to underscore the reality that issues of race are always already about power. I also do this to emphatically demonstrate that any and all local configurations of race and racialization are structured in and through global hierarchical relationships. While the need to prove the reality of global White domination is unfortunate, I want to establish that it is the *conditions* of White supremacy that continue to make racialization significant.[4] Yet, the research presented here is not specifically about "Whiteness" or "Blackness" per se. It is instead about how a local site is structured through racial meanings and how such meanings—while reflecting the saturation of White racial hegemony as it has been secured as a process of domination—are variously mapped onto individuals, communities, and nations.

This book is not about the ideologies and practices of racism or isolated racist incidents.[5] It is about the various processes—historical, economic, political, and cultural—that have worked to create and structure racial meanings in Ghana. Here, I take David Goldberg's (1993) position that the concept of race can only be understood in terms of how it is signified. Race is so embedded in prevailing cultural and scientific conceptions and in the everyday that it is malleable to many forms. Thus, it is better to understand race in terms of how its discourses and practices structure lives in time and space. And though there is no doubt that racism remains an important and cruel part of the structure of global society, the analysis here focuses on the construction, constitution, and maintenance of racial categories and meanings—the processes of racialization.

Key to this conceptualization of racialization—and racial formation in general—is the idea of race as a process that is always historically situated, and of racial categories and meanings as fluid, unstable, decentered, and constantly transformed by changing historical, social, and political relationships (Omi and Winant 1994). These conceptualizations are in place even as we recognize that the construction of race through the establishment of an overdetermined hierarchy still defines the concept and its meaning. Racial formation is, therefore, a set of racialization processes—processes that give race its constant and shifting social, cultural, and political meaning and that determine how such meaning is deployed ideologically and through various practices and institutions. In addition, processes of racialization are multiple and entail the interplay of often contradictory "racial projects,"[6] each of which works to advance its own conceptions of race in contemporary society. In other words, "racial projects" are the building blocks of racialization processes (racial formation). My approach in this book is to focus on some of the "racial projects" that work to continue to give race meaning and therefore contribute to the terrain of racial formation[7] in Ghana. Of course racialization processes are not the same everywhere; rather they are a family of forms that are subject to local articulations and incarnations. At the same time, I am arguing that while processes of racialization are multiple and varied, they are all interconnected through the broader historical reality of European empire making.

In making the case both for the deployment of racial analysis in postcolonial Africa and for understanding the analogous relationship of continental and diasporic African communities, I am proposing a theory of racialization that recognizes its global import, its contemporary significance, and its relative overdetermination in structuring (Black) identities and experiences. I want to be clear that this theory takes as given the historical, political, and contingent realities of racial categorization; at the same time, it recognizes that racialization has "served to fix social subjects in place and time, no matter their spatial location, to delimit privilege and possibilities, to open opportunities to some while excluding the range of racialized Others" (Goldberg 1993, 206). Yet, to argue for an analysis focused primarily on the racial contours of Ghanaian identity and community formation is not to deny or diminish the significance of other processes of identification such as ethnicity, nationality, religion, gender, and class. It is, however, to establish how, even in independent Africa, race is the modality through which many of these identifications continue to be structured (Hall 1980). The very production of "Africa"—its colonial history, its geographical, political, and cultural mapping, as well as ongoing discursive configurations of the continent's incorrigible difference—occurs through ideas of race. We cannot, therefore, understand how notions of ethnicity, nation, or culture are deployed in racialized-as-Black African communities without recognizing the ways they are refracted through processes of racialization. The overall scholarly interest in "ethnic conflict" or indigenous cultural traditions belies the continent's relation to global racialized hierarchies against and through which these local events develop. Without analyses that also cover racial processes, scholars lose the ability to fully grasp the way broader social and political relations of global White supremacy continue to "create the conditions for the Black Atlantic dialogue over collective identity" (Matory 1999, 38). Indeed, the question for scholars should be: Why *not* race and racialization?

## Writing Ghana, Mapping Africa[8]

From pre-independence to modern times, Ghana has been at the center of Pan-African politics and culture. At the same time, Ghana has been a key place in both the histories of the transatlantic slave trade and colonialism: it was a key node in the commercial routes of the traffic in Africans, a fact verified by the country's identification as a UNESCO world historical site for the distinction of having more precolonial European-styled forts than any other country in Africa, including the three largest former slave-trading castle-dungeons. This is a legacy that dates from the earliest articulations of Black racial consciousness in which, along with Liberia, Sierra Leone, and Nigeria, the Gold Coast was the staging ground for a robust cosmopolitan intellectual vanguard seeking to challenge racist ideologies of the day and to vindicate African society. A. Adu Boahen calls this a "real intellectual revolution" that generated African racial consciousness and identity as well as the ideologies of Ethiopianism, Pan-Africanism, and the notion of an "African personality" (1987). These earliest movements helped shape the internationalist framework of anticolonial revolt and postindependence nationalism, and we can see this long legacy in the state's historical and contemporary deployment of its various cultural practices. Ghana was the first nation below the Sahara on the African continent to gain political independence, and it is therefore at the center of major political shifts in the modern world. We find in Ghana a country with the historical predicaments and contemporary realities that resonate across the various fields of African, African diasporic, and postcolonial studies. It is also a site with legacies that epitomize the cross-cultural and cross-political currents of peoples, ideas, and movements that urge us all to, in effect, race back and forth across the (Black) Atlantic.

*The Predicament of Blackness* takes global racialization processes as a point of departure and explores various local acts, objects, and ideas that contain within them diverse representations that relate Ghanaian racial formation to the international politico-economic and cultural arenas. As I argued above, Ghana is hardly unique in its historical confrontation with global processes of race and power. For example, we will see in chapter 1 that even racial apartheid—often considered South Africa's domain—was the norm rather than the exception in a continental Africa under colonial rule (Mamdani 1996). This has great implications for helping us rethink the ways we have approached Africa's relationship to racial colonialism, colonialism's intimate connection to slavery and racial terror, and Africa's relation to the Black diaspora. It is Ghana's banality that opens up the theoretical and methodological space for us to also consider Ghana's experience as a metaphor for postcolonial Africa.

## A Note on Methodology

*The Predicament of Blackness* is an ethnography of racialization that is based on more than five years of accumulated formal ethnographic research in Accra and Cape Coast, Ghana, as well as archival research in Ghana and in England. It is also the result of insights gained from my engagement with Ghana spanning almost two decades, beginning with my first experience as an undergraduate exchange student, followed by a sponsored independent research project that allowed me to live in Ghana for a year before beginning formal graduate studies, and continuing over the years with near-annual trips.

I want to stress that my aim was not to produce an anthropological project in the traditional sense. While my research trajectory more or less follows the expected methods of anthropology, combining participant observation and open-ended and semistructured interviews with archival research and reviews of secondary sources, some of my most profound insights emerged not during "formal" research moments, but rather in random events and interactions and in heated arguments with friends. Moreover, I focus on racialization as my site of study and therefore examine the various ways that it occurs and continues. There are no day-to-day details of the religious, political, or family lives of small bounded geocultural groups. Nor do I focus (at least not explicitly) on the micropolitics of particular contradictions and controversies within a small, localized community as such. Instead, I cast my net wide, exploring the multiple settings and relationships in which individuals, social groups, and the state actively participate in constructing, transforming, and challenging the various competing and overlapping racial projects within Ghana's cultural and sociopolitical field. As an ethnography of racialization, *The Predicament of Blackness* brings together analysis of a selected set of sites—competing "racial projects"—that serve to delineate the various and contested nature of racecraft in Ghana.

## Chapter Synopses and Outline

Together, the chapters of this book examine the historical forces and contemporary practices that shape the terrain of struggle, the prevailing racial order, within which Ghanaian urban communities and identities are constituted. Four of the seven chapters are ethnographic and focus on different sites of racialization. The first, second, and sixth chapters are historical and theoretical in content and work to bring into dialogue the fields of anthropology, African studies, postcolonial studies, and African diaspora studies. Chapter 1 uses the context of the formalization of colonial rule in the Gold Coast to present a theoretical discussion of "nativization" as "racialization." The goal here is to locate racialization as a key process in the long historical arc of Europe's relationship with Africa and Africans. Chapter 2 extends the historical analysis from colonialism to the political economy of racialization at the dawn of independence and establishes, in detail, the relationship between decolonization and racialization, and the impact on the contemporary moment.

The following four chapters each focus on a particular racial project and on distinct sites of Ghanaian racial formation. Chapter 3 examines the position of Whites/Europeans and the discourses and practices around notions "Whiteness." Chapter 4 interrogates the practice of chemical skin bleaching and attendant local dynamics of light-skin color privilege. Chapter 5 considers the Ghanaian state's active promotion of "heritage tourism" and "diaspora relations" through a discursive deployment of its Pan-Africanist history. And chapter 6 maps out local Ghanaian interactions (in Accra) with populations of African descent from the diaspora. The ethnographic chapters are ordered in a way that demonstrates the necessarily complex, uneven, and incomplete nature of racial formation in Ghana. For example, the study of White positionality, the discourse of Whiteness, and skin-bleaching practices work to demonstrate (and reinforce) the effects of (global) White supremacy in Ghana. At the same time, however, the Ghanaian state's conscious affirmation of Blackness through its rearticulation of Pan-Africanism and Black racial pride as well as the ongoing interaction of Ghanaian and diaspora Black populations (in Ghana) work to challenge the very hegemony of White racial privilege. As they struggle for hegemony in the cultural and political fields, these individual racial projects are never complete. It remains to be seen, therefore, how the interplay of these projects under study—along with various other projects—will continue to shift the terrain of Ghanaian racial formation. *The Predicament of Blackness* reveals, nevertheless, that Ghanaian politics and culture continue to be structured in a way that works to (re)inscribe Ghana's marginality within various racialized global hierarchies.

The seventh and final chapter, along with the first chapter, serves as a theoretical bookend of my analysis. Chapter 7 brings together the book's thesis on global processes of racialization with my two primary fields of engagement: African studies and African diaspora studies. Beginning with a discussion that explores the interlinked historical development of these two fields, the chapter interrogates their subsequent theoretical and epistemo-logical isolation from one another and concludes with a call to rethink our conceptions of Black internationalisms.

At this historical moment of increasing globalization, along with persist-ing racialized forms of inequality that continue to structure community and nations hierarchically, race remains an important site of analysis for anthro-pologists, Africanists, and African diaspora scholars. Africa in particular—both imagined and real—has historically occupied an explicitly racialized space in the global political imaginary. I hope that the research and analysis presented in this book can place postcolonial African studies' relative lack of engagement with race in conversation with African diaspora studies' lack of concrete engagement with contemporary African societies. Indeed, by bringing a postcolonial African society into a sociohistorical dialogue about race, processes of racialization, and the interlinked transnational construc-tion of identities, this study also offers one of the many ways to confront modern Africa and the multifaceted nature of transnational Black identity formations.

# ONE

# Of Natives and Europeans: Colonialism and the Ethnicization of Racial Dominance

[T]he racial category "black" evolved with the consolidation of racial slavery. By the end of the seventeenth century, Africans whose specific identity was Ibo, Yoruba, Fulani, etc., were rendered "black" by an ideology of exploitation based on racial logic—the establishment and maintenance of a "color line." . . . With slavery . . . a racially based understanding of society was set in motion which resulted in the shaping of a specific racial identity.

—Michael Omi and Howard Winant, *Racial Formation in the United States*

The premier Gold Coast nationalist [John Mensah] Sarbah by ethnic identification was Fanti; colonial legislation enacted in 1883 also classified him as a Native, one of several million such in the Gold Coast (and beyond).

—Kwaku Korang, *Writing Ghana, Imagining Africa*

[C]olonialism is one of the elements that subtends the construction of white identity.

—Richard Dyer, *White*

This chapter's epigraphs refer us to a particular consolidation of identity that results from the interrelated histories of the transatlantic slave trade of Africans and the formal European colonization of the African continent. The first epigraph charts how various African groupings were, through capture and enslavement, rendered "Black"—racialized through cultural and social distinctions into a scarcely differentiated mass. The second epigraph points to how African groupings were, through colonial legislation and practice, rendered "native"—a dual process of first constructing and then flattening ethnocultural difference and belonging into a racialized collectivity. This racialized "Black" and "African" collectivity was then contrasted to a racialized White European colonial power. Thus, the third epigraph demonstrates the other side of the racializing coin—the homogenization of European groupings and the making of colonial Whiteness. In juxtaposing these epigraphs, I am explicitly marking the overlapping processes of a racialized New World "Blackness" and a continental-colonial "nativeness," processes constructed through and against those of the "Whiteness" of the broad imperial project. The delineation of these overlapping processes also serves to make the obvious, though underexplored, link between the transatlantic slave trade and colonialism—two key moments in the long historical arc of European empire making. By examining the various ways that European empire making created and then variously confronted the "native question," I capture the local dimensions of the global designs of the coloniality of race and power (Mignolo 2000).

The legal and de facto construction of nativeness was a key structuring principle of the local racial terrain forged under colonial rule in continental Africa. Nativization was racialization. My discussion here follows a particular historical genealogy that presents the establishment of formal colonialism in the Gold Coast/Ghana—and West Africa more generally—as the foundation both for the consolidation of racial/civilizational distinctions and racial rule, and the structuring of a local racialized cultural and political terrain from that moment to the present. This analysis takes as a point of departure Mahmood Mamdani's contention more than a decade ago (1996, 1999) that the contemporary moment in Africa is informed by the core structural legacy of the colonial strategy of "indirect rule." Indirect rule was in fact the establishment of formalized racial thinking rationalized through the practice of apartheid. Thus, apartheid—"with its racially-defined democracy alongside its ethnically-demarcated Native Authorities" (1999, 862)—is neither exceptional nor solely a South African predicament; rather, it is the *generic* form of colonial rule in Africa. In the Gold Coast, as in other European-controlled territories in Africa, racialization was embedded institutionally, built into the particular structure and practice of colonial rule. The making of the native depended upon the racial configuration—both through official recognition and artificial invention—of a loose constellation of mutually exclusive and antagonistic "tribal" groupings. This fact affected local identity and politics in profound ways. Tribal affiliation, as opposed to a comparable racial distinction based on Black subordination and White advancement, was the overwhelming fact of life for the average colonized African. Significantly, the joint processes of "native" and "European" identity making were such that the active production of racial ideology on the ground was rendered simultaneously absent and imminent.

The formal nativization of African identities was a result of a shift in British colonial ruling policy and concomitant Europeanization. Under indirect rule, colonial policy racialized the African as native, crucially displacing a prominent local professional elite of so-called Europeanized Africans. Alongside this displacement was the practical enactment, on the ground, of the social, political, and juridical racial and cultural apartheid that separated natives from Europeans. Thus, the official procedures and consequences of indirect rule allowed for the consolidation of a thoroughly racialized social and political structure in the Gold Coast. This same structure would, ironically, create the conditions of possibility for the emergence of a collective and "national" racial consciousness—intellectual and political movements from Pan-Africanism to anticolonial nationalism and independence. It would also inform the ongoing contradictions between this racial consciousness and enduring ethnocultural loyalties that persist even in the present moment.

This chapter interrogates the structure of colonial rule—indirect rule—as an important racialization process in the Gold Coast/Ghana. Indirect rule enabled the implementation and development of a particular set of new racial, ethnic, and cultural regimes throughout the West African territories ruled by England. I begin with an examination of indirect rule's general features, particularly the simultaneous making of "natives" and "Europeans" through the pattern of differentiation based on assumptions of radical racial and cultural difference. There are, of course, many important projects of structural racialization (and racism) in the colonial Gold Coast. These range from discriminatory economic practices and political mandates to African-specific educational policies that depended on the belief in African intellectual inferiority. I briefly review two of these projects here. First, I examine the political and economic practices of the colonial state and concurrent demise of the class of African educated commercial and professional elite. Second, I look at the establishment of apartheid through urban planning and residential segregation. While the scope of this discussion does not permit an exhaustive treatise on all colonialist racializing processes, these examples serve to reveal not only the inevitable hierarchical racialization of the local community but also the consistent efforts of the colonial regime at consolidating Whiteness. The chapter ends with a contextualization of this discussion of nativization and racialization by prefiguring the trajectories and tragedies of postindependence reform.

## The Modes of Colonial Power

The categorical distinctions between "native" and "nonnative" represented a fundamental method of ordering colonial society. These distinctions were conceived in terms of absolute physical difference within a racial frame and consolidated through cultural discourse, legal practices, and social convention. Official and unofficial colonial correspondence about Africa is replete with references to "the natives." From deliberations on the "native question" to disputes over how to define a native, such conversations point to negotiations around particular distinctions of race, culture, and hegemonic power. One of the clearest descriptions of the African subject population, the natives, comes from a commissioned survey of "race relations" in the colonies toward the end of British rule.[1] Referring to the various British colonies on the African continent, the document reports that there is an overlap between the use of the terms "native" and "African," against those of "European" and "nonnative."[2] While there was great variation in how the terms were applied in distinct spaces, the authors came to the following conclusion: "The normal meaning of 'Native' or 'African' is therefore seen to be a member of an aboriginal African tribe or community who lives among and *follows the customs* [italics added] of such community."[3] In particular, "native" not only indicated a strictly biological identity, but such reference was only significant inasmuch as it was linked to a distinguishing set of cultural practices and customs. "Native," therefore, is more than just a category marking a subject of rule; it is a distinction of ethnological proportions linking beliefs about the subjects' physiological, emotional, and mental character to, ultimately, capacity for rule.

Through colonial discourses about the native and practices of native making, the institutionalization of racialized rule came to be hidden beneath local articulations of power. Colonial domination in Africa was distinctive. It was the site of a significant shift in British colonial policy from the "zeal of a civilizing mission" to a hegemonic cultural project of incorporation, "harnessing the moral, historical, and community impetus behind local custom to a larger colonial project" (Mamdani 1996, 286).[4] With the expanded focus on the notion of the "customary," we see the marshaling of indigenous culture (real, perceived, and invented) for authoritarian rule. In dealing with the "native question"—that is, the most effective way for a small of number of conquerors to rule a majority—colonial powers followed two paths: direct rule and indirect rule. Direct rule came first and was aimed at providing a small local elite access to European "culture" and "civilization" in return for strong allies in the colonial enterprise. Indirect rule, on the other hand, was premised on the perceived diffusion of colonial power through "native custom." Thus, where direct rule sought to "shape the world of the elite amongst the conquered population, the object of indirect rule was to shape the world of the colonized masses" (Mamdani 1999, 865). And indirect rule emerged as a way to reform the contradictions inherent in direct rule—how to justify the exclusion of the small elite group of subjects who, by virtue of their cultural assimilation into "European civilization," expected to be granted full "civilized" rights. Indirect rule shifted this concern and instead established the legitimacy of rule through the incorporation of the masses through what was considered their own organic institutions.

Key to this incorporation, and to indirect rule, was the configuration of racial and ethnic (or tribal) identities—for Africans as well as for Europeans. The colonial state had a two-tiered structure: on the ground, the subject population was ruled by a constellation of ethnically defined native institutions that were, in turn, supervised by nonnative/European officials "deployed from a racial pinnacle at the center" (Mamdani 1996, 287). But this two-tiered rule constructed and reproduced these two sets of identities in a dual move for Africans. In the first instance, there was the distinction between native and nonnative (or European)—and later, others such as those of "Asiatic origin"—that was based on notions of absolute racial and cultural difference. In the second movement, the native, while categorically representing the racialized mass of subjects under rule, was further subdivided into distinct (and presumably culture-bound) tribal and/or ethnic groupings. The native in this configuration was actually fragmented from a *singular* subject group; in practice, each ethnic or tribal group was understood to be governed by its own set of rules framed under its specific cultural patterns, however defined. Moreover, tribal or ethnic identities were associated solely with the natives. The European, in fact, was racialized but not ethnicized. The native, on the other hand, was both ethnicized and racialized—but her racialization was subsumed under her tribal/ethnic affiliations. In this social patterning, there emerged a dual set of consequences. Whereas the European/nonnative political, cultural, and civic identity presented itself as a singular racial power controlling the group of natives, the force of this power was diffused through the various cultural "authorities" of the native tribal groupings. In practice, this worked through the distinctions between "civil society" and "customary society," juridically enacted through notions of civil law/rights and customary law, respectively.

Similar to native identity, customary law was not singular; it was a set of laws based on a varied set of customs and practices believed—and often rendered—by colonial authorities to be customary.[5] Each tribe purportedly

had its own set of customary laws that would be enforced by its own colonially established "native authority." What "customary" meant, how the
native authority enforced a set of customary laws, and how these were set
up against the "civil society" comprising the European group all reflected
the solid racial structure of colonial power as well as assumptions of the native's cultural alterity. Also at the heart of this structure was the dual system
of justice and punishment, one set for the colonial rulers and one for the
native authorities. The power of the native authorities was seen to reside in
the chief, the authoritarian ruler and enforcer of tribal customs (Crowder
1968; Killingray 1986). And unlike civil law, customary law was never written[6]—the colonial-sanctioned native authorities had full control over the
interpretation of "customs." Most significant, however, was that the crude
violence of colonial rule was also disseminated through the native authorities, and "custom" became the language of force in everything from land
distribution to forced labor and direct taxation to the colonial state.[7]

It is important to highlight the overlapping, and at times unstable, inflections of race and culture at the heart of the decentralized rule of the
colonial state through indirect rule. The split between the Native Authority
and civil or colonial authority—a clear legal and political distinction—was
racially framed and based on a crude biological understanding of race as
encompassing physical, somatic, genetic, and cultural differences. Europeans—and, later, Arabs and Asians—were considered racially distinct from
the subject "tribal" African populations. Indeed, by the time of the formal
colonization of continental Africa, scientific racism and ideas about the
African or "Negro" had already been consolidated from the early period of
the transatlantic slave trade and the establishment of chattel slavery in European colonies in the New World. In late nineteenth- and early twentieth-
century thinking, this biological and racial distinction was also a cultural
one, and it would define political status since race identity was assumed to
determine behavioral as well as cultural tendencies (Stocking 1992). If the
native was rendered racially distinct from the European ruler, it also meant
that she was culturally distinct, further marked by the difference between
"custom" and "civilization."

In particular, assumption of British national, racial, and cultural superiority provided clear justification for its imperial ventures in Asia and Africa.
This sense of superiority had been honed through justifications for British
plantation slavery in the Americas, rapid industrialization, and a growing
nationalism that was linked to imperial conquests. By the time of Britain's
formal conquest of parts of the African continent, English beliefs about the

native's retarded development were commonplace. For Frederick Lugard, the chief architect of indirect rule, colonial control depended on the absolute racial difference between the White European and the Black African. And Africans were naturally predisposed to occupying certain positions in the hierarchy of human evolution and civilization (Táíwò 2010). Lugard believed the "typical African" to be a "happy" and "excitable" being, "full of personal vanity, with little sense of veracity, fond of music. . . . His mind . . . far nearer to the animal world than that of the European or Asiatic, and exhibits something of the animal's placidity and want of desire to rise beyond the stage he has reached'" (Lugard 1922, 69).[8] Britain's dual mandate therefore was to impart culture and civilization to the African "primitive" while availing itself of the continent's resources, which such "primitives" were incapable of managing.

This is why the group of educated and "Europeanized" Africans and the racially mixed Euro-Africans proved especially problematic for the colonial government, and for Lugard in particular. As a culturally and often racially mixed group, these Africans stood starkly apart from the African masses in education and social class and political status. They also posed a challenge to nineteenth-century racial assumptions of African inferiority and intractable cultural backwardness. On the one hand, they were crucial allies to Europeans in their early imperial adventures—"middlemen" on the coastal frontiers with cultural and matrimonial access to the interior. On the other hand, they were economic, political, and often cultural competitors. The formalization of colonial rule necessitated racial and cultural reclassification: this African elite had to become "native" and therefore "African" and "Black" so as not to challenge White European racial superiority and political hegemony. "However strong a sympathy we may feel for the aspiration of these African progressives," Lugard asserted about the Euro-African elite, "sane counselors will advise them to recognize their present limitations" (1922, 80). Michael Crowder underscores this point in his discussion of West Africa under colonial rule: "For the British the educated African was a gaudy, despised imitator of European ways. For them the 'real' Africa was the peasant or the traditional chief who, unlike the educated African, did not challenge their supremacy. The 'real' African had no ambition to enter the world of the British" (1968, 397–98). Within the hierarchical scaling of cultural systems the Europeanized Africans were suddenly limited by their presumed racial characteristics. And where there continued to be confusion about racial classification and cultural identity—as in the case of West Indians of African descent in the colonial service[9]—the colonial office maneuvered legal proclamations in defense of European cultural and racial superiority (Ray 2007).

The migration of Lebanese and Syrian populations to British colonial territories in West African further consolidated this racial and cultural hierarchy. Tied to British colonialism, this group came to play a significant role as "middlemen" in West African commerce partly because of European late nineteenth-century racialism. As Emmanuel Akyeampong asserts, "In the age of scientific racism, whiteness certainly had its advantages and race may have paved the way for the commercial role of the Lebanese." Many European firms followed the racial protocols of the time and preferred Lebanese traders to Africans, "whom they distrusted." This enabled the growth of Lebanese and Syrian wealth and population and effectively made this group "beneficiaries of British imperialism and colonial capitalism, and targets of indigenous west African hostility" (2006, 308).[10] Yet, while colonial rule spawned a hierarchically structured multiracial West African society, this multiracialism rotated on a European-native axis that depended simultaneously on a race-culture conflation and a race-tribal distinction.

The conflation of race and culture/ethnicity deployed within the structure of colonial rule also meant that, on the ground, the actual contours of White racial power were often obfuscated. Colonial power was diffused through various native authorities—with seemingly disparate groups of tribes enacting individual and unique sets of laws. In other words, the racial character of colonial rule was hidden beneath constructed ethnic or tribal differences. Both in official documentation and among tribalized subjects, this ethnicization of racial rule ensured the deployment and maintenance of racial structures of power without an explicitly raced referent. Thus, the European-African racial dualism was "anchored in a politically enforced ethnic pluralism" (Mamdani 1996, 7). The obvious effect, which is significant for analyzing contemporary racial formations in politically independent Africa, is that, first, the color of actual colonial domination, though powerful and explicitly racialized, remained quite distant from subject populations. Instead, the natives—which, as a whole, were racially unified but ethnically distinct and fragmented—were under the management of a Black local (native) authority (led nominally by a "chief"), which ruled through "culture," "tradition," and "custom."[11] Second, the bottom tier of the colonial order, the native, was key to stabilizing indirect rule because it was institutionalized in such a way that made it difficult to present a collective and effective challenge to the upper tier. As Kadiatu Kanneh reminds us, "the deliberate fragmentation of a colonized people into separate spaces . . .

results in a 'native' collectivity which is radically diverse, cultural and mutually antagonistic" (1998, 87).

The structure of rule, therefore, obscured the colonial state's top-down racial inequality while potentially retarding the growth of a consolidated resistance against its power. Even as there were various forms of local challenges to this kind of racialized ethnogenesis among a prominent group of natives, the structure endured, having fully been traditionalized, adapted, and rationalized as the *natural* outcome of *cultural* differences among now-distinct ethnic/tribal groupings. Indeed, various liberal responses to colonialism, particularly those sensitive to African demands, often accepted these tribal or ethnic identities both as precolonial and primordial. This kind of understanding also worked to construct such ethnic, tribal, or cultural identities as seemingly distinct from racial formation. Later, new independent African states would have few options but to adopt such tribal-ethnic-cultural paradigms in ways that both challenged and upheld the structure of their composition.

In an incisive critique of Africanist historians' refusal to engage the relationship between race and empire, Nigerian scholar Christopher Fyfe reminded his peers that the manifestation of authority in colonial Africa was simple: "White gave orders, black obeyed. . . . It was an easy rule to understand and enforce, and it upheld colonial authority in Africa for about half a century" (1992, 15). Though Fyfe was making a seemingly obvious point, it is clear that the workings of race (and Whiteness and otherness) had not been adequately addressed in conventional historical analysis of colonialism. Yet Fyfe also made the more important point that "the underlying strength of British racial rule was that its existence was regularly denied. . . . A barrier of race rigidly separated white from black in colonial Africa. But the separation was never explicitly formulated as part of British colonial policy. There was no need; everyone understood it" (23–24). I would argue, however, that it was not that racial rule was not explicitly formulated; it was rather the way it was operationalized. "Everyone understood" the rules precisely because the major institutions and relationships of colonial rule—law, political organization, economic relationships, segregation, and so forth—were structured *in* and *through* the process of the establishment of its racial order, that is, in and through White supremacy.

The colonial state's racecraft was integral to the colonial project. Its major strength lies in the ways that its architects were able to construct a system in which racial ideology was embedded through institutions and restructured (indeed, renamed) in a way that hegemonically incorporated the colonized. In this sense, *indirect rule was a racial project*, established through the racializing process that constructed the Black native—culturally, racially, and juridically—against the White European and the Asiatic middlemen (Omi and Winant 1994; Winant 2001; Akyeampong 2006). This rigid racial distinction was hardly lived as such by the majority of the colonized, however, because in practice it worked not as a form of exclusion, but rather as incorporation—as hegemony. Nativization was racialization, but this racialization worked through *ethnicization*—the constitution and organization of a constellation of tribal groupings whose incorporation into colonial society depended on mediating its racial and cultural separation from the "civil" and "civilized" society of White European colonizers. Naturally, this also demanded ongoing Europeanization, the simultaneous process of White racial identity making.

The racialization effected by the establishment of an indirect colonial rule would shape, irrevocably, the contemporary local cultural and sociopolitical terrain. What we see in the example of the Gold Coast, below, is the official structuring of nativeness—against that of Europeanness—with the onset of a formal racialized colonialism. This occurs in many ways, including the economic and political displacement of the educated and cosmopolitan local (African and African-descended) elite and residential and cultural segregation in the urban areas. At the same time, the form of rule shaped the form of revolt against it. Nativization—in the language of the tribal customs and institutions—would become the first front in the fight against colonial rule. Ironically, the struggle for a consolidated national, and thereby racialized, consciousness would also depend on a difficult relationship with such native institutions. It would also pave the way for a postindependence racecraft.

## The Gold Coast and Colonial Racecraft

There is growing up in Ghana a generation which has no first-hand knowledge of colonial rule. These boys and girls, born since Independence, will find it difficult to believe that there was a time when Africans could not walk in certain parts of town, unless they had business there as servants. . . . It is cheering to think that when they meet a European it will never occur to them to touch the imaginary forelock, or bow in servility, as some of our older men still do, so hard is it to break long-established habits. . . . The social effects of colonialism are more insidious than the political and economic. . . . The Europeans relegated us to the position of inferiors in every aspect of our everyday life.

—Kwame Nkrumah, *Africa Must Unite*

These remarks by Ghana's first president, Kwame Nkrumah, were meant to remind his audience of the racial indignities of colonial rule in urban Ghana. While indirect rule depended on the belief in a two-tiered racial hierarchy that rested on residential, social, and economic segregation, this apartheid was simpler to deploy when the locus of the Native Authority was the "local state"—rural areas where individual customary laws could be bound to tribal practices. But in the towns, the urban seats of colonial power and the resident European population as well as homes to many natives, the racial hierarchy had to be strictly institutionalized and constantly maintained. In fact, older Ghanaians still recall the days when certain sections of Accra were reserved for European missionaries, colonial administrators, and other White residents. Mr. Proven,[12] who was one of Nkrumah's close friends at the dawn of independence, told me that racial apartheid during those days was not so much formal as it was naturalized. "We knew where we could and couldn't go," he said, "The colonial masters did not have to use force to keep us out of their areas; we learned our place early on in life."[13] Mr. Proven's recollection demonstrates that once authority was institutionalized through racialized practices, it did not necessarily need to be enforced through the use of force. As Fyfe reminds us, "District Officers did not have to flourish revolvers to carry on their day-to-day routines. White women did not need a gun to take them to the front of the queue. Their white skin was warrant enough to confer authority and privilege" (1992, 19).

Racial apartheid was the result of an explicit shift not only in British colonial policy, but also in the nature of European and African interaction in the Gold Coast. Because the African and European interaction on the West African coast dates back to the late fifteenth century, the late Ghanaian historian Adu Boahen tells us, "the most surprising aspects of the imposition of colonialism on Africa were its suddenness and its unpredictability" (1987, 1). Others would argue, however, that the transatlantic slave trade and slavery—spanning the fifteenth through eighteenth centuries—had already transformed the landscape of West Africa (and the continent more generally). This catastrophic practice brought about a restructuring of social and political relations on the coast and inland, where local practices of "domestic slavery" converged with those of chattel slavery to forge a peculiar situation in which human beings vacillated between full-scale humanity and commodity. It is telling that both (racialized) chattel slavery and (nonracialized) domestic slavery existed within the same time and space (see Crowder 1968; Ajayi 2002; Perbi 1997; Lovejoy 2000). Chattel slavery in West Africa expanded the demand for domestic slavery, intensified and expanded wars, and ultimately left behind a tumultuous environment in which race, power, culture, and religion structured relationships.[14] By the time of the suppression of the slave trade and European partition and control of the continent in the mid-1880s, there were already considerable transformations in the relationship between Africans and Europeans on the west coast. Commercial integration of European and African societies and economies, particularly along the costal regions, also depended upon political negotiations and complex social interactions. An important aspect of this integration was the development of a middle stratum of elite Africans[15] and Euro-Africans—merchants and middlemen, a wage-earning class, a crop of educated clergy, intellectuals, and barristers—who were differentiated from the local indigenous population in part because of their cultural and economic links to European merchants and religious leaders on the coast (Boahen 1987; Buah 1980).

This elite group was part of a new generation of wealthy African intellectuals and merchants that became a political and economic force during the waning decades of the transatlantic slave trade. Mostly located in the coastal towns of Cape Coast, Accra, and Takoradi, this diverse group quickly consolidated power. From the late seventeenth century through the end of the nineteenth century, members of this group served as teachers, clergy, doctors, civil servants, law clerks, journalists, and academics within the growing European imperial project in West Africa. They were also responsible for a flourishing journalistic and intellectual tradition with a cosmopolitanism that would continuously challenge the emerging colonial state and its excesses (Buah 1980; Baku 1990; Gocking 1999). It is significant that many of these intellectuals took advantage of opportunities on the coast and served also as merchants. Roger Gocking has argued that this dual role reflected more than just economic specialization; instead, "as trading activities became more complex, entry into the more lucrative levels of the capitalist system depended on mastering some degree of Western education." Here, the role of the Christian missions in expanding this group is significant, providing the critical link between Christianity, civilization, and commerce—the "Three Cs" (1999, 58).[16] Throughout the nineteenth century, the African elite formed the backbone of the establishment of European enterprise on the cost. In fact, in the immediate aftermath of the establishment of formal colonialism in West Africa, Africans staffed many junior-level posts and half of the senior posts. In the Gold Coast, Africans were members of the legislature from the 1850s; in Lagos (Nigeria) and Sierra Leone, it was much the same (Fyfe 1992). In the 1880s, the Gold Coast's most senior judge and medical officers were Africans, often enjoying the same pay scale as their European colleagues (Gocking 2005, 41). Some scholars have even argued that the relationship between Europeans and this educated and wealthy elite at this time was one of relative equality and stability (Táíwò 1999; Boahen 1987).

By the closing of the nineteenth century, however, this relationship would be radically transformed as the formalization of colonial rule in the Gold Coast depended on the establishment of official and institutional racism. Consolidation of British power on the coast came after the departure of the Danish and Dutch in 1850 and 1868, respectively. In 1874, the Crown Colony was created with the transfer of colonial headquarters from Cape Coast to Accra in 1877 (Parker 1998). By the 1880s, Britain's new imperialism facilitated the shift from direct to indirect rule, whereby "British imperial ideology discarded its charter of an African civilizing mission and began to adapt itself to law and order administration under the formal colonial order" (Korang 2003, 43). In the new colonial grand scheme of things, there were "now only two salient distinctions: European and Native. Europeans were white, natives were anything not white; and to be a nonwhite 'Euro-African' was to share with the 'African' . . . the same inferior exchange value as *native* compared to a superior white caste" (40). The African educated and business elites, now rendered homogeneously native by the incorporation of indirect rule, were quickly stripped of once-prominent positions in church and state and replaced both by a new crop of European administrators and their new local agents, the chiefs.

Colonialism, of course, is a system that depends on the administration's commercial, financial, educational, and military institutions. Some of the important areas through which we see the institutionalization of the colonial racial order were the colonial service and economic enterprises, among others. The prominence of Gold Coast elites was directly tied to the small number of Europeans in West Africa. With advancements in medicine in the mid-1800s came improving health conditions for Europeans and thus an increase in their population on the coast. The colonial state Europeanized the upper positions in the civil service, expelling both local African officers and West Indians of African descent.[17] Gocking gives the examples of Dr. John Farrell Easmon, the chief medical officer in the Gold Coast, and Henrick Vroom, a district commissioner for the British. In 1894, Easmon was unceremoniously removed from his position and run out of the Colonial Medical Service; the new British governor demoted Vroom "on the grounds that he was a native of the Gold Coast" (1999, 84; see also Patton 1989). While employing Europeans instead of Africans in West Africa was a more expensive undertaking for the colonial government, it seemed justifiable given the views of Africans as inferior and untrustworthy (Padmore 1969).

Arguably the most far-reaching consequence of formal colonialism and racialized indirect rule was the near complete control of the Gold Coast's emerging economy and its trading relations by European firms. As entrepreneurs and agents for European trading firms, Africans were integral to this expansion. Gold mining and trade in timber were rapidly growing, and the Gold Coast became the leading producer of cocoa as an export crop. Meanwhile, large scale trading companies and banks, such as the British Bank of West Africa and Barclays Bank, greatly expanded their portfolios. With discriminatory loans and concessions from the colonial government, European trading firms and mining and timber companies quickly created an expatriate oligopoly controlling all wholesale trade and retail (Howard 1978). Throughout the colonial years, European companies that joined forces and formed close contacts with European banks and shipping companies monopolized the Gold Coast economy. Except for a very few individuals, the class of African entrepreneurs, who usually owned small-scale companies, were excluded from the major economic activities on the coast. They could not compete with the large European monopolies that, because of their economic and political influence in the metropolis, freely obtained credit lines as well as access to local and international markets. They were also specifically refused credit because of racist assumptions about African trustworthiness and lack of business acumen.[18] In the economic field that was open to Africans—cocoa farming and harvesting—farmers had to contend with their inferior bargaining positions vis-à-vis the European-controlled international cocoa exchanges. Moreover, while European businesses had full access to exploit the territory's ample natural resources such as gold, timber, bauxite, and diamonds, they paid token compensation in rents and royalties (Howard 1978).

Howard has convincingly argued that had Ghana been a nation-state rather than a colony, "the expansion of European monopoly control over its economy might not have been so rapid or so complete" (1978, 22). Europeanization depended not only on the racial-cultural demotion of Africans to natives but also on the Africans' political and economic underdevelopment. Colonial economic and political control was key to the racialization process and the establishment of White supremacy. In the Gold Coast, as elsewhere, it was imposed through a system of inequality based on racial difference that granted differential access to goods, services, property, opportunity, and even identity. This racialization was tied to juridical and constabulary apparatuses of colonial administration. For example, in addition to preferential treatment in business concessions, the colonial state "acted as a mechanism to maintain law and order in Ghana, preventing any rebellion

The Royal Pavilion at Accra Palaver.

1.1 Visit by Edward, Prince of Wales (later Edward, Duke of Windsor), to the Gold Coast in 1925. Source: The National Archives, UK.

against the Europeans; as the agent of the metropolitan bourgeoisie; and as a moderator in conflicts between the different sections of the metropolitan bourgeoisie" (23). White racial privilege and European supremacy pivot on the structural racialization of the colonial project. The many institutional arrangements based on this racialization were soon understood and experienced as common sense, dominating public and private relationships and constantly reinforced by established practices.

Indirect rule enabled these structural racialized relationships of power. They came to be regarded as part of the natural order of things. But because the "natural order" was not so natural, it had to be continuously maintained on social and cultural levels. For example, the popular staging of grand durbars in the colonial Gold Coast worked to reinforce the structural positionings of nativeness and Blackness versus Europeanness and Whiteness. Grand durbars demonstrated the spectacle of imperial posturing that depended on the explicit visual representation of Whiteness and its tropes. In these stagings, British administrators orchestrated elaborate public ceremonies to contrast the symbols of White, European imperial rule with the display of Africans as tribal subjects (Shipley 2003). For example, the durbar to commemorate the 1925 visit of Prince Edward to the

The Ga Manche.

1.2 "Great Palaver of Head Chiefs" on the Accra polo grounds, at which Prince Edward is introduced to the chiefs. Source: The National Archives, UK.

Gold Coast revealed the White racial spectacle of colonial administration. The prince was impeccably dressed in an all-White naval uniform with pith helmet and accompanying sword, and he stood on stage with other similarly dressed Europeans, facing down the multitude of erratically dressed "natives," including the native military forces whose members were dressed in shorts and were left barefoot (ibid.). In these and other ceremonial roles, Europeans and Africans are inscribed in their racially hierarchical positions. At the same time, these ceremonies evoked what the British colonials felt to be a moral duty to God, Crown, and country—a duty used to justify colonialism's racial and cultural hierarchy. It is a duty that was directly linked to the "hegemonic discursive frames" of Whiteness—such as notions of civilization, modernization, progress, development, and, importantly, the divine.

Nativeness and Europeaness were also simultaneously constructed and enforced through spatial segregation. Here, we can turn briefly to the ex-

ample of the planning and development of the city of Accra and the consequent formalization of racial apartheid through zoning laws and strictly
enforced rules of segregated socialization. Accra was chosen as the seat
of colonial power in the Gold Coast because it was considered a safe ha-
ven for Europeans who sought a place away from what were considered
"native-born diseases" (Parker 2000). The main catalyst for this designation was the 1862 earthquake that destroyed large parts of the city and
therefore created the opportunity for colonial reorganization and planning.
Colonial administrators moved their headquarters from Cape Coast and
set about to create a "piece of England grafted into the townscape of Accra" (MacDonald 1898, 199–200). From 1877, the city was redesigned and
planned by the British based on the principle of rigid (racial) residential
segregation. Colonial Accra was divided into three distinct areas: the European town and administration area (collectively, the Jamestown, Ushher
Town, and Victoriaborg neighborhoods); the European residential area
(the Ridge and Cantonments neighborhoods); and the native town (the
Adabraka neighborhood). The European town, also known as the European
Central Business District, was spatially organized around a port at James
Town that was to connect the Gold Coast economy to England. This area became the main commercial district of the colonial period, with docks, ware-
houses, headquarters of foreign (multinational) companies, banks, railway
terminals, and so on. Zoning and building codes were strictly enforced
to maintain what administrators believed to be a "European feel or atmosphere." Most of the colonial administration buildings and military bases
were located in the immediate vicinity to the east, in the neighborhood of
Victoriaborg.

The rigid enforcement of the policy of residential segregation also meant
clearly demarcated areas for European residences. The European residential
areas were built on the elevated parts of Accra; they were filled with large
houses on spacious lots, surrounded by parks and "green spaces." European
homes were also located near social services, such as the Ridge European
hospital, and outdoor recreational lots, spaces that doubled as clear physical enclosures of the residential areas. At the same time, the designated
native areas—particularly Adabraka and New Town—were, by established
law, to be separated from the European residential and commercial areas.
This de jure segregation was specific: European residential areas were to be
separated from the native ones by at least 440 yards of clearance through
what authorities called "building free zones," zones that stood as "an open
space, and . . . utilized for golf courses, race courses, cricket and football
grounds."[19] The green and open spaces were strictly reserved for European

View of the European Residential Area, Accra, across the Race Course.

1.3 Government photograph of a European residential area in Accra. Date unknown. Source: The National Archives, UK.

NATIVE VILLAGE, JULY 1911

1.4 Government photograph of a native village from an unknown area
in the Gold Coast, 1911. Source: The National Archives, UK.

extracurricular activities and sporting events. Thus, this spatial segregation "physically enforced racial boundaries and minimized 'racial pollution'" (Bush 1999, 76).

This segregation was often not pursued in an explicit *racial* language. Instead, as the colonial archive demonstrates, spatial planning and segregation were often justified in the languages of health, hygiene, and sanitation, as well as sociocultural preference. In his *Dual Mandate*, for example, F. Lugard would presage this justification with the argument that: "what is aimed at is a segregation of social standards, and not a segregation of races" (1922, 150). Yet, colonial authorities worked especially hard at maintaining what they considered to be the integrity of the European residential areas and, in the process, protecting the integrity of racial Whiteness. Through the position of the medical officer of health, for example, explicit rules were drawn up for residents in the residential areas of the Gold Coast. These included restrictions on the native population—especially children and "servants' wives"—within the residential areas, even as members of this population were needed for labor.[20] Directives from the colonial medical department also required that male domestic servants' children be "rigorously excluded from the [residential] area . . . and that petty trading by wives should be specifically prohibited."[21] These requirements were always made from a "principle [that was] exceedingly simple—from a sanitary viewpoint."[22] Significantly, Europeans who did not uphold the residential color bar were often fined.

Residential segregation was bolstered by discrimination in the provision of education and healthcare and through the development of a social color bar. The colonial health infrastructure was segregated and linked to the need to limit contact between Europeans and natives. Hospitals and other health and social services were segregated. Even later colonial progressive educational policies depended upon indirect rule's racialist distinctions between African educational needs compared to those of Europeans. For example, the British colonial administration sought the aid of the Phelps Stokes Commission to establish a blueprint for primary and secondary education in its West African colonies. The object of establishing a specialized educational program was based on the dictum of indirect rule whereby the presumed radical racial-cultural difference of Africans determined colonial policy. Thus, for the governor, the object of education for the natives was "not to denationalize them, but graft skillfully on to their national characteristics the best attributes of modern civilization" (Kay and Hymer 1972, 279). Moreover, the plan was to discourage "literary education"—which was seen to be responsible for a "glut of clerks" and for the "false sense of values [in Africans] in which the dignity of labour is lost sight of" (280)—in favor of vocational and technical training based on the model promoted by African American Booker T. Washington at the Tuskegee Institute in Alabama.[23]

While there were no blatant signs forbidding Africans to enter establishments or to be served in them, European-run clubs, bars, hotels, and churches all operated under the color bar and practiced segregation. This was often "justified on the basis of the undesirability of too much 'social intercourse'" (Bush 1999, 77–78). During the interwar years in the Gold Coast, for example, it was not considered appropriate to invite Africans into European homes, and only a few rare and exceptional men were accepted as "honorary Europeans." The bars and social clubs of athletic teams and sports clubs were the most resilient in the years immediately before political independence because they were considered private and not subjected to the laws of the colonial authorities. Yet, Colonial Office policy on what would soon be understood as "colour discrimination" was never explicitly

ACCRA. New European Hospital.

1.5 Government photograph of a European hospital in Accra. Date unknown.
Source: The National Archives, UK.

codified. Indeed, most colonial officials would have denied the existence of a racially structured apartheid even while condoning it in practice and while holding views that "assumed different racial capacities and . . . required different policies for different 'races'" (Wolton 2000, 35).

Studies on colonial racism have recounted the numerous ways that the colonial state apparatus established White supremacy and maintained power (Bush 1999; Frederickson 1982; Young 1995). Yet it remains important to explore how the creation of the native and the European depended on the racecraft of indirect rule that set the foundation both for a structural White supremacy and anticolonial racial consciousness among Africans. At the same time, it enabled the obfuscation of the enduring legacy of White supremacy in the political and economic structures of the Gold Coast because African racial consciousness was ultimately expressed in the language of "tribe" or "ethnicity."

1.6 Coronation Day garden party at the Government House, Accra. Date unknown. Source: The National Archives, UK.

## Of Natives and Blacks: Responses to Indirect Rule

The colonial state's hegemony, though formidable, was never complete. But because indirect rule established and reinforced ethnicized (and religious) collectivities, for example, dissent by the colonized often took the form of revolt against local hierarchies—and, in particular, against the Native Authority. Thus the various forms of unrest throughout the Gold Coast and other British colonies came first within various ethnic (or tribal) settings, with protests against, among other things, forced labor, totalitarian chiefs, local taxation, and land disputes. We find a powerful example of the deployment of local laws in the rise of the influential the Gold Coast Aborigines' Rights Protection Society (ARPS). Established in 1897 in protest of the British Crown's proposed lands bill—a bill that would give the colonial authorities full claim to all local lands deemed, by such authorities, open and unused—this society used the customary law of property in the Gold Coast to make the claim that all lands were communally owned and held in trust either by family heads or by the chief (the native authority) for the local people. The deployment of customary law and the claiming of an ethnic legitimacy in this way worked to reinforce both localized (ethnic or tribal) affiliation and a racialized nativity. Among other prominent organizations that emerged within the displaced African educated elite was the National Congress of British West Africa (NCBWA), organized by Gold Coast intellectual and politician John Casely Hayford. The NCBWA's leadership first sought to exert direct influence on colonial administration. They demanded African participation within colonial legislative councils and equality in employment appointment, compensation, and advancement for similarly qualified Africans and Europeans. The group also exploited indirect rule's bifurcated ruling system to make the case against colonial influence over "traditional" indigenous customs (Buah 1980).

Both the NCBWA and the Aborigines' Rights Protection Society sought to ensure local rights while acting as representative to natives as a racial *collective*. It was, of course, the practices of racialized categorization and exclusion that fueled a racialized collective consciousness. We see this rise in racial consciousness particularly among the growing numbers of urbanized natives "who were beyond the lash of 'customary' law but were excluded from the regime of 'civilized' rights [and kept] on the margins of a racialized civil society" (Mamdani 1999, 875). Thus, the educated class of Africans, "legislated by race" and "colonially constructed as undeservingly native," but "ethnoculturally as not native enough to be deserving" of political status, would soon arrive at a collective self-consciousness about their

"Africanness" (Korang 2003, 45). Significantly, members also charted a return to Africa and the claim to an African identity or African personality—both simultaneously appropriating the colonial discourse and claiming an African autochthonous cultural past—that reflected the interplay of localized nativity and collective racial solidarity.[24]

The development of a parallel reaction of race consciousness resonated with the response of educated African and diaspora elites to late nineteenth-century scientific racism. These reactions included the development of Ethiopianism, a form of African religious nationalism, and, later, a cultural, intellectual, and political Pan-Africanism that ranged from an intellectual revolution that centered on a vindicationist tradition to the various Pan-African Congresses (1900–1945) to the development of branches of Marcus Garvey's United Negro Improvement Association throughout Africa and the diaspora (Boahen 1987). Key nodes in this powerful anticolonial reaction were the West African press and intelligentsia, whose major players, as we will see in chapter 4, insisted on the internationalism and cosmopolitanism of a collective African identity.

African response to the structures of indirect rule occurred, then, on two fronts: tribal/cultural and racial/national. These two fronts clearly point to the interrelation of local and global forces in the making of African and Black identities. The logic of indirect rule was that Africans belonged naturally to "tribes." And the creation of tribes was bound up with the reification of White supremacy such that tribal Africans were uncivilized and governed by custom while Europeans were of civilized *nations* and governed by law. While working within the local tribal language of custom to challenge colonial rule on the ground, the African Gold Coasters were also forging a national and international self-consciously racial movement. As Akyeampong rightly observes, "The opposition of nation and tribe transformed African nationalism into a struggle by Africans to be recognized as a race, as 'Africans,' and as a race to gain access to the world of rights, to the community of *civilized societies*" (2006, 313; italics in the original). With direct links to groups of African descent—many from British colonies in the West Indies and Africa, and from both throughout West Africa and the metropolis—educated Africans were drawn into the structures of global White supremacy and forced to respond. Practices of racial discrimination in Britain, the Caribbean, and the United States were directly connected to racialized colonial rule and fueled a radical, transnational critique of oppression while forging Black racial unity (Adi 1998). While this unity would eventually enable a successful anticolonial movement, its ambivalent and unresolved tensions with the "customary" ultimately resulted in the inability to address and dismiss the structures of White power and privilege.

The examples of some of the key practices of racial colonialism in Ghana should demonstrate that we cannot understand how popular notions of ethnicity, nationalism, and culture are deployed in African communities without recognizing the ways they are refracted through ongoing processes of racialization effected by the practice of indirect rule. My specific aim in this chapter has been to demonstrate the ways that the racializing process of nativization powerfully impacted African sociopolitical and cultural fields in ways that uphold the structures of race.

## Racialization, Nativization, and Decolonization

Colonialism in Africa was based on a concept of indirect rule that was structured through racial apartheid, separating White Europeans from a Black constellation of tribes, ruled by their individual traditions. Unlike many who understand this racial apartheid to be a process of exclusion, Mamdani demonstrates for us that it was rather a form of *incorporation*, pulling the racially constructed natives into the fold of colonial power. But the strength of indirect rule was the fact that its power was concealed within the structure of the local native authorities, rendering the racial despotism of colonial rule almost invisible and hidden behind a constructed local one. This holds true even for the "urbanized" natives in the towns, who endured racialized spatial and social segregation because they continued to be sorted and treated in terms of the "customary." In this sense, racial dominance was hidden beneath identities and arrangements deemed "tribal" and hidden beneath local articulations of power. Colonial racecraft institutionalized White supremacy while attempting to diffuse a racialized counterhegemony through the operationalization of tribal differences. While the racist practices of Europeanization enabled a form of racial transcendence of these tribal differences, this transcendence would not diminish the significance of such differences. After political independence these differences became the locus of discussion in the formation of a new national identity, effectively leaving intact the economic and political structures supporting White supremacy.

The historical processes of nativization allow us the room to understand how discussions about race and identity in Ghana are both absent and imminent. Nativization concretized the shifting modes of self-conception that had begun at the moment of contact and submergence within the forces of European empire making (the slave trade and formal colonialism); it gave Africans race and shaped them culturally, politically, and materially as "Black" within a global hierarchy of privilege and powerlessness. At the same time, the mode of implementation in the process of nativization localized and fragmented that self-conception; Africans were also (and primarily) "tribal" or "ethnic," with seemingly autochthonous traditions that cemented and naturalized the idea of ethnicity. Forcibly locked within the quotidian materiality of a localized ethnicity, the nativized, with prominent exceptions, had to articulate her or his needs in local terms. But making sense of these local terms—and the nature of postcolonial societies more generally—requires a particular fluency in the broad language of race, empire, and domination.

# TWO

# "Seek Ye First the Political Kingdom": The Postcolony and Racial Formation

Seek ye first the political kingdom and all other things shall be added unto you.

—Kwame Nkrumah, *Ghana*

It may be fairly easy to understand that new nation-states, emerging from imperial or colonial oppression, have to modernize their institutions, their modes of government, their political and economic structures. Very well. But why then adopt models from those very countries or systems that have oppressed and despised you?

—Basil Davidson, *The Black Man's Burden*

Political independence is inadequate when it is accompanied by inherited and continued economic dependence for markets, goods, capital, technical skills and personnel on one or a very few economically larger states and their firms.

—Reginald Green and Ann Seidman, *Unity or Poverty?*

Colonialism has greater and wealthier resources than the native.

—Frantz Fanon, *The Wretched of the Earth*

In launching the state-sponsored biennial Pan-African Cultural Festival (PANAFEST)[1] in Accra in 2001, vice president Alhaji Aliu Mahama proclaimed: "The NPP government attaches importance to these celebrations for various reasons. Ghana's role as the beacon of hope for the Black Race cannot be compromised for Ghana has, since independence in 1957, served as the catalyst for regaining the dignity of the Black race" (Mahama 2001). Mahama continued by reminding his audience of the "pioneering role

Ghana played just after independence [in] encouraging other African and Black countries then under colonial rule to struggle for political emancipation" (2001). Ghana's "role in the emancipation struggle was not limited only the African continent," he said, but to all frontiers in the world where the Black Race suffered discrimination and oppression." Mahama's Pan-African rhetoric and racially conscious narrative has a long history in Ghanaian politics. It dates as far back at least to the rise of the "middle stratum" in the nineteenth century, the traditional intellectual elite, and the emergence of African racial consciousness in the context of a stifling and shifting colonialism. At the dawn of independence this was given renewed meaning as African racial consciousness was linked to postcolonial self-determination. It signaled a shift in the colonial racial project: "Africanization," in the broadest political sense, was to gain a new valence. Kwame Nkrumah was the first to bequest Pan-Africanism official status within the newly independent state. He sought to harness the cultural politics of racial consciousness for national unity and development. But what was the purpose of deploying Pan-Africanism when Ghanaians had, in Nkrumah's words, already gained the "political kingdom"?[2]

This chapter takes this question as a point of departure to explore certain vectors of racial formation in the postcolonial state at independence. If colonial rule depended upon a racial hierarchy that "nativized" Africans through the simultaneous consolidation of "tribal" difference and White racial and cultural and political supremacy, what happens to this structure at independence? In other words, what happens to racial processes at the end of formal colonial rule? I contend that we have to view Nkrumah's and the new Ghanaian state's racialist Pan-Africanist ideological orientation alongside, if not as a response to, the continuation of institutional White privilege on the ground through economic and cultural domination within a global political hegemony. There is hardly a doubt that, for the postcolony, political independence never meant full economic or even political control. But if colonial political and economic structures—structures that enabled the institutionalization of a racial hierarchy and attendant White supremacy—were carried through to the postcolonial moment, then it must follow that the racialized practices of such structures did not disappear with independence. This chapter argues that at independence, the social and political field enabled the coexistence of a number of often competing racial projects, with two of the most prominent being, first, the racial and cultural dynamics that emerge from sociopolitical and economic relations between the former colonialist government and the new independent state, and, second, the emerging state ideology of Black self-determination. In this way, Ghanaian racial formation at independence was a complex set of sociocultural and political projects, whereby a new postcolonial African racial renaissance struggled against the realities of persistent local ethnogenesis, racialized foreign economic dominance, and an undoubtedly disadvantaged global political positioning.

This discussion is about the complex nature of racial politics at the dawn of independence. It focuses on two of the main competing racial projects at the time. On the one hand, there is the colonial racial project of indirect rule that had to be dismantled upon independence. On the other, there is an African national and Pan-African racial consciousness that served as the ideological motor of independence. How did the new state—and its peoples—navigate these two projects? At independence the Ghanaian state had to deal with both the ideological and structural racecraft of the colonial state while it simultaneously attempted to affirm an African and pro-Black self-determination. But one of these tasks appeared easier than the other. Because of its deeply structural nature, the racialized sociopolitical and economic power of the colonial state proved almost impossible to extinguish. The legacy of its inequitable practices was also buoyed by the demands of Cold War politics and the emergence of a powerful United States. Consequently, the Pan-Africanist ideals of the Nkrumah government, and perhaps African racial consciousness and self-determination, seemed only nominally powerful. At best, this Pan-Africanism became a discursive response to a structural postcolonial dilemma.

My examination begins with a brief theoretical discussion of the shift from indirect colonial rule to independence and the transformation of state racecraft. The point here is to explore the available options for full decolonization and subsequent democratization. I then focus on the negotiations of Nkrumah's government, run by his Convention People's Party (CPP), with the postcolonial realities of global politics and the effects of such negotiations on local ideas of race, ethnicity, and governance. This account is hardly exhaustive. But I hope to demonstrate how racialization processes directly informed the new postcolonial state where: (1) institutional White power and privilege were structured into the neocolonial relationship with Britain, the United States, and the West in general; while (2) Pan-Africanism and African racial self-determination served as ideological and cultural, but ultimately ineffective, responses. These processes, and the other racial projects that they inevitably spawned, continue to shape the contemporary Ghanaian social, political, and cultural fields.

## Racialization, Ethnogenesis, and Decolonization

At the dawn of independence African societies had a tripartite agenda of deracialization, detribalization, and economic development in an unequal international context (Mamdani 1996, 287). As we saw in the previous chapter, the colonial state was bifurcated based on a dual racial-vertical and ethnic-horizontal structure—a group of indigenes ruled by an ethnically defined native authority, himself under the rule of White officials "deployed from a racial pinnacle at the center" (287). Thus, colonialism took on two forms: one, a "civil society" based on notions of civil and human rights (available only to the European colonial rulers); the other, a society based on custom and culture (available only to the nativized subject). With indirect rule, African racial difference was built into the variegated native identities and experienced on the ground as such. At the same time, White racial power and supremacy were built into the colonial state apparatus through economic, cultural, and political edifices and practices. In this context, decolonization would have to mean the dismantling of these racial projects: White racial supremacy (Europeanization) and the concurrent tribal/ethnic fragmentation (nativization). Once dismantled, these projects would then allow for a truly democratized postcolonial state, the strength of which would eventually enable African parity in the global political economy.

None of this three-part decolonizing agenda for postcolonial Africa was completed. The fact that African bodies replaced European ones in the state political apparatus is often read as "Africanization," with the implication that African access to the political realm removed racialization as an important factor in the postcolonial social field. Yet, the appropriation by Africans of certain administrative positions did not fully mean the erosion of the accumulated privilege of Whiteness in the former colonies. To understand this point we have to recognize that the racial character of colonial rule extended beyond the European control of administrative apparatus. It was, as I demonstrated in chapter 1, institutionalized in economic and social relationships. Thus even the attainment of political positions by Africans was by no means a complete exchange of power. The decolonization process in Ghana was gradual and depended on the retention of some of the most important structures of colonial rule. In this context, deracialization—which would necessitate the full replacement of foreign businesses and industries, as well as their primarily European staff and economic advisors, with local enterprise and staffing—could not be fully pursued.

It was the same with the second vestige of colonial rule: tribal affiliation or ethnic differentiation was neither reconfigured nor dismantled in the making of the nation; in some cases it was reaffirmed. Because the form of colonial rule (indirect rule) determined the form of dissent against the system, ethnic/tribal affiliation came to be entrenched both in the anticolonial struggles and later in the process of nation making. According to Fanon, decolonization was supposed to unify people "by the radical decision to remove from it its heterogeneity, and by unifying it on a national, sometimes a racial, basis" (1967, 46). Yet nativeness—and the ethnic or tribal authorities it represented—continued to be significant to the new national identity, often in unproductive ways. Full de-ethnicization, therefore, failed to take hold, and its reassertion made it difficult to present a united challenge to the carryover structures of White racial power. The failure to detribalize—that is, the reassertion of ethnicity—also meant that the structure of the bifurcated state remained in place, with power diffused (and contested) through a "multiplicity of ethnically defined Native authorities" who maintained the top-down political structure and agenda enforced on the peasantry (Mamdani 1996, 288). In most postcolonial states the chiefs retained their role as the enforcers of "customary" law, reproducing "tradition" while at the same time ending up at odds with the new nations' centralized style of (electoral) government. Some postcolonial states, such as Ghana, either attempted to both recognize the chiefs and curtail their power in the new governing structure, while others, such as Kenya under Jomo Kenyatta, tried to modernize tradition (Shaw 1995, 129). Ultimately, however, these approaches split national governing strategies into an uneasy friction between "traditional" and "modern" forms of power while replicating the "decentralized despotism" of the colonial state. These were tough odds. Without democratization—that is, bringing the various native authorities into the fold of a national (and racial) collectivity—then, the new states would be unable to establish effective rule that would benefit the colonial state's inheritors. Consequently, these new nations did not have the necessary structures to manage the realities of the global political economic hierarchy and the new states' marginalized position within it.

True decolonization in postcolonial Africa demanded no less than the full uprooting of the bifurcated colonial structure: decoupling Whiteness and power (a "de-Whitening" or Africanization) *and* dismantling or reformulating the basis of ethnic identification (detribalization). What we see happening in Ghana and other postcolonial states, however, is a shift in focus with the emergence of the new state. Where once the colonial state's practices—and in particular its racial and social hierarchies—were the targets of social justice and decolonization movements, these were now associated with the newly independent state's governing apparatus and, in particular, the political party. At the same time, the fact that the new state now had African leadership meant that the government's practices could no longer be challenged in explicitly racial terms. This was the case even if certain state apparatuses still reflected White European foreign economic and political domination. Independence therefore ushered in a new moment during which the effective economic and, specifically, racial imbalance (and White privilege) of the colonial period was hidden beneath the new politics of the state. Meanwhile, the new state's ideological promotion of Pan-African politics further hid any discrepancy.

In the following section, I briefly examine some aspects of the process of decolonization in Ghana to demonstrate their relationship to racialization. Focusing on Nkrumah's prominent role in the ideological and political making of the new nation-state, I discuss how his actions—within the context and constraints of a colonial legacy and postcolonial global politics—simultaneously challenged and enabled the retention of key aspects of the colonial apparatus. In the process, I show how he left a particularly contradictory legacy of racial and state formation that would reverberate through to the present.

## Nkrumah and the Political Kingdom

Ghana marked its fifty-year independence in a 2007 year-long "Golden Jubilee" celebration. The festivities were launched with a media blitz, with an official website that covered everything from Ghana's history to instructions for foreign dignitaries, media, and tourists. By the time I arrived in Ghana in mid-February 2007, the celebration was well under way. From the road leading out of the Kotoka International Airport into the city of Accra, some commercial billboards were plastered with congratulatory messages from businesses, while others invoked the historical import of this anniversary with pictures of the "Big Six"[3] and, in particular, of Kwame Nkrumah. Many of the government-sponsored billboards mounted staged pictures of president John A. Kufuor either in conversation or posing side by side with Nkrumah. The message seemed clear: Nkrumah and Kufuor were counterparts in the triumphant journey of African independence and self-determination. The paintings and calendars in artists' corners throughout Accra carried a similar message. In addition to the abundant artworks honoring the fathers of the nation and Pan-Africanism, there were many representations of Kufuor's symbiotic relationship to Nkrumah. Street vendors hawked calendars and other products reflecting similar themes. Accra itself was awash in the tricolors of the national flag (red, gold, and green) and representations of the flag's black star on cars, on light posts, on the tops of buildings, and in trees. The official "Ghana@50" symbol was conspicuous—it appeared on billboards, on commemorative anniversary cloths, on dishes, cups, and mugs, on television commercials, and in newspapers.

The Ghanaian government seemed not to spare money or detail in demonstrating its role in "Championing African Excellence," the anniversary's theme. Planned official events included marches by the Ghana Armed Forces, musical concerts, academic conferences, films, and a reenactment of the parliamentary motion for independence in 1957; unofficial events were almost innumerable. The state-sponsored events were scheduled throughout the country—but mostly in Accra—for the entire year, with each month under the banner of a specific subtheme: February was "Towards Emancipation"; April was "Our Nation, Our People"; June and July were "African Unity Month" and "Diaspora Month," respectively. What emerged for me throughout these weeks in Ghana was the official and popular deployment of the political ideology of Pan-Africanism through reclamation of the memory of Kwame Nkrumah. Accra was remembered as Nkrumah's Pan-African capital, and, more importantly, Ghana was the gateway to African self-determination and the rising "African personality." In this sense, the subthemes of "African Unity," "Diaspora," and even "Our Nation, Our People" all continued to resonate with Nkrumah's legacy.

For the ruling National Patriotic Party (NPP) to claim this legacy was of no small consequence. Its members are descendants of Nkrumah's formidable opposition, a group with roots in the traditional elite and marked by cultural and political allegiance to the British. They presented perhaps the greatest challenge to both Ghana's new nationalism and Pan-Africanist politics.[4] For elderly members of Nkrumah's Convention People's Party and other Pan-Africanists familiar with this history, it must have been jarring to see billboards with President Kufuor's picture superimposed over Nkrumah's with Pan-Africanist slogans. The contemporary CPP boycotted the festivities, while other former members expressed embarrassment over the indiscriminate use of Nkrumah's legacy. Despite these misgivings, it was clear that Ghanaians embraced not only Nkrumah but also his message of Pan-Africanism, racial determination, and African unity. And this message seemed to saturate the charged celebratory atmosphere of Ghana's fiftieth anniversary.

Few personalities have had as much broad appeal and influence on African self-determination as Kwame Nkrumah. All across the world, and particularly among Black intellectuals and politicians, Nkrumah's political significance and ideological legacy have spawned a near cult following

2.1 Osagyefo Kwame Nkrumah, first president of Ghana.
Source: The National Archives, UK.

during and after his rule. In Ghana, Nkrumah's popularity waned after the 1966 coup d'état but resurged in the late 1980s with the military government of John J. Rawlings. Rawlings was able to capitalize on Nkrumah's Pan-Africanist rhetoric, deploying it against the national political malaise spawned by the realities of economic underdevelopment and policies of rapid liberalization. I contend that Pan-Africanism worked in similar ways for Nkrumah. While he genuinely believed in African progress and self-determination and the role of his new state in the fight for continental freedom, Nkrumah's Pan-Africanist rhetoric ultimately obscured the reality that Ghana's nationalist ambitions were severely constricted by the predicament of postcolonialism: an underdeveloped and bifurcated polity within the context of an unequal and racialized global political economy.

As with the anticolonial struggles and contemporary politics, Nkrumah's nationalist Pan-African rhetoric provided the necessary *racial* counterbalance in the face of consistent African marginalization. As Frantz Fanon reminded us, "The lack of culture of the Negroes, as proclaimed by colonialism . . . ought logically to lead to the exaltation of cultural manifestations which are not simply national but continental, and extremely racial" (1967, 217). Nkrumah's speech at independence demonstrated exactly what was at stake for Africa and Black people: "Today, there's a new African in the world, and that new African is ready to fight his [sic] own battle and show that after all the black man is capable of managing his own affairs. We are going to demonstrate to the world, to other nations, that young as we are, we are prepared to lay our own foundations" (Ankomah 2006, 4). He correctly articulated the mood of global Black communities. This was a reckoning, of sorts, he seemed to proclaim, and Ghana was leading the way. And in the process, its Pan-Africanist nationalism would help to dictate some of the terms of racial formation on the ground and in relationship to the outside world. Through both rhetoric and action, the newly independent Ghanaian state became the site of a continental and racial Pan-Africanism as well as the center of Black liberation.

Because Ghana's independence offered a symbolic racial redemption for Black populations worldwide, diaspora Blacks, in particular, flocked to Ghana at independence (a story I take up in chapter 6). The important examples here are the Trinidadian George Padmore and the Black American W. E. B. DuBois. Padmore organized, with C. L. R. James, the International African Services Bureau in London, and he is known as the "father of African emancipation" (James 1977). It was the bureau that first sponsored Nkrumah's trip to the Gold Coast in 1947 to begin preparations for an African revolution. While in London, Nkrumah worked with Padmore to organize the Fifth Pan-African Congress in Manchester, England, in 1945. This congress was significant in that, for the first time, it included an increased participation of Africans and its agenda was primarily focused on the question of colonialism on the continent. It was at the congress that Nkrumah became close to DuBois. He would later bestow Ghanaian citizenship on DuBois in his waning years. Nkrumah's government also agreed to sponsor DuBois's project, the Encyclopedia Africana.[5] Beginning in London, Padmore was a close advisor to Nkrumah. He later became Nkrumah's special advisor on African affairs and his most trusted confidant until Padmore's untimely death in 1959. During that time he had a particular influence on the new state's foreign policy. Some historians interpret Padmore's role as being to carry through Nkrumah's policy "for the emancipation of those parts of African still under foreign rule and therefore to work with nationalist movements and political parties, an area of activity which it would be inappropriate for civil servants to engage in at the time" (Adu quoted in

Afari-Gyan 1991, 4).[6] Padmore's work, thus, was to direct affairs in line with his and Nkrumah's vision of Pan-Africanism (Afari-Gyan 1991).

When Ghana first became independent, Pan-Africanism took on new meaning. It was part of official state ideology as well as the state's practical programs and symbols of self-representation. In particular, state symbolism reflected Nkrumah's admiration of Jamaican-born activist Marcus Garvey. In his biography, Nkrumah recalled that "of all the literature that I studied, the book that did more than any other to fire my enthusiasm was *Philosophy and Opinions of Marcus Garvey*. Garvey, with his philosophy of 'Africa for the Africans' and his 'Back to Africa' movement, did much to inspire the Negroes of America in the 1920's" (1957, 45). The black star symbol of Garvey's organization, the Universal Negro Improvement Association and African Communities League (UNIA), became ubiquitous, synonymous with Ghanaian independence: Independence Square was adorned by a large black star; the star was also in the center of the nation's new flag, which adopted Ethiopia's tricolors of red, green, and gold; and later, the national soccer team was nicknamed the Black Stars. Moreover, Nkrumah's government established a national shipping corporation under the name of the Black Star Line, recalling the transatlantic shipping line established by Marcus Garvey to promote global Black trade and commerce.[7]

Nkrumah's view of Pan-Africanism was one that balanced the *political* imperatives of newly independent African states with recognition of racial dimensions of global Black identities. The very institutions and ideologies of the postcolonial Ghanaian state, then, were produced through recognition of the need to maintain the links between African politics, emerging nation-states, and the Black diaspora (Pierre and Shipley 2007). This understanding no doubt emerged from Nkrumah's own experiences as he moved throughout the Black world on both sides of the Atlantic. As Kevin Gaines recently noted, "Nkrumah's route to the leadership of postindependence Ghana was steeped in the circuitous routes of diasporic black modernity" (2006, 39). In this Nkrumah was not alone; his predecessors, Edward Blyden, J. E. Casely Hayford, and James Aggrey, all early twentieth-century African promoters of African self-determination, moved through intellectual and political Black Atlantic circuits. Yet, although Nkrumah's Pan-African nationalism was clearly reflected in both his promotion of continental independence and his relationship with diaspora Blacks during his administration, he held a position that was "race conscious in appealing for the assistance of diaspora blacks for nation building yet maintaining a principled commitment to nonracialism in solidarity with the struggles of Africans, peoples of African descent, and colonial peoples the world over"

(157). He was also very practical in his relations with diaspora Blacks. In a visit to the United States shortly after he became prime minister, Nkrumah was explicit about how he envisioned Ghanaian-diaspora Black interaction. Treated to a hero's welcome in U.S. Black communities, Nkrumah recalled the "bonds of blood and kinship" binding Ghanaians (and Africans) to African Americans. He would later tell an audience: "Back at home . . . we think of them still as our brothers, and we can assure them of a warm welcome whenever they chose to visit the land of their forefathers" (*New York Times*, July 29, 1958). Yet he specifically appealed to "doctors and lawyers and engineers to come and help build our country" (*New York Times*, July 28, 1958).

On the ground in Ghana, Pan-Africanist ideology was also given pragmatic form in the Nkrumah government's foreign interactions. Because Nkrumah's dictum was that the independence of Ghana was meaningless while the rest of the continent remained under colonial rule, his government sought to help in the continent-wide fight against colonialism. He sponsored the All Africa People's Conference in Accra in 1958, which brought together for the first time anticolonial forces and freedom fighters (Afari-Gyan 1991) to work for the demand of a resolution to colonialism and imperialism and to promote an agenda for continental political unity. But the new country's quest for African liberation was not only limited to hosting conferences. Nkrumah established the Bureau of African Affairs[8] to monitor and aid in emerging anticolonial uprisings, and a national security council that was responsible for the military aspects of Pan-Africanism, including training camps for African freedom fighters. Nkrumah's government also offered asylum to refugees from South Africa and Portuguese Africa and to militants from the Black world, and it provided education for students from across the continent (Apter 1972). At the same time, Nkrumah's dedication to continental African independence led to major national expenditures abroad, including the notable example of a £10 million loan to Guinea at independence when France abruptly withdrew from its former colony with all equipment and services.

In many respects, Nkrumah's—and Ghana's—early Pan-Africanism, both ideological and practical, is a well-rehearsed story. The effort here is to highlight some key moments in the making of the new postcolonial state that have heretofore been neglected: the structural and racial counterpoints to ideological Pan-Africanism. Indeed, it is to the credit of Nkrumah and other nationals that the memory and practice of Pan-Africanism is the recognized national story. Ghanaian governments since Jerry John Rawlings's have held on to this narrative of the nation's identity as emerging from a radical, humanist, and at times socialist Pan-Africanism. But how does this Pan-Africanism merge with Nkrumah's consistent railing against the dangers of neocolonialism? It is this relationship that demonstrates the context of postcolonial racial formation: an ideology of Pan-Africanism against both continuing foreign—and predominantly White—economic control and persistent ethnic differentiation in an unequal global world.

In his discussion about Ghana's transition from colonial to self-rule, historian David Apter makes a telling observation: "At a rally on a Sunday, Nkrumah may damn the 'imperialists,' but on Monday he sits down to work with them in the sleek modern offices of the secretariat" (Apter 1972, 293). Apter's analysis of the decolonization process reminds us how the new nation's transition to independence was more politically and culturally conservative than radical. Barbara Calloway and Emily Card echoed many others in arguing that "despite Nkrumah's flamboyant denunciation of imperialism and his avowedly socialistic statements, his actual policies were clearly pragmatic and conciliatory" (1971, 66). This is an important point to remember because it forces the question: What where the parameters of political and economic choice for this new African state? More directly, what were Nkrumah's options and how did his government manage them? A description of the process of transition, if partial, is important for our study because it provides a counternarrative both to the usually emphatic assumption of full Africanization—at all levels of society—and to impressions of the diminishing significance of race at independence. To begin with, Ghana's transition from colony to nation was not borne of revolutionary anticolonial struggle, military or otherwise.[9] It occurred through a long process that moved from what some called a diarchy beginning in 1951, when Nkrumah shared power with the British, to full political independence in 1957. During this period, Nkrumah's position and relative power was fully dependent on the British colonial authority and its associated administrative apparatus. The "shared" government worked with the White European staff conducting the majority of quotidian administrative details, an arrangement that, even with African members in the now integrated cabinets, ensured British control. But this "shared" period served to satisfy nationalist calls for African self-determination only by masking continued colonial control, even with Africans in key positions. In truth, the material and symbolic colonial apparatus remained in place. Apter describes the political and symbolic environment of this transition period in this way:

> It can hardly be forgotten, however, that the Gold Coast is still a British colony. The picture of the queen is found in government offices. The secretariat

is still full of an expatriate complement. . . . The governor drives to the hall
in his Rolls Royce, wearing a plumed helmet. . . . Preceding the governor's
car, mounted troops on black horses canter down the processional route carrying plumed lances, wearing green or red Zouave jackets, while a military
band drawn up on the green strikes up "God Save the Queen." . . . It is impossible to measure just what meaning such symbols do have upon Gold
Coasters in any wide numerical sense, but there is little doubt that they have
helped to maintain the prestige value of British and parliamentary authority.
(1972, 277)

The process of decolonization, in effect, "was designed to protect the
institutions of colonial domination" (Marshall 1976, 50). The first way in
which this was done was through the maintenance of the cultural and racial symbols of empire, the "prestige and value" of British rule prominently
expressed through the formal spectacle of racialized White pomp and pageantry and the promotion and performance of European competence. The
second protective measure of these institutions was through the parliamentary structure and the party politics. With the colonial staff as the technical
and electoral tutors within this shared-power arrangement, there was never
a complete break from British influence. This was perhaps most crucial in
the economic field. In particular, as Judith Marshall demonstrates, decolonization worked not only to protect state and foreign companies from any
radical challenge but also to "bring the commercial and bureaucratic bourgeoisie into alliance with imperialism" (ibid.).

In seeking the political kingdom, Nkrumah and his political party,
the CPP, made compromises that reflected the contradictory nature, and
compromised position, of a nonrevolutionary transition mediated by and
through the terms of the former colonial master. It is true that the CPP
emerged through Nkrumah's split from the earlier nationalist group, the
United Gold Coast Convention (UGCC), because of that group's timid demands for independence. The CPP was known as the radical party that was
impatient with the conservative demands of the UGCC. It supplanted that
group's slogan of "independence within the shortest possible time" with
"self-government, now!" By the time the CPP actually gained power—importantly through the electoral process initiated and directed by the colonial government—that radicalism had already been co-opted. At the end of
the day, the "nationalist movement was skillfully channelled [sic], via the
conciliatory posture of the colonial administration, into narrowly political
solutions" (Marshall 1976, 51). The gradual transfer of power through an
imbalanced diarchy was contingent on the expertise of the colonial staff

and an assemblage of other European expatriates—not only those serving as consultants and advisors, but also the business elite who controlled broad sections of the country's extractive and trading economies. The CPP, and Nkrumah specifically, depended on the British administrative apparatus: they planned and supervised elections, thereby conferring legitimacy to the new party. In this way, the British not only added to the force of their symbolic presence in the Gold Coast, they also maintained their handle on material power. And they used this power as a bargaining tool against nationalist demands.[10] In short, the nationalist demands of the CPP were, from the start, effectively defanged. When qualified control of this political kingdom came, Nkrumah and the CPP spent as much time consolidating the party's electoral power as they did attempting to transform the entire colonial system, particularly its economy.

In truth, British imperialism "could cede the 'political kingdom' in order to maintain the substance of economic domination" (Marshall 1976, 51). And Nkrumah was quite aware that political independence and economic dependence were incompatible and would never lead to his ultimate goal of making Ghana the modern industrial center for the African continent. It was because of this—as well as because of his strong belief in the need to vindicate African dignity—that he sought to fast-track the state's modernization schemes. But he took over a new Ghana that, economically, was a paradigmatic colonial society. The economy was an extractive one, dominated by the export of one major crop, cocoa. The other extractive raw materials, gold and diamond, were under private foreign ownership. There were no other industries; manufacturing was almost nonexistent. In addition, the colonial state had controlled cocoa production as a means of tax revenue.[11] As a result, while private businesses were able to operate within the global capitalist market, cocoa farmers suffered extremely low prices for their goods because the colonial—and, later, the Nkrumahist—state determined the margins, often against the gains of the global market.[12] Because of the consolidation of European firms, along with the concomitant disenfranchisement of Ghanaian businesses during colonialism, foreign expatriate firms fully controlled Ghana's business community by independence. Indeed, "90 percent of import trade was controlled by foreign firms; 96 percent of timber concessions were owned by foreign firms, all of the country's gold mines and half of its diamond concessions were foreign-owned, and banking and insurance were overwhelmingly dominated by foreign firms" (Handley 2008, 152; see also Esseks 1971). Accordingly, the business community formed what Handley calls a "pyramid structure," with large multinational European firms at the top; medium-sized Indian, Lebanese, and

Levantine businesses at the middle; and small-scale African traders in large numbers at the bottom. This pyramidal structure, we should remember from the previous chapter, emerged through racially inflected practices that enabled monopolization by European companies through denying local businesses necessary credit and effectively keeping Africans out of the local and international markets. Thus, the racial implications of having White expatriate control of business is clear, as these business structures reflected an institutional arrangement that privileged White Europeans and Levantine populations at the expense of Africans. And because these European multinational companies were tapped into the global market, they ultimately, though arguably, had more clout than the new state. The racial dimensions of this arrangement, while hardly a point of discussion for scholars (at least beyond their recognition), is important to keep in mind as we explore the Nkrumah government's attempts to both Africanize and industrialize the new Ghana.

In Nkrumah's Pan-Africanist vision, Ghana was to serve as the leader of a gradually industrializing Africa. This meant economic independence with African control of both the state and the political economy. It is for this reason that "his Pan-African policy was intimately tied up with his plans for Ghana's internal economic development" (Callaway and Card 1971, 76). The first step, then, to a developed, economically independent, and ultimate socialist Ghana was industrialization. This was distinct from merely replacing European bodies with Africans, as "Africanization" sometimes narrowly implied (though that too remained an issue). For Nkrumah, foreign expertise could be used—as long as it led, ultimately, to full state control of political and economic enterprises. His government embarked on massive development projects that sought to industrialize and modernize Ghana in the shortest possible time. As a Ghanaian government economic consultant pointed out, "Nkrumah was a politician in a hurry" (Anin 1991, 10). There was enormous growth in infrastructure, roads, the provision of electricity, the founding of commercial banks, and a number of manufacturing enterprises. There were also more schools, hospitals, first-class roads, better prices for cocoa, and, with increasing Africanization in the civil service, more money for a better standard of living for many (Owusu 1970). But while Ghana had a relatively large monetary reserve at independence, it was primarily based on cocoa, and it would certainly not be able to support the massive industrialization schemes of the government. Moreover, the "absence of large accumulations of private capital in Ghanaian hands meant that only the state or foreign sources of capital could promote the basic services and industries" (Callaway and Card 1971, 77).

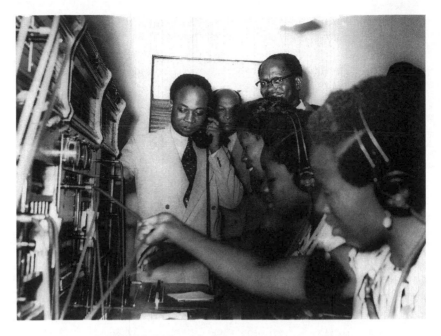

2.2 Prime Minister Nkrumah at a communications center in Accra.
Date unknown. Source: The National Archives, UK.

Nkrumah's government recognized that these facts were the result of colonial rule and felt that it could resolve them through massive state involve-
ment and investments in the provision of these services. At the same time,
the forces of neocolonialism—which Nkrumah often decried (1965)—were
apparent in the ways that the banking and commerce industries, with the
blessing and assistance of Western powers, were able to both manipulate the
Ghanaian economy and influence politics. It is important to recall here that
during formal colonial rule British and other European firms formed monopolies that fixed prices that engulfed trade in the Gold Coast to squeeze
out African middlemen. For example, British companies—with government
sanction—secured complete monopoly of the country's gold reserves. Representatives of these companies exploited the colonial state's structures of
indirect rule and worked through local chiefs to gain virtually unlimited
mineral concessions, paying very little royalties on their profits (Padmore
1967). Moreover, the extraction of resources and revenue from the colonies
continued unabated through the postcolonial period. Basil Davidson em-
phasizes this point: "the extraction of wealth from an already impoverished
Africa was in no way halted by the 'transfer of power.' A transfer of pov-

erty continued as before, even while the means of transfer were modified or camouflaged. When the boom in raw material prices collapsed . . . the direct political control of territories in Africa could be safely passed to the colonized while at the same time ensuring that these territories remained subject to the overall financial and commercial domination of . . . the West, meaning essentially the United States and its European partners" (1992, 220). The new state's financial reserves and monocrop economy—both inherited from the British—could not afford to undertake the massive industrialization projects it promised the people without private investment. In the absence of an effective local Ghanaian capitalist class to invest, the foreign private sector, local and international, came to play a commanding role in Ghanaian economics and ultimately impacted local political developments. Moreover, the government failed to attract much foreign investment or to find alternative sources of funding. Thus, very early on, the new state's restricted options and its own political strategies together placed it at the mercy of creditors. As Callaway and Card point out, this meant "more influence for foreign capital than ever before in Ghana's history. This is particularly true in view of the fact that most debts of private capital in Ghana were *guaranteed* by [foreign] governments" (1971, 85; italics in the original). A perfect example of this predicament is the Volta River Project, the centerpiece of Nkrumah's grand scheme for Ghana's rapid industrialization.

The Volta River Project (VRP) was part of a comprehensive scheme for Ghanaian development and industrialization. It consisted of a hydroelectric dam on the Volta River in conjunction with the building of an aluminum smelter and bauxite processing plant in nearby towns. In the 1920s, the British colonial government found large deposits of bauxite, which it wanted to exploit for Gold Coast development (and which also would have provided Britain with a cheap source of aluminum production in the context of rising global demand). Upon coming to power, Nkrumah seized on this project as a means to bring his industrialization plans to fruition and began the journey down the long road to development under African control. Once it was complete, the VRP would enable Ghana to produce its own power, and the associated refinery would convert the raw bauxite into aluminum for export. But the costs for such massive investment were great. During the period of the diarchy, Nkrumah and the CPP partnered with the British government; the British government would provide some funding alongside some private firms. But the British pulled out of the scheme right after independence, citing rising economic difficulties in the metropolis. By the time he took over political control of the new nation in 1957, Nkrumah was in a bind. His campaign to power promised industrialization and development, and now he was desperate to have something to show the people. More-over, he strongly believed that the dam was the key to Ghana's industrial, and truly independent, future.

In an important and ironic twist of fate, the VRP gained renewed life af-ter a racist incident involving Nkrumah's finance minister, K. A. Gbedemah. Gbedemah was on a private visit to the United States in 1958 when he and his secretary, Bill Sutherland, were refused service in a restaurant in Dover, Maryland, because they were Black. The incident with Gbedemah made it into a Washington newspaper and caught the attention of U.S. President Eisenhower. Since the United States had come under increasing worldwide attack—particularly by Russia and the communist block—for its Jim Crow policies and the disenfranchisement of Black Americans, officials were wary about the backlash of this event.[13] Moreover, Eisenhower recognized that as the first of new African states, Ghana would present an opportunity for the United States to have a stronger presence on the continent. Gbedemah was issued an official apology from the U.S. State Department and invited to breakfast with President Eisenhower and vice president Richard Nixon. As a result of this breakfast, the United States became involved with the VRP. In later correspondence with Nkrumah, the U.S. government made a dual offer. It would first act as a catalyst to bring together interested private firms to finance the aluminum smelter and bauxite mines; then, it would make a substantial loan to power the project (thereby underwriting the investments of the U.S. private companies). With loan guarantees from the U.S. govern-ment, two firms, the Kaiser Corporation and Reynolds, took on the project. They would invest money in the dam and build the smelter, which would, in turn, be powered by the electricity generated by the dam. However, rather than use Ghana's large bauxite deposits, Kaiser insisted on importing baux-ite from the United States; moreover, it demanded and received a below-market rate for the plant's power supply, guarantees that its taxes would not be increased for a substantial period, and the retention of full convertibility of all net profits for at least thirty years (Green and Seidman 1957). By the time Nkrumah learned of these conditions, his government had invested so much time, energy, and political capital in the VRP—while simultaneously having little access to other foreign investors—that it had no choice but to proceed under these extremely unfair conditions.[14]

The Volta River Project was either a curse or mixed blessing. Nkrumah's political opposition thought it was too large and costly; contemporary ana-lysts view it both as a symbol of Nkrumah's bold vision of industrialization and as a reason for Ghana's delayed development potential. Most agree that the project's contractual arrangement was an exploitative one, with the foreign companies accused of riding roughshod over Ghana's cowering marginal position in the broader global political economy.[15] However, the VRP also provides the clearest example yet of how the complex mix of options available to the newly independent state—and the concomitant circumscribed strategies employed by its first leadership—inevitably led to an intractable neocolonial predicament. Ghana was effectively at the mercy of foreign interests from the first years of political independence, with foreign capital and its foreign personnel having a greater influence than ever on the ground. What this means, additionally, is that the structural legacies of foreign—and primarily White Western—control remained virtually intact in the postcolonial era. In fact, at the formal inauguration of the Volta River Project, Nkrumah noted this irony. After thanking all the parties involved in the scheme, especially the United States and the Kaiser Corporation, he conceded:

> We live in a world of contradictions. These contradictions, somehow, keep the world going. . . . Ghana is a small but very dynamic independent African State. We are trying to reconstruct our economy and to build a new, free, and equal society. To do this, we must attain control of our own economic and political destinies. Only thus can we . . . free [our people] from the legacies and hazards of a colonial past. . . . In such a world we certainly need great friends. The United States is . . . the leading capitalist power in the world today. Like Britain in the heyday of its imperial power, the United States is . . . adopting a conception of dual mandate in its relations with the developing world. This dual mandate, if properly applied, could enable the United States to increase its own prosperity and at the same time assist in increasing the prosperity of the developing countries. (Nkrumah 1965)[16]

To compare the U.S. dealings with Ghana in this project with the British colonial policy of the dual mandate is to recognize an important reality of the postcolonial predicament. Nkrumah's words seemed melancholic; at the very least, they reflect a certain acceptance of a situation, a circumscribed postcolonial condition, in which the protuberant power of colonial control underwrites the euphoric present of independence.

Indeed, by the time of Nkrumah's fall in 1966, foreigners dominated most large-scale commercial ventures in the country (Handley 2008). For his part, Nkrumah enabled, if not promoted, the Western "expert" in the pursuit of Ghana's industrialization. Many of his advisors—in government, education, on the economy, and even his personal secretary—were holdovers from the colonial government. In the realm of business development, the CPP government, attentive to its ideology of socialism, virtually impeded the growth of a local private sector, even as it courted and subsidized foreign private investment (see Anin 1991 for examples). And as Handley argues, even as the Ghanaian government "began to shift its strategy and to foster a home-grown set of private enterprises, state and foreign interests had already been accorded deciding dominance of the economic terrain" (2008, 157).

As a matter of no small importance, this dominance was also reflected in the racial politics tied to the issue of personnel working in these foreign enterprises. In the industrialization scheme, both state and foreign private firms often argued that the skilled workforce of the foreign investors was an attractive part of the deal. While the Gold Coast, and later Ghana, boasted of one of the most highly educated and skilled populations in Africa at the time of independence, in 1960 non-Ghanaians made up 48 percent of the skilled workers employed by foreign firms (Callaway and Card 1971, 79). If we combine that percentage with the obvious saturation of foreigners involved in Nkrumah's government and many industries, the numbers are staggering. While there is no official tally of the racially White upper administrative and commercial positions, the fact that there was a consistent demand to Africanize (or "indigenize") these industries in order for Ghana to have more political and economic control is testament to the reality of this issue as an important problem. Moreover, Stephanie Decker points out that while the public sector had a considerable local Ghanaian presence soon after independence, the private business sector kept a significant expatriate presence well into the 1980s (2010, 794). In reviewing the corporate archives of five major British firms practicing in Ghana and Nigeria that had considerable prominence in their respective sectors, Decker found that Africanization in the private sector was much slower than in the civil service. At the same time, the new independent governments were reluctant to use legal means to coerce foreign companies to diversify their personnel. In addition, foreign companies that did begin to diversify their staff did so primarily to appease new parties and in the most superficial ways, for example, by promoting Africans to prominent, but nonexecutive, directorships (Decker 2010). These directors were no more than figureheads, often serving as a front for the foreign business to improve its local image in the face of local demands for Africanization: "Without necessarily being aware of it, foreign companies had not really opened their internal professional networks for development and promotion to most African employees, as the significant gatekeepers in the firms still found it difficult to identify 'potential' or 'character' in recruits whom they perceived as fundamentally different from themselves. The result was a 'glass ceiling,' albeit one that shifted upward over time" (800).

Significantly, the attitudes of the White managers of foreign firms consistently betrayed their racialized defense, however understated, of their slow and often unsuccessful efforts to Africanize their companies. In particular, White managers charged that the African could not be trusted and needed fundamental changes in character, or, more popularly, they questioned African ability to truly advance. Thus, even as there were no overt discussions of African racial inferiority (at least recorded), it is noteworthy that Africans were assumed to be fundamentally different and unable to reach the standards of trustworthiness and competence. Even in the postcolonial context, it was obvious that this focus on African competence reflected the pervasive racist bias against Africans from colonial times. At the same time, it was also difficult for British foreign managers to measure African competence or trustworthiness because they had very little social contact with them—especially since Africans had little access to systems through which they might socialize with expatriate staff members. The expatriate staff in Ghana comprised primarily White, middle-class men who, because of their expatriate status, often socialized only with one another and whose movements were controlled by their companies (Decker 2010, 801). And they were also better compensated. This made for an inherently differentiated employment pattern, one that rotated on the axes of race, economics, and nationality. But it seemed that the new postcolonial state had its own justification for not redressing this situation. As Wallerstein argues: "The political leadership was furthermore reluctant to Africanize the bureaucracy totally because of its suspicions concerning the potential political role of this group. This reluctance to eliminate European personnel was reinforced in many cases by the fact that their salaries were not met out of the local budget, so that Africanization would have been all the more expensive" (1971, 29). In later years, the social and cultural distance between European expatriates and some of their African colleagues lessened, if only marginally. Owing in part to the constant pressure on these foreign companies to train locals, Africans gained more prominent administrative positions. Ironically, this also broadened the gulf among the Ghanaian classes, particularly through the rise of what can be considered a local technical bourgeoisie. Nevertheless, structural and racialized differences remain, even as Ghanaians have been able to infiltrate some of the administrative positions in private companies. While there is little research that examines the correlation between this uneven diversification, the increasing number of African managers, and continued foreign dominance of the economy, the point is that this foreign dominance has significant cultural and racial consequences. I explore some of these consequences in the next chapter; in particular, I focus on the privileging of Whiteness and White bodies as they are constructed through ideologies of White competence and technological superiority.

If there were alternatives to the expatriate technical and economic supremacy, they were not easy to define. The overwhelming constraints on effective deracialization—and the attendant displacing of White European economic and political hegemony—demonstrated the overall difficulties in establishing a fully independent nation that did not carry vestiges of colonialism. If full deracialization was configured within the compromised and conscripted nature of independence, what of detribalization? The answer lies partly in Nkrumah's relationship to both the local Ghanaian business community and his dealings with the inherited political structure of the Native Authority. With a political ideology that saw Ghana as a rapidly industrializing African nation on the way to a socialist society, there was a case to be made against the growth of a national bourgeoisie. It was assumed that such bourgeoisie would reinforce a certain tribalism through clientelism and, even if inadvertently, the sedimentation of the powers of the Native Authority. Nkrumah saw both of these institutions as impediments to national consolidation and, ultimately, continental Pan-African unity. His engagements with these two institutions are telling, and they further explain the ways that postcolonial Ghana ultimately retained and reinforced colonial patterns.

In the effort to curtail the growth of a national bourgeoisie, Ghana's industrialization schemes focused on foreign monetary and technical support at the expense of a local equivalent. Some scholars have argued that Nkrumah felt it safer to deal with foreign private business interests than local ones because he feared the challenge to his political control (Esseks 1971; Anin 1991). Others insist that Nkrumah was focused on industrialization through which the state, rather than the private sphere, would eventually lead Ghana's economic decolonization (Card and Callaway 1971). Nkrumah believed that foreign private investment was first necessary to transform Ghana's economy into a mixed one. Once this was achieved, expanding state enterprises would be able to compete with foreign firms, gradually restricting their access to, and privilege in, Ghana's markets. But we have to keep in mind that the colonial administration had already enabled the marginalization of the local Ghanaian business class through its support of the monopolization of its firms from the metropolis. Thus, there were few local firms available to participate in the large-scale industrial schemes undertaken by the new independent state. At the same time, both the state's leading role in joint state-foreign private agreements with foreign firms and its early reluctance to promote the local private sector worked to impede local enterprise. On top of this, Nkrumah's administration had the tendency to give more privileges to expatriate than to indigenous firms (Handley 2008; see also Akinsaya 1982).[17] The state, under the CPP, instead focused on expanding its own role as the main engine of the Ghanaian economy, even as European- as well as Syrian- and Lebanese-owned businesses flourished (Handley 2008).

Chieftaincy and its institutional base, the Native Authority, also posed a major constraint on decolonization efforts. As we saw in the previous chapter, a clear feature of the colonial program of indirect rule, the institution of the chief and attendant native authority, was difficult to incorporate into the new national identity. The new independent state developed through parliamentary party politics and the rise of the CPP, but in a context where it needed to overcome the tribal or ethnic groupings and cleavages that were the foundations of indirect colonial rule. The early nationalist movement, directed by educated middle-class professionals, often used prescribed nativeness as a tool against colonial rule. At the same time, according to one view, these professionals viewed themselves to be "the logical heirs to colonial rule." For this Westernized middle group, "their vision of an independent Ghana was one in which they would play the same paternalistic role as the colonial administrators before them, instituting a black 'indirect rule' over their less educated brothers" (Callaway and Card 1971, 68). In this scenario, the chiefs would maintain roles similar to those allotted them under British colonial rule. The rise of Nkrumah and the CPP, however, transformed this vision; its goal of the complete dismantling of colonial political and economic structures and modernizing Ghana meant, of course, that the Native Authority and attendant chieftaincy would have to be reconfigured, if not dismantled.

By its very composition, the early CPP stood to transform the narrative of local power. The CPP cast its net wide to embrace the masses, claiming among its supporters the youth, low-income workers, and farmers (Buah 1980). The masses also existed outside of the means of traditional power and had no access to the accoutrements of the traditional elite. In this vein, unlike most Ghanaian nationalists before him, Nkrumah had no royal lineage (ibid.). Members of the UGCC, however, were considered elitist and conservative in their demands for self-government. But the CPP propaganda machine worked to promote the need for a national movement to ensure the complete dismantling of the colonial system. In this sense, loyalty was to be to the emerging nation-state and against the key site of colonial rule, native rule, and tribal affiliation. Many saw chieftaincy as corrupted by colonial rule. Where chiefs and kings existed before the advent of colonialism, indirect rule accorded them more power than before; because they served as "sole native authorities" for the colonial power, they were only beholden to the British power structure (Crowder 1964). For the CPP leadership and its supporters, many of whom considered chieftaincy to be the site of their general malaise, immediate dismantling or reform of the institution was necessary for full decolonization.

From the start of its shared power during the diarchy, Nkrumah's CPP sought to "rid the country of what many of their activists regarded as the anachronism of chieftaincy" (Rathbone 2000, 158). Moreover, once the CPP began to gain power during the diarchy, its members saw chiefs as competitors for sovereignty, which was similar to their view of local entrepreneurs. The Local Government Ordinance of 1951, passed by the colonial authorities, and with the support of the Nkrumah government, allowed for dismantling the Native Authority by eliminating its treasuries and transferring its assets to newly created urban and local councils (van Rouveroy van Nieuwaal and van Dijk 1999, 57). In this way, the administration of the revenues of the former Native Authority was transferred to the state, which then distributed them through local councils. The ordinance allowed for elected local councils to replace native authority. The Chiefs Act of 1959 empowered the central government to have full control over recognizing or deposing chiefs (Boafo-Arthur 2007). Thus, from the beginning of full political independence in 1957 until its overthrow in 1966, Nkrumah's government "minimized the political and judicial roles of traditional rulers, broke their financial backbone and made them passive appendages to the central government" (Brempong 2006, 30).

Yet, in the process of dismantling the Native Authority by defanging its chiefs and centralizing its functions, the CPP surreptitiously acted similarly to the colonial government. The CPP undermined chieftaincy through local government reform. This made sense because the CPP wanted a centralized government in order to create a unified country (Rathbone 2000). But the problem was that local committees, often filled with CPP members, worked to undermine customary authority through the party (Brempong 2006). In other words, the CPP seemed focused on party loyalty as a means of reorienting the former Native Authority toward a new unified and fully democratic state. The CPP, in effect, lost itself in the party and also to the state.[18] It did not help that, from the time of the diarchy until the consolidation of Nkrumah's one-party state, there was a wide range of regional (and ethnic) opposition. The British had ruled Togoland, the Northern Territories,

Ashanti, and the coastal territories as separate regions. In the drive toward independence, Togoland and the Northern Territories were not necessarily keen on rule by a CPP party that they felt favored the coastal and urban regions of the south. But crucially, the traditional elites from Ashanti were to become the most effective opposition to the CPP through their party, the National Liberation Movement (NLM). The NLM was a regional and ethnic organization, and its opposition to the CPP was to demand a measure of regional autonomy. According to Buah (1980), the NLM was not only perturbed by the CPP's popularity, but it also did not agree with Nkrumah's push for a unitary government. Its leaders saw the CPP's push for too much centralized administration as a clear sign that Nkrumah was leaning toward a dictatorship. Moreover, the NLM as well as the Northern People's Party (NPP)[19] and the Togoland Congress (TC) sought to access national political power through regional and ethnic positions and loyalties. Thus, the entrenchment of chieftaincy and "native" distinctions during the colonial period ultimately created the conditions for the deployment of these distinctions as the basis for political opposition.

While Nkrumah did manage to dismantle large aspects of the Native Authority and diminish the power of the chieftaincy, the "CPP-fication" (Owusu 1970) of local government and, more importantly, Nkrumah's ever-tightening grip on the central government actually reinforced those divisions. In an essay on the shifting relations between a modern postcolonial government and the "tribal consciousness" developed and consolidated through indirect rule, St. Clair Drake argued that while these colonial powers carved out new political identities and manipulated ethnic differences to "divide and rule," it is "only in the period of nation-building that these differences become a matter of supreme concern. If not handled with skill," he continued, "ethnic solidarities can make the consolidation of new states very difficult" (1963, 13). The CPP was, of course, hostile to regional federalization; nation formation under the promise of economic socialism depended on a unified country. Moreover, the CPP rightly believed that these regional differences reinforced colonial tribalism, and it was concerned to dismantle all of its unprogressive elements. But as the new state sought to contain such political parties and attendant regionalism, it became increasingly despotic with Nkrumah declaring a one-party state while persecuting his political enemies. Until the very end, Nkrumah believed that only a fully centralized government could rid Ghana of its colonial ethnic vestiges while preparing it for a socialist, and therefore more equitable, communism.

Thus, in the same way that the attainment of the political kingdom did not bring economic independence and instead left the country more beholden to foreign capital and its agents, it also did not remove the structures that encouraged ethnic differentiation or tribalism. One of the key problems of Nkrumah's and the CPP's actions was that the effort to deal with the colonial structures of nativism was not made in relationship to those of foreign White racial economic domination. If decolonization necessitated the dismantling of colonial structures, the tribal or ethnic articulations of indirect rule should have been tackled as part of that process. In this way, the racial distinctions underwriting economic differentiation between the foreign (White) population and the grouping of Blacks would have broken down. But then again, these efforts were pursued in an environment where the pressures of a new state, internal and external, were tremendous. The reality, as C. L. R. James reminds us, is that in the transfer of power, "the British government gave nothing, handed over nothing, fought to the last second to retain everything that it could, and when it was forced to retire, left the Gold Coast tied up in knots which Ghana will have to spend a long time untying" (1977, 150). And, while Nkrumah was combating the implosion of the CPP and rising local discontent, events such as the worldwide fall of cocoa prices in 1965, the consequent shortage of foreign exchange (as well as a freeze on credit by Western financial institutions), and Cold War politics quickly made the compromises of shared power and Ghana's neocolonial status apparent (Marshall 1976). Nkrumah felt increasingly entrapped by converging complications in his plan to industrialize and fully decolonize and modernize Ghana; he came to rely more on the rhetoric a radical Pan-Africanism. No doubt this was influenced by Cold War politics and the increasingly imperialist response to African decolonization (particularly Western complicity in the assassination of the Congo's Patrick Lumumba).

In the context of rising national economic crisis, such calls to Black racial solidarity against an encroaching new—and White—imperialism were difficult rallying cries. For despite its constricted options to redress the country's mounting problems, it was the Ghanaian state—and not the colonial administration—that was in charge and would bear the burden of a mass backlash. African self-determination was now African responsibility. The takeover of control of the economy held by foreign interests, while a constant reference for Nkrumah, could not fully materialize in the context of an increasingly repressive state apparatus, economic malaise, and marginalization in the global political economy. Moreover, as Judith Marshall has rightly argued, the CPP did not capitalize on the opportunity to establish a "revolutionary transformation of popular consciousness for real decolonization of the state with all its institutional, cultural and political consequences" (1976, 51). In truth, there was also not much more beyond the rhetoric of socialism and Pan-Africanism. People were not shown how theory could be operationalized.

But even before this turn, which would eventually lead to a CIA-backed coup,[20] Ghana's failed attempt to fully decolonize and become truly post-colonial with "all other things" to be added to it was already evident. In the end, European economic supremacy and structural privilege, and na-tivization in the form of persistent regionalism, were the true victors in the decolonization experiment. Perhaps a more important victory for neo-colonialism was the fact that the reconsolidation of European power and influence on the ground were no longer treated as the major culprits in Gha-naian economic and political marginalization on a global scale. Ultimately, "Direct military interference from international capitalism was unnecessary in Ghana. The quiet pressures through economic destabilization measures and through the cultural imperialism of Western-trained Ghanaians and of Western experts and volunteers sufficiently exacerbated the internal contra-dictions of the [CPP's] left option as to make a right-wing coup inevitable" (Marshall 1976, 55).

## After Nkrumah

It is not possible to give more than a sketch of Ghanaian state politics—and racecraft—after the overthrow of Nkrumah's government. Suffice it to say that with the military governments that followed Nkrumah's, at least un-til the PNDC under Jerry Rawlings, state rhetoric of Pan-Africanism waned while dependence on international capitalist interest grew. The coup spon-sors and victors, the National Liberation Council (NLC), imposed military rule and began issuing decrees to reverse CPP policies (Rathbone 2000). The NLC also sought to purge all relations with socialist countries and end talk of continental African unity. It banned national party politics, and it also attempted to rehabilitate chieftaincy by destooling[21] chiefs whose in-stallments were believed to have resulted from CPP patronage (Rathbone 2000). More significantly, the NLC was willing to manage the economy in the interest of foreign capital, selling off state industries to private capital and reopening the economy to transnational companies with liberalized import policies and fewer exchange controls (Marshall 1976). It is no sur-prise then that Apter describes the regime's administration as having "the character of a colonial system" (1972, 384). In other words, the first military government, in its quest to destroy the material and ideological imprints of the CPP, effectively established a mode of rule and social structure very much similar to that of the country's colonizers.

The three-step process of a proper decolonization—deracialization plus detribalization to lead to democratization—seemed a faraway option. And the ultimate failure of democratization further exacerbated the problem of an incomplete decolonization (deracialization and detribalization). As this postcolonial state with its monocrop economy and depleted national reserves confronted the international economy, its weak positioning provided an opportunity for further encroachment from outside. This resulted in "an externally defined structural adjustment" that stressed more privatization by foreign Western parties. "The result," as Mamdani rightly argues, "was both an internal privatization that recalled the racial imbalance that was civil society in the colonial period and an externally managed capital inflow that towed alongside a phalanx of expatriates—according to UN estimates, more now than in the colonial period" (1996, 288)![22]

In the immediate years after Nkrumah, there was no official state rhetoric of African renaissance or calls for self-determination and Pan-African unity. This would be the case until the rise of J. J. Rawlings and his "populist" government. But it is significant that the explicit critique of colonial (and neocolonial) structures through direct economic and political action is no longer part of the contemporary program of Ghana's rhetoric of national development. In the current climate state rhetoric touts a successful, modern, and democratized Ghana by linking the struggle for self-determination with the advocacy of IMF-style market liberalization (Ferguson 2005). Indeed, Ghana's liberalizing shift was foreshadowed even before Nkrumah's demise, as the economic downturn in the world markets in the late 1960s quickly helped to diminish the euphoria of political independence. The economic deterioration particularly dealt new African states a harsh blow as these nonindustrial states, reliant on the colonial economic structure of agriculture and mineral extraction, saw the deterioration of the global terms of trade and the beginnings of an unending debt crisis. It is a deterioration from which no postcolonial African state has recovered, and it continues to set the terms of engagement between rich Western countries and African nation-states.[23] The quick shift from political and economic independence to relative debt peonage and the consequent loss of real national sovereignty for African states is significant. It is not clear if Nkrumah could have avoided the liberalizing shift enforced by the Western racial capital elite that swept world economies in the 1970s. Nevertheless, successive administrators of the Ghanaian state increasingly framed national development in the neoliberal speak of creating conditions for foreign investors, the growth of the private sector, and, significantly, not in terms of explicit Pan-African political and economic cooperation.

One of the key consequences of the fall of Nkrumah's administration is that Pan-Africanism became less central to Ghanaian (and African) political practice and ideology. With time, the acknowledgment of explicit links between African politics and global racialized inequality was bracketed. Two decades later, the Rawlings administration revived the memory of Pan-Africanism and replaced Nkrumah's explicit *political* Pan-Africanism with a distinctively neoliberal and depoliticized version (the specifics of which I discuss in chapter 5). The current government has not strayed far from Rawlings's—and his successors'—program. Today, official state Pan-Africanism emerges primarily through a depoliticized rhetoric about cultural heritage and development tourism, such as the PANAFEST and Emancipation Day festivals.

## ". . . and all other things shall be added to you"?

In 2010, the Ghanaian government organized a year-long set of activities for Kwame Nkrumah's centenary celebrations. "Hundreds Troop to Ghana to Celebrate Nkrumah!," a *Daily Guide* headline proclaimed. The African Union and the government of Ghana jointly sponsored the main celebration program, which ran from May 22 to May 25, 2010. Under the theme of "Contemporary Relevance of Kwame Nkrumah's Contribution to Pan-Africanism and Internationalism," the celebrations were set to promote Nkrumah's "ideas, visions and policies" (*Daily Guide* 2010). It is fitting that the African Union should honor the man who never wavered in his call for African unity. Whether the African Union represents that power that Nkrumah envisioned is another matter. In official statements, state officials waxed eloquent about Nkrumah's role in the making of national identity. Nkrumah "opened the doors of Ghanaian politics, previously the exclusive domain of the educated elite and wealthy merchant class, to the ordinary people. . . . Above all [he] bequeathed to Ghanaians a sense of self-worth, national pride and dignity, and also embodied and promoted Ghanaian identify far beyond the shores of the African continent" (Sackey 2010). And indeed, across the Atlantic, in New York, African American state senator Bill Perkins proposed and led "Senate Resolution Celebrating the 100th Birthday of the late Kwame Nkrumah" "for his contributions to Pan-Africanism."

In the current moment, it is Nkrumah's Pan-Africanism and calls for an African renaissance and political unity that emerge most prominently.

This is a point that I take up in chapter 5 in my discussion of contemporary state racecraft. In the meantime, however, I want to point out how the celebrations of Nkrumah do not incorporate the other aspects of his legacy, namely, the call for economic independence and the forceful critique of neocolonialism. In the context of Ghana's position as a highly indebted impoverished country, this is significant. In truth what the focus on a rhetoric of African renaissance and unity—as opposed to Ghana's neocolonial predicament—reveals is that Nkrumah's expectation that "all other things shall be added" to the political kingdom did not come. Indeed, for some even the control over the political kingdom seems weak. While compared to other countries in Africa, Ghana continues to boast peaceful, secure, and democratic transitions of power, the various governments since Rawlings's Fourth Republic have only differed in name and flag, for they all have been feeding the population on a steady diet of structurally adjusted neoliberal economics, privatization, and state retreat from social responsibilities. It seems clear that we are far, far away from Nkrumah's promised "socialism" and African economic independence.

As a racial project, state-sponsored Pan-Africanism remains a key aspect of the Ghanaian social field. But it is definitely joined by other potent and contradictory ones. Economic dominance is very much racialized; as we saw above, and as we will see in the ethnographic example in the next chapter, one of the consequences of neoliberalism and the search for foreign private investors is the workforce of mostly White expatriates it brings into the country. But this neoliberalism and continued rising poverty in the developing world has also spawned what some are calling the "Non-Profit Industrial Complex" (INCITE! 2007) and the proliferation of foreign nonprofit agencies throughout the developing world, where many such organizations have undue influence on the local scene. There are other relationships and structures that point to the complex nature of racial formation in modern Ghana. Colonialism, of course, was an entire sociopolitical, economic, and, importantly, cultural regime that affected every aspect of the life of the dominated. While most of these institutions—education, law, religion, moral regimes—do not come under scrutiny in this chapter or this book, it must be assumed that they were erected to uphold racialized despotism, and colonial culture shaped them in its own Eurocentric terms (Comaroff and Comaroff 1992). But the two-faced character of rule—based on European civil society and African native society—also delineated a multifaceted response from Ghanaians. Pan-African racial unity and national consciousness is once again providing the call for racial consciousness. But this is at the expense of pointing out its link to a continuing and persistent neocolonialism.

This is occurring in the context of broader politics of race and power, privilege and subjugation. I have dealt with political and economic manifestations of racialization processes, but what of cultural and social responses? The next four chapters address this question through an ethnographic reading of Ghana's contemporary racial landscape. As I stated in the introduction, my focus on race does not mean that other aspects of identity are not important. The racial projects covered here, however, reflect not only Ghana's (and Africa's) relationship to a long history of slavery and colonial rule, but also the surviving colonial economic and political structures and "colonial cultural footprints" (Leonard 2010, 9) that these make on local relations. Indeed, the discourse of race in Ghana is a direct legacy of the structure of colonial rule that concealed racialized power beneath constructed ethnicized identity and politics. Through this history, racialized processes and power appear Janus-faced. On the one hand, colonial power elicited a racial response; on the other, it depended on a communalism based on ethnic differentiation. This is why we see in the Ghanaian local terrain that some racial projects challenge White racial power, while others affirm it. Thus, in Ghana, everyday mundane relationships may take on meaning and structure unequal power relations without an explicit reference to race. Nevertheless, there are other processes—such as the Ghanaian state's location within a transnational Pan-Africanist history—that are explicitly articulated as racial. These distinct, contradictory, and powerful "racial projects" articulate together to produce, sustain, and reproduce Ghanaian society in a "racially structured form" (Hall 1980).

# THREE

# "You Are Rich Because You Are White": Marking Race and Signifying Whiteness

But what on earth is Whiteness that one should desire it? Then always, somehow, some way, silently but clearly, I am given to understand that Whiteness is the ownership of the earth forever and ever, Amen!

—W. E. B. DuBois, *Darkwater*

It is evident that what parcels out the world is . . . the fact of belonging or not belonging to a given race. . . . The cause is the consequence; you are rich because you are white, you are white because you are rich.

—Frantz Fanon, *The Wretched of the Earth*

In nearly every aspect of my family's life in Ghana in the mid-1990s, our Whiteness mattered, for foreigners with light skin are accorded enormous privileges and status. . . . The ideology of white supremacy appeared to me to be pervasive in Ghana.

—Catherine Cole, *Ghana's Concert Party Theatre*

I remember the first time I walked into Champs, a popular sports bar in Accra known for its Mexican cuisine, its broadcasting of major international sporting events, its karaoke nights, and its lively clientele. It was a late Saturday evening in the summer of 2006, and I had accompanied a Ghanaian friend, Kemi, who was meeting a business acquaintance. I had not heard of Champs before Kemi mentioned it, even though, as I would later find out, it is well known among many inside and outside of Ghana. My first reaction as we ducked through the front door and stepped down into the basement-like venue was shock. This shock was quickly followed by extreme discomfort. Kemi, sensing my reluctance to move beyond the front door, put his arm around my shoulders, laughed heartily, and said, "Welcome to the expats' hangout!"

Champs is a boisterous place. Its patrons are primarily expatriates and overwhelmingly White. Although I was aware that such places exist in Ghana as well as throughout postcolonial Africa, and although I had been to other specifically "White" expat hangouts, this scene was much more intense than any other I had encountered in Accra. I stood by the door for a few more seconds and took stock of my surroundings. Across from the front entrance was a large, well-stocked, T-shaped bar with two bartenders, a young Black (presumably Ghanaian) man and a White woman rushing about and serving clients.[1] Around the bar were stools occupied by White men, many of them chatting with young Black women. At the back of the room, to the right of the bar, there were several pool tables and gaming machines—that area, too, was filled with people. In the back left corner was a kitchen bustling with Ghanaian cooks dressed in white shirts, pants, and hats, hurrying to hand out plates of food to the White waiters. Most of Champs' patrons were seated immediately to the left of the bar facing a large screen that was broadcasting a soccer game. They were sitting at a series of booths set along the wall or at tables that seemed to take up every square inch of the space. The place was packed with people and activity, and it was loud!

Champs Sports Bar and Restaurant is described online and in travel guides as the place where, in the words of a White British study-abroad student in Ghana, "you forget that you are in Accra." Perhaps it is its out-of-the-way location: you arrive through a nondescript entrance at the back of the Paloma Arcade, a Lebanese-owned hotel, restaurant, and gaming complex fronting Accra's busy Ring Road. But it is also the diversity of its predominantly White clientele. There are other expat hangouts in Accra catering to specific clienteles; Ryan's Pub, for example, serves mostly businessmen (and sometimes women). But Champs is different. There one can find Peace Corps volunteers stealing away from the village to "find civilization" in the city, European and Australian backpackers salving a nostalgia for home, anthropologists temporarily leaving their premodern ethnological sites, study-abroad students looking for real "American" food, UN and NGO workers spending their stipends, and foreign businessmen and, occasionally, businesswomen satisfying an after-work thirst. National, class, and professional differences among these expats seem to evaporate in Champs. Indeed, they seemed to have evaporated as quickly as the Accra streets I left outside, crowded with Black bodies.

My general unease about walking into a place like Champs stemmed from a contradictory sense that the scene was both familiar and peculiar. My very first thought after Kemi and I walked in was that, as a young woman who *looked* Ghanaian, I did not want to be mistaken for a prostitute. Indeed, Champs seemed familiar precisely because it was an expats' hangout—a relatively all-White space with few Ghanaian patrons and with the too-common feature of older White men accompanied by very young Black women who are often assumed to be prostitutes. But Champs also felt strange to me because such an exclusively White space should not make sense in a predominantly Black African city without a history of European settlement. As a Black subject and researcher, encountering a Champs in postcolonial Ghana was disturbing to me also because it was a local articulation of a historical global political economy of race and power. The scene at Champs provides a window into the forms of White power in postcolonial Africa. It is a power that stretches back to racialized colonial rule, was carried through to contemporary international economic and political dominance, and is solidified through unofficial racial, cultural, economic, and spatial segregation.

In chapter 1, I discussed how the structure of colonial rule consolidated a racialization process that began with a European presence on the West African coast and continued through the transatlantic slave trade. This racialization was operationalized through the construction of natives and ethnics: indigenous African groups were nativized through juridical and practical ethnogenesis constructed through the tropes of custom and tradition. The goal of this colonial racial project was to establish a bifurcated state in which a constellation of diverse and mutually antagonistic "tribes" would be ruled by a consolidated racialized-as-White European grouping. The consequences of this method of rule would have lasting impact not only on the structure of the postcolonial state, but also in the ways that it would enable an enduring racialized sociocultural and political field. But while in that chapter I focused primarily on nativization and the construction of Black Africanness, I made clear that this was only one side of the racializing colonial process. The other was the consolidation of Whiteness. The discussion in this chapter takes this colonial Whiteness as a point of departure to explore a key racial project in contemporary Ghana: the interdependent relationship between the trope of Whiteness and White positionality.

My discussion of the local dynamics of racialization in contemporary Ghana begins with an ethnographically informed analysis of the contours of modern Whiteness. I focus on the mutual constitution of the ideology of Whiteness and the positionality of those persons racialized as White. By "Whiteness," I mean historical, cultural, and social practices, as well as ideas and codes, which practically and discursively structure the power and privilege of those racialized as White. I argue in this chapter that though the White population in Ghana is mostly transient, and White positionality is hardly rigid, Whiteness has retained its undisputed, if contested, power of position. Moreover, I demonstrate the ways that Whiteness continues to have currency in this nominally Black postcolonial African nation, revealing a clear discourse of race that is articulated through practices that both reflect global economic, political, and cultural hierarchies, and that reinforce White privilege on the local level. To explore the mutual constitution of Whiteness and the positions of White people in Ghana is to first distinguish between Whiteness—historically as ideology, trope, and cultural practice—and actual racialized White bodies. Indeed what is important for this analysis of the signification of race through Whiteness is the recognition that racialization occurs both in tandem with and *in excess* of the corporeal (Hesse 2007). In other words, race (in this case, Whiteness) articulates with racialized-as-White bodies, all the while moving beyond such bodies and expressing itself in other representations of itself—such as culture, aesthetics, wealth, and so on. The effort here, therefore, is to understand the *meanings* attached to Whiteness and how those so racialized are positioned within these sets of meanings and are often, but not always, enlisted into the servicing of Whiteness, projecting and performing its attributes with "varying degrees of consciousness, unconsciousness, coercion, seriousness, and parody" (Frankenberg 1993, 13).

Although articulations of Whiteness clearly have distinctive manifestations in Ghana, we cannot read its configurations solely in terms of the local context precisely because notions of local Whiteness, the local position of Whites, and Ghanaian racialized consciousness are all linked to a broader sociopolitical and cultural field that extends well beyond the borders of the nation. Structured as it is within a worldwide hierarchy of race, Whiteness is global *and* local in scope and impact. The argument in this chapter follows the larger thesis of the book that racialization processes in various locations are interlinked and occur in relation to one another within the global context of White supremacy. As such, to understand the significance of Whiteness is to recognize what Ruth Frankenberg calls the "fundamental co-constitution of Whiteness and racial domination" (1993, 4). It is the historical and contemporary, and therefore structural, position of racial Whiteness in Ghana that allows a place like Champs to become a space of White privilege and White social distance from Blacks. Moreover, the Whiteness enacted through the space of Champs is a metonym for the reality of Ghana's—and Africa's—global racialized position vis-à-vis the racially "White" Western north.

The analysis in this chapter is in two parts. In the first part, I explore the various ways that the ideology of Whiteness is deployed. To do this, I revisit some of the colonial tropes of Whiteness and extend them to contemporary representations and understandings among some Ghanaian groups. And I consider conceptualizations of Whiteness as they appear in everything from religious iconography to language. In the second part of this chapter, I focus on the actual positions of Whites as they are primarily perceived by Ghanaians and as they impact the local landscape. This section explores the ways that local distinctions made between "development Whites" and "Peace Corps Whites" allow us detailed views of the range of White positionality and experience and the meaning of Whiteness in the contemporary moment. I want to stress here that this chapter does not necessarily analyze the group recognized in Ghana as "White people" as such. Rather, it is an attempt to show how Whiteness (as trope and physical "visual regime") operates in everyday Ghana in the construction of local meanings of race and the simultaneous (re)articulation of global White supremacy (Mills 1998).

## On the Trope of Whiteness

[W]e tend to treat . . . Whites . . . in a much better way than we treat our fellow Ghanaians. . . . [Even] in the midst of mistrust and the negative perceptions we have of them, I personally believe that . . . because they are advanced—technologically, in education, and things like that—we tend to lean on them more for knowledge and things . . . so the way we see them as advanced and leading everything in the world we try to adopt their ways, we learn their culture. . . . In the midst of all this mistrust of them, we still count on them.

[I]t appears that they [Whites] work in industries and in high positions. And those industries are prospering. And it seems that those who work under Whites are doing very well. So it means that they [Whites] are honest.

I think because we view them as "minigods," as "demigods," we tend to value them more than our own people.

[I]t comes from the fact that most of what we are doing now, they brought it here. We've got technology, they brought it; we've got industry, they've brought it. So we assume that because they are the pioneers they should have advantage. Most Africans believe that . . . they'll say, "You know, the White man brought school," "The White man brought the computer."

[W]e also see them as supernormal human beings, something close to the demigod or so.

In these comments by Ghanaian university students, we clearly see the mutual constitution of White positionality and the ideology (trope) of Whiteness. Whites in Ghana—and throughout the world—represent modernity, technological advancement, industry, innovation, economic success, political leadership, and cultural superiority. There is also a moral economy that emerges from such "advancement"—hence, the student that says that Whites seem more honest because they succeed in their business ventures and industry. Yet, what is significant here is that this understanding of Whites—of Whiteness—is almost forced, something that has to be accepted by students, however grudgingly. These statements emerged out of an often contentious discussion about Whites in Ghana at the University of Ghana, Legon campus. It was evening, and a group of twelve students and I were sitting in a lounge discussing various issues when the topic arose. The responses were uneven—at times a certain student would praise some aspect of Whiteness only to quickly be rebuffed by another. Most often, the comments reflected what the students assumed the general Ghanaian response to Whites would be, and it was often difficult to draw the line between individual belief and the assumptions they had of the general population. While many of these students were enumerating the "negative" attributes of White/Whiteness, they nevertheless seemed forced to admit White superiority because of the presumably overwhelming examples of White success. How could the White man be so bad if he is part of the group that gave so much to the modern world? Look at his industry! Look at his success! Look at how ordered his society is, how beautiful and clean his streets and neighborhoods are. The White man must be doing something right.

In 1920 W. E. B. DuBois asked, "What on earth is Whiteness that one should desire it?" (DuBois 1999, 18) We can begin to find an answer to this question in the comments of these university students. Whiteness to these students is a trope, a metaphor, a metonym for a wide range of structures and relationships; it is a set of "assumptions, privileges, and benefits that accompany the status of being white" (Harris 1993, 1713). Thus, Whiteness is at once development, modernity, intelligence, innovation, technology, cultural and aesthetic superiority, and economic and political domination. These are all things that denote value in today's world; they are what dictate the terms of membership—humanity—in modern society. These are also things that many Africans believe have been created and perfected in a "white, non-African elsewhere" (Ferguson 2005), and, as such, they are a valuable set of assets that remain to be obtained. Because the Whites in Ghana (and Africa) are generally believed to come from this elsewhere, naturally endowed with all of the gifts of Whiteness, they do indeed come to occupy a privileged position in the racial consciousness of local communities. This occurs, of course, in tandem with their actual (superior) structural location within Ghanaian society, which, in turn, is directly connected to historical relations and global traditions and practices of race and politics.

Yet, although it has a physical referent, it is clear that this is not only about individual Whites and their positionality in Ghana. As I argued at the beginning of this chapter, race exists and is always expressed in excess of the corporeal (Hesse 2007). Whiteness cannot be properly understood outside of the context of the development of the political, cultural, economic, and social structure of White supremacy (Harris 1993, 1725). Race—in this case, the category "White" as the position of power—was defined and constructed through the brutal history of European conquest and domination. It is in this context that we have development of the political system of "global White supremacy," the "particular power structure of formal or informal rule, socioeconomic privilege, and norms for the differential distribution of material wealth and opportunities, benefits and burdens, rights and duties" (Mills 1998, 3). In this sense, Whiteness represents unearned privilege for the group racially designated as White, as such racialized persons do not have to work to attain race-induced respect; instead, respect and honor are attributed to their positions and they are expected to personify this role (Harris 1993). If we reconsider the relationship between the historical construction of White people and the attendant structural power of "Whiteness," it is no wonder then that those so racialized (and therefore powerful) could be understood—albeit grudgingly—as "demigods." Indeed, the terrain of relationships that inform Ghanaian racial consciousness is filled with conceptualizations of Whiteness (and White people) that acutely reflect its (inevitable?) valorization. I must stress here, however, the well-known reality that the valorization of Whiteness in not unique to Ghana or postcolonial Africa. It is, rather, a worldwide phenomenon because, as DuBois so succinctly put it, "Whiteness is the ownership of the earth." Thus, what is unique is the *content* and distinctiveness of the valorization of Whiteness in the Ghanaian context. This valorization of Whiteness and its embodied agents (racialized as White peoples) takes on many forms, from religious iconography to language.

Before I give some contemporary examples in Ghana, it is important to remember the various ways that such tropes of Whiteness were constructed and consolidated by the laws and practices of the colonial state. As we saw in the first chapter, in the same way that nativeness was constructed and re-inforced, Whiteness also had to be structured and maintained. This took on many forms, one of which was the spectacle of imperial posturing through the staging of grand durbars and construction of "frames" of Whiteness. These frames were based on a discourse of Whiteness as civilization and racial progress. I contend that it is not too difficult a jump to the present to see these frames (and tropes) at work in Ghana and elsewhere. That the university students linked Whiteness primarily to these hegemonic discursive frames speaks directly to their familiarity with them, particularly as embodied by Whites and lived through their experiences.

In a conversation about race in Ghana in early 2001, Kwame Dompi,[2] a professor at a U.S. university, asserted: "The most important thing for me is the perception of God as White that [Ghanaians] and others are promoting. If you think of God as the good of all good, then you will think of Whites in the same way." This conversation was initiated in part by a major campaign by some Christian groups in Ghana to cover prominently placed billboards with pictures of Jesus along with Bible verses. For a few months these bill-boards could be seen all over Accra. But I was struck by how much the picture of Jesus contrasted with the majority of Ghanaians. Jesus was depicted as a White man with long blond hair and a blond beard. Scholars have well documented the ways in which Christianity was a productive site of racialization for the colonial project (Dyer 1997). For me, the irony of the White Jesus billboards in Ghana was palpable but not surprising. It resonated with the broader associations of Whiteness with divinity, morality, and ethical goodness. There is no doubt that White Christian imagery—which remains prevalent throughout the world—continues to elevate the status of Whites and the valorization of Whiteness in a very religious Ghana. Combined with other images of White merit and technological superiority that construct Whites as "supernormal human beings" and close to being "demigods," the statement reveals the deeply naturalized and continuous strength of the (often unconscious) belief in White goodness. As W. E. B. DuBois once remarked in response to the hegemonic dominance of cultural Whiteness: "Everything great, good, efficient, fair, and honorable is 'white'; everything mean, bad, blundering, cheating, and dishonorable is 'yellow'; a bad taste is 'brown'; and the devil is 'black.' The changes of this theme are continually rung in picture and school book, until, of course, the King [white] can do no wrong" (1999, 25).

Another example of the naturalization of the trope of Whiteness is found in language. One potent illustration is the signification of the word *obruni*.

Taken literally, *obruni* means "foreigner" and is a term that has been used historically to identify White Europeans in Ghana. The word, however, has a complex set of meanings. Over time, *obruni* has been used to refer to foreign Whites, foreign Asians, and lighter-skinned and often brown-skinned diaspora Blacks; it has also been applied to Ghanaians returning from abroad who are perceived to be affluent and are often derided as dressing, walking, talking, and acting White. Indeed, this popular understanding of *obruni* has led many people from outside of Ghana to make the now very popular case that Ghanaians consider diaspora Blacks to be White. As we will learn in chapter 6, this is not exactly accurate. Indeed, we see this clearly when we review the underlying meanings of the word. To be considered *obruni*, even if jokingly, is to be associated with the class and cultural standing of Whites (and Whiteness) in Ghana. Significantly, because the term is also employed in describing seemingly rich and culturally different *Ghanaians* and other Blacks, it signals a clear association made between Whiteness as racialized identity and Whiteness as a particular class status, cultural standing, education level, and outlook. Here, as Fanon reminds us, the cause is the consequence: "you are rich because you are white, you are white because you are rich" (1967). Indeed, analyzed within an African diaspora racial-formation framework, *obruni* does the same work that *blanc* does in the francophone Caribbean, that "Oreo" does in the United States, or that the phrase "money whitens" does in Latin America. All of these references clearly point to the ways that Whiteness assumes privilege and is deployed as identity, status, and property. A non-White can, at times, become an "honorary White" if she possesses some of the cultural, political, and economic accoutrements of Whiteness. In this sense, it is easier to understand the popular Ghanaian critique of diaspora Blacks as those with "too much money" (see chapter 6), whereas the same critique is not made of U.S. or European Whites, who presumably have the *right* to be rich.[3] The deployment of *obruni* therefore signals a thoroughly racialized discourse in Ghana, and it is a discourse about Whiteness and the articulations of White power and privilege.

Obruni—as a trope and signification of Whiteness—is also sometimes used as an indicator of goodness or attractiveness. A reference to one's child or family member as *mi bruni* works to point out the child's attractiveness or the family member's cultural or educational advancement, respectively. In a similar vein, a good or tasty mango is sometimes preceded by the word. We see, thus, the normalizing effects of White discourse imbued as it is with representations that continuously construct and affirm a racialized hierarchy that permeates society. As Dyer reminds us, this type of White power "habitually passes itself off as embodied in the normal" and is peculiarly seductive because of the way Whiteness "seems rooted, in common thought, in things other than ethnic difference" (1988, 44). But this grammar of Whiteness is upheld and consolidated by the consistent and structurally elevated position of White bodies in the local terrain. Here actual White men and women are enlisted in its service. I turn now to this part of the discussion.

## The Physical and Visual Regimes of Whiteness

One early weekday morning in the spring of 2001, my friend Paul and I waited for a red traffic light to turn green at a busy intersection in the Dansoman area of Accra. We noticed an interaction that seemed peculiar to me. In front of our car was a sport utility vehicle—the preferred car of official international foreign-aid workers, diplomats, Ghanaian officials, and members of the elite. The SUV's windows were shut; in the front seat was a Black driver, and in the back was a White woman and her two young children. On the sidewalk near the car was a young Ghanaian street vendor, a girl who appeared to be the same age as one of the children in the car. Although such young vendors usually took advantage of stalled traffic to make their sales, this young girl seemed unaware of the early morning bustle of other street vendors, pedestrians, and cars around her. Instead, she stood still, scarcely wincing under the weight of the large container filled with small ice-water bags on top of her head. Her gaze was fixed on the back seat of the SUV; she was staring at the White family, timidly waving, attempting to get its attention. It was clear that the young girl was not trying to offer her wares to the family. Instead, she kept waving at the people in the back seat, and with each small wave, she would smile shyly, seemingly in anticipation of acknowledgment. For at least a couple of minutes, the young girl stood patiently waving until the traffic light turned green and the SUV sped off in front of us. She had not been acknowledged, of course. However, the interaction piqued my interest and sparked a commentary from Paul. He suggested that the young vendor would not seem so awed if the family in the car had been Black and/or Ghanaian, Lebanese, or Indian. "She probably would have been mad," he said, "especially if there were kids her age in the car." After a pause he continued: "They have so much respect for the Whites—the poor especially." Paul went on to say that he believed that the wealth and prestige of Whites were often taken for granted by many in Ghana, and that people associated Whites with privilege and money much more than I could imagine. As we overtook the SUV further down the street, we recognized the printed logo on its side doors as representing one of the many UN-affiliated organizations in the country.

While numbers are difficult to confirm,[4] Ghana's White population seems to be predominantly made up of officially recognized "experts"—affiliated with donor agencies and international nongovernmental organizations, missionary efforts, Peace Corps and other volunteer groups, and academic institutions—whose presence, though transient, makes for a highly visible part of urban life. Within the context of a global inequality that structures relations between the racialized north and south, this is hardly surprising. The emerging literature on the racial politics of "development" has begun to address the reality that "development relies on expatriates and . . . the majority of these are white" (Crewe and Fernando 2006, 47). "Official" status for whites in Ghana therefore is a given. In Ghana's sociopolitical and cultural landscape, as well as in popular imagination, this White presence and positionality denote the complex interaction of race, economics, and politics. White people are understood, by definition, to occupy particularly high positions in Ghana—positions that also signify political, economic, social, and cultural capital. This means that Whites occupy a range of powerful positions that, though internally heterogeneous, reveal a radical distance from the local population (Hale 2006). "Official" status also means a particular placement in the local context—distinctive locales and groups for socializing, as well as the establishment of private subcommunities.

A recurring conversation among my group of Ghanaian friends is how to describe White presence in Ghana. In general, these friends see Whites as economically privileged, socially distant, and politically powerful actors on the local scene. At the same time, they often joke that Whites, as they are positioned and perceived in Ghana, can loosely be grouped into two categories: "development Whites" and "Peace Corps Whites." While this framing was conceived in jest, it reflects a certain reality that is well recognized throughout Africa (and other parts of the developing world). A colleague once gave me an article that spoke directly to this kind of perception of Whites. It was an amusing editorial from the Ugandan *Sunday Vision*, complete with an accompanying cartoon (see fig. 3.1), entitled "Bazungu Different from Whites." "Today there are the different categories of whites," the editorial announced, "one of which will be the whites, the other will be the *Bazungu*."[5] The editorial goes on to list the differences between a White man and a *Bazungu*: the White man dresses in suits and shiny shoes, drives around in a Pajero (a type of SUV), and is well fed and well bred, while the *Bazungu* looks dirty and confused, but is "the real tourist":

3.1 Cartoon accompanying the article "Bazungu Different from Whites,"
*Sunday Vision* (Uganda), October 29, 1995, 12.

The white man is here on a consultation job with some NGO or, God forbid,
the World Bank and the IMF or is doing research on the possibility of cross-
breeding Ugandan rabbits with French ones. . . .

. . . The *Muzungu*, on the other hand, is a peace-loving citizen of his country who gets bored easily and one day decides that he should get up and see
more of the world. . . . [So] he comes to Africa . . . where Amin lived, where
the Gorillas are.

This tongue-in-cheek satirical piece represents rather popular local sentiments around Whiteness and White presence. The White man in the editorial is linked to the "development" industry; he is assumed to be in the
country officially, and he needs CNN, business news, and a working telephone service. This man is directly linked to the IMF and World Bank—a
clear sign of economic power. Indeed, even when it is not true, Whites are
assumed to hold such positions—for what other reasons would a White
man have for being driven around in his Pajero and heading to the nearest
"respectable place"? In the end, the White man in the newspaper piece is
seen as the extension of mechanical Western hegemonic capitalism, as he
is described as a "stiff-necked boardroom bureaucrat . . . not [a] human
being." On the other hand, the *Muzungu* is the adventurer, whose carefree

(and presumably oblivious) existence in the country elicits mostly bewildered amusement. Yet, although this White is deemed "human," at least, it is clear that this *Muzungu* is also a stranger, one who is believed to be too naive to bother learning much about the specific local context. To the *Muzungu*, "Africa" is a construct—a dream, an invention, and, most importantly, a place of life-defining adventure somewhere in the deep jungle, "where the Gorillas are." Thus, although the two sets of groups are clearly differentiated, their individual engagements with their local (African) contexts are presented as not only inauthentic, but, importantly, this engagement is seen through the assumption of White privilege—either by official status or by the ability to be indifferent to the specificities of African life while in search of the next adventure.

Though amusing and generally reductive, I contend that these images emerge directly from the perceived positionality of Whites on the ground in postcolonial Africa: Whites are either technocrats on official stays in the country or they are adventurous and oblivious students who use "Africa" as a stage for their self-discoveries. Not only do these images reveal White positionality, in the most explicit ways, they also come together to reveal a uniquely racialized process in this postcolonial moment. More importantly, there is a way in which these images point to how they are both informed by and inform local racialized consciousness. The term "development Whites" refers to a diverse group of people made up of the professional Europeans/North Americans who are in Ghana as development experts or as World Bank, IMF, or UN officials. They are in the country to work on its many foreign-funded projects, projects that are the cornerstone of the country's dependent and highly indebted neoliberal economic structure. Specifically, development Whites are part of the transnational expatriate class of workers that represent the West and privilege, and whose positions denote the conflation of race, class, and nationality (Leonard 2010). Peace Corps Whites, by contrast, represent the many exchange students, recent college graduates on short-term volunteer trips to (mostly) rural areas, others who are independently taking backpacking trips across West Africa, and academic researchers. While not all of these people are Peace Corps volunteers (though a great number are), many nevertheless represent a particular perception. Together, these two groups cover the spectrum of the understanding of White positionality in modern-day Ghana. Of course, I am aware that the various White populations in urban Ghana are heterogeneous with a number of differences—gender, class, and nationality, among others—as well as often competing values, beliefs, and loyalties. My goal here is to focus on how, even in heterogeneity, perceptions of White positionality in contemporary

Ghana remain peculiarly stable, indexing a set of relationships that involve a consciousness of history, politics, race, and power.

In urban Ghana, particularly in Accra and other major cities, development Whites seem to be shrouded in a veil of mystery and awe. Importantly, they are thought by many to be associated with money, power, intelligence, and modern Western development. In an extensive survey that I conducted with Ghanaians in two areas with a high concentration of foreigners—the Osu neighborhood and Labadi Beach—respondents often (and only) distinguished between Black and White foreigners.[6] The majority of the 150 people surveyed categorized these foreigners differently. Blacks (diaspora Blacks in particular) were often considered to be tourists who were visiting Ghana to "find their roots." And not all were considered wealthy. Respondents described Whites, on the other hand, as being associated with one of the following: business enterprise, mining and factories, and exchange programs. All were considered wealthy and with connections. I would argue that this view of Whites emerges from the reality that the group's existence is quite pronounced; we see its members mostly in their official vehicles being driven around town by Ghanaian drivers, and, by virtue of their professional status in Ghana, they receive considerable media attention. In fact, it is rare to read local newspapers or watch the evening news in Accra without reference to foreign missionaries or NGO workers donating supplies to rural communities, or to foreign experts engaged in certain development projects, forecasting on the country's economic trajectory, or waxing assuredly on its political shortcomings. This visibility and what it represents (and what it has always represented in terms of high socioeconomic status and privilege), also brings with it certain amounts of unqualified respect. These Whites embody the prestige and power of the dominant West.

Generally, the local population knows little is about development Whites beyond their professional engagements and business relationships, a fact that shrouds the group in mystique while reinforcing its power. In addition to their highly visible professional profiles and work, the leisure and personal lives of members of this group are usually observed from afar. Whites in Ghana live only in certain neighborhoods, patronize particular clubs, bars, and restaurants, and socialize primarily with one another. On any given Sunday afternoon, we can find some members of this group leisurely spending time by the poolside at one of the top hotels in the city. We can also find them dining at exclusive restaurants and socializing in places such as Champs. This patterned differentiation is not unique to Ghana, and this rather active racial segregation is often reinforced by various rituals that work to also regulate (White) identity—through language, comportment,

3.2 Ivy Coffee Shop in Accra, 2005. Photograph by the author.

and cultural events. As Crewe and Fernando demonstrate in their article on the relationship between race and development, White expatriates' "position of power relies in part on a degree of separation between nationals and themselves," and it is strengthened through a tendency to congregate in "particular bars, invite each other for dinner, toddler groups or to 'ladies lunches,' [and] hold . . . sport events" (2006, 48).

Often, discussions of the racially exclusive practices of development Whites occur in the language of class, and it is generally understood by many that certain places are open to all who have the necessary resources. This analysis is accurate insofar as members of the Ghanaian upper class (or Ghanaians visiting from abroad) have the resources to access these places. When I have been to such exclusive places as Monsoon (a Japanese restaurant in Osu) or Ivy Coffee Shop,[7] it was to meet with other U.S.-based scholars and professionals (from varying national and racial backgrounds), diaspora Blacks, or young Ghanaians from the diaspora. Non-Whites nevertheless remain the minority population at these sites. The more important point, however, is that such class distinctions are invariably racially structured such that *all* Whites in Ghana have (or are assumed to have) access to these places, where only a few privileged Ghanaians do. It is understood, for example, that there are no poor White people in Ghana, and because their socializing spaces are typically off-limits to the average Ghanaian, economic distinctions are institutionalized—naturalized through the linking of White racial and cultural identity to particular spaces and places.[8] We see then the operationalization of White power through this convergence of race and class positions.

The naturalization of White skin with economic and sociopolitical privilege is, importantly, bolstered by the *assumption* of White people's veritable right to this wealth and status. I remember well an event that solidified this point for me. In the spring of 2007, I was in Ghana to participate in fiftieth-anniversary celebrations. There were numerous events in the months and weeks leading up to and following Ghana's March 7 anniversary. The celebrations attracted powerful and popular figures from all over the world; they also attracted a number of academics, particularly those interested in Ghanaian history and society. It was a pleasure to be with many of my academic colleagues in Ghana for the first time. But on the night of March 7, I found myself with a colleague and friend, a Black woman anthropologist, outside the gates of the Kwame Nkrumah Mausoleum, locked out of the main events of the anniversary for lack of proper "official" identification. As we stood pleading with the guard to reconsider our case, we remembered that another friend, a fellow anthropologist from the United States, was already inside the gates. He had accompanied his friends who were to perform at the opening ceremony later that night. We immediately contacted him on his cell phone, assuming that his Whiteness would aid in our predicament. When our friend reached the gate, he simply told the guard that the two of us, Black non-Ghanaian women anthropologists, were with him. After a slight hesitation, the guard relented and let us in without a word. This experience left the three of us giddy, because the scene developed exactly as we assumed that it would. It must be noted that no one was allowed to enter the premises without an invitation card. This was the case even if one had official acquaintances inside. Thus, our White anthropology colleague's ability to gain entrance for us into this event clearly was linked to assumptions about his status and position. And at the moment, it did not matter whether or not he was acting in any official capacity.

My Ghanaian colleague Kodjo relayed a similar experience. During a conversation with him and his wife, Nancy, he recalled a scene at Ghana's Kotoka International Airport. Kodjo had gone there to await Nancy's arrival from England. Because of the various construction projects throughout the airport at the time, a new set of regulations forbade awaiting passengers from entering the airport lobby. As Kodjo stood waiting by the door of the airport lobby, a number of Ghanaians came up to the officer stationed at the door, pleading with him to be allowed in. In all these cases, the officer refused. However, Kodjo said, a White man with two kids came from the crowd and walked straight through the door, both without stopping to ask for permission *and* without being stopped by the officer at the door. Kodjo said he became extremely angry and asked the officer why he allowed the White man to go through the door. The officer did not have a direct response and instead told Kodjo that if he too wanted to go through the lobby, he could very well do so. Kodjo quickly replied no and began to loudly admonish the officer for his actions. In relating this story, Kodjo theorized that the officer "just assumed that the White man was important." He added, "And I have no tolerance for such foolishness." Kodjo was eventually let into the airport by the guard, no doubt because he threatened to report him. Indeed, the common sense of White merit (and therefore power) is something that is not lost on many Ghanaians and non-Ghanaians. This is an issue that is often undertheorized in anthropological renditions, particularly within discussions of the relations of White researchers and Ghanaians. With few exceptions (Cole 2001a), the practices and discourses indexing assumed White merit are presented as mere anecdotes, with no direct engagement or analysis. The special treatment afforded Whites is directly linked to the reality of White positionality in Ghana and beyond, and to assumptions about the status of White people in the country (as foreign experts and professionals). In practice, this privilege is literally embodied in their White skin (Fyfe 1992).

This point certainly was not lost on the students who participated in a set of interviews I conducted at the University of Ghana in the fall of 2004.[9] In a conversation about general perceptions of Euro-American Whites in the country, a young female student offered, "We see Whites as the people who have money. Most Blacks [Ghanaians] who associate with Whites, they just want to go somewhere." A male student continued, "I think that Ghanaians think that because the White is rich, I might get close to that person and become rich." The young woman responded in turn that Ghanaians, in general, "feel that the [Whites] are so important, because of their color and maybe their social background, and also because of the kind of [technological] advancements in their country. So [Ghanaians] want to get closer, much closer to them." What is significant about this exchange is the almost seamless shifts between notions of race (Whiteness), class (wealth), and status, as well as the linking of this race and class to modernity and technological advancement. In fact, in perception (and probably in reality), there are no poor Whites in Ghana. Indeed, there could not be within local racialized consciousness—they simply couldn't be imagined. This point is brought into clear relief when students describe people's sense of fascination, cognitive dissonance, and even discomfort with some Whites—particularly young college-exchange students—who challenge this race/class arrangement. Aba, another female student at the interview, said that because Ghanaians see Whites as those who are rich, it is difficult to see them in a different situation: "Economically, we see them as people who are rich. At times we find a White man or a White woman in a *tro-tro*; we see a White struggling [fighting] with people in a queue [line] and we are surprised." The surprise, of course, comes from the fact that *tro-tro* riders are only the working poor, and, given the choice, most people would not willingly ride one.[10] Thus, since Whites, because they are White, cannot be poor, a White riding a tro-tro brings not only stares, but a complex combination of feelings that include surprise, dismay, and even respect.

To make the point more explicitly, one only has to examine the relationship between race and class for a Black Ghanaian or a non-White person in Ghana. Whereas Whiteness and wealth are inevitably linked, the case is not the same for Blackness and wealth. Thus, an upper-class Black Ghanaian or any other African—with similar class status to White development expatriates—has to *perform* his status in order to be read as upper class. This often entails the conspicuous display of class and status—from type of car, the presence of driver/chauffeur, dress, language, modern or Western "air," and the comportment worthy of "big men."[11] At other times, the display is unwitting and may entail the ability to frequent certain social spots or afford the right kind of education for children. For Whites, however, such a performance is not necessary, as class (and political and cultural) status is not only already a given, but understood as a merit and a right (a point to which I will return shortly).

I am not attempting to characterize White racial positionality as unrestrained privilege. To be sure, negotiations of identity in this contemporary urban postcolonial space rest on a complicated set of historical realities, assumptions, and relationships that work, often, to structure a hierarchy of positions that is by no means completely rigid. White positionality in Ghana often does not go unchallenged. It is challenged in the most mundane of instances, from local stereotypes of Whiteness ("The White man is selfish" or "The White man is greedy"), to assumptions about unrestricted White wealth as well as White gullibility in Ghana, to blatant and active denunciations of White privilege by various individuals and groups.

Yet, the average Ghanaian generally does not have direct contact with development Whites. What stood out for me, for example, in my conversation with the university students was how few of them had actually had direct conversations or interactions with any European or U.S.-born racialized White person. This makes their views of Whites even more remarkable. Many students linked White economic and political superiority in Ghana directly to the history of colonialism and the country's current predicament of marginalization in the global political economy. John proffered:

> I don't have interaction with Whites. Some come and say hi, but I don't want to have interactions with them due to my personal beliefs. Personally, come to think of history, . . . when I look at the White people . . . no matter how they present themselves, it's not how they show up. [They always have] something up their sleeves. . . . When we read history books, I learned that the doom of Africa is because of Whites; they colonized us and other things. The things they do to us . . . Now, come to think of the policies of Whites toward Africa, it's just not fair.

John went on to discuss the discriminatory IMF policies toward Africa, saying, bitterly, that Whites control Africans because they "are giving us this money."

The Ghanaian professionals I knew that had direct contact with development Whites bitterly lamented the unfairness of White positionality in Ghanaian society, often radically challenging the general perception of White superiority. Paul, for example, told me that as an electrical engineer working for a Ghanaian telephone company in the summer of 2000, he was placed under the supervision of a White electrician from England. He was extremely outraged and frustrated about being placed in a subordinated position to someone educationally below him and with significantly less professional experience. Yet, the fact that he was being supervised by someone with a lesser technological skill set was soon overshadowed when Paul discovered that this British electrician earned a salary that was literally ten times greater than his.[12] Many of Paul's friends relayed similar tales of unequal remuneration compared with that of White expatriate workers. During a discussion one morning with some young Ghanaian engineers working in the Volta region of Ghana, the young men angrily cited several examples of White American or European "experts" receiving exorbitant salaries compared with the wages earned by similarly or more highly trained Ghanaians. These young men argued that this situation has historical antecedents in the colonial days, when British "experts" were imported into the Gold Coast to take up technical and other positions for which Ghanaians were not deemed competent or qualified. They also expressed anger that the disparity in remuneration between them and mostly White expatriate professionals was accompanied by the elevated status enjoyed by Whites in Ghana.

My conversations with these young professional men, the university students, as well as a number of other people confirmed a recent discussion in the international-development literature that forces us to acknowledge how the development industry is structured by a set of explicitly racialized practices that affirm Whiteness as power position. Indeed, the idea that "notions of Whiteness and the west provide symbols of authority, expertise and knowledge" (Kothari 2006, 10) is generally recognized globally, even if it is rarely interrogated or challenged. Within the context of the modern world, where the developing world continues to be ruled politically, economically, and culturally by the developed West, it is also clear that this distinction and power relation is deeply racialized. Uma Kothari further argues that there is the "often unacknowledged and unconscious assumption of white superiority and expertise within development as part of the wider global distribution of racialized power" (15). Thus, there is the inevitable race/ Whiteness-knowledge-expertise connection in which "it is not always *what* is known but *who* knows that signifies 'expertise'" (16). The young people I spoke with clearly articulated the truth of this trend with the recounting of their experiences. Similar to Kothari's demonstration of how such connection works on the ground, where the appointment of a White consultant is seen to proffer a higher status than that of a non-White local person, these young people also gave specific examples—from complaints about the long list of White European football (soccer) coaches to the turning over of management operations of Ghana's large formerly state-run telephone company to Norwegians. There was no shortage of such examples. My friend Paul also described how the Ghanaian owner of a private technology firm for which he worked announced how much his company had advanced because of its ability to afford to hire a White British consultant with the requisite expatriate compensation package and benefits. This consultant, according to Paul, was often given a visibility within the company and in its dealings with other businesses such that the firm would be perceived as more competent and "modern."

Along with the superior professional, economic, and political status granted to development Whites in Ghana, there are also the ways that this group reinforces this hierarchy through its socializing patterns. As the editorial in the Ugandan *Sunday Vision* described for us, the White man's time in the country is spent not only in the comforts of his air-conditioned Pajero and stays in hotels that "must have some CNN and business news," it is also spent as far away from local places as possible. As we saw with Champs, and with Crewe and Fernando's (2006) characterization of the White expatriate community, the modern racial segregation that arises from the practices of Whites in Ghana stems the contemporary reality of Africa's postcolonial/neocolonial predicament in which race, class, development, and aid are all structured through the long historical durée of colonial rule and persistent political and economic dependency. In the contemporary moment, it is more significant that wealth and aid continue to be intimately tied to race and Whiteness. As James Ferguson (2005) reminds us, even though explicit racial hierarchies are illegitimate in this day and age, they continue to be constructed through the very actions that work to legitimate White positionality at the top of a political and economic hierarchy. Development Whites, in this sense, perform their positionality through varying forms of consciousness and unconsciousness—but in a set of performances that nevertheless structures institutional as well as individual power (Frankenberg 1993). In other words, it is the access to generally inaccessible resources, political power through "official" positionality, *linked* with the distancing from the local scene (and local people) that such access and officialdom enables that gives Whiteness its power. White positionality in Ghana in this context indexes what George Lipsitz (1998) calls the "possessive investment in Whiteness," an often unwitting, yet nevertheless strongly guarded

3.3 A group of young white people in Accra, July 2007. Photograph by the author.

privilege that allows racialized-as-White people and groups to possess status and power.

At the other end of the spectrum, Peace Corps Whites are conspicuous precisely because they do not behave in ways that are associated with "official" Whiteness. Unlike development Whites, this grouping of young Whites is seen more as a haphazard collection of people either seeking adventure or with altruistic intentions. I would argue, however, that this group performs and inhabits Whiteness in ways that result in a positioning that does not challenge the supremacy of development Whites. These Whites dress differently, they often travel by tro-tro or walk around in groups, they buy food from vendors by the side of the road, they shop at the outdoor markets, and they have developed a certain rapport with some ordinary Ghanaians. Furthermore, this group often seems oblivious to its positionality within its surroundings, and there is a general sense of amusement when its members are seen walking along the streets of Accra. Often, Ghanaians will describe this group as disheveled or "dirty" and yet at the same time with a measure of bemusement and familiarity. Perceptions about Peace Corps Whites are similar to the description of the *Bazungu*, as members of this group appear to be more at ease with living life in Ghana. And their apparent ease with working-class Ghanaian lifestyle and custom has gained members of this group a particular kind of respect.

I remember well a discussion that emerged as I sat in a barbershop in tourist-heavy Osu, chatting with friends on a Saturday afternoon in the summer of 2000. We had been curiously watching the stream of foreigners, mostly young White visitors, passing by on Oxford Street. Most of the comments were in the form of jokes about their backpacks, sandals, and the ever-present water bottles. The discussion, however, suddenly turned to Black Americans. After a group of Blacks presumed to be African American[13] passed by, Eddie, one of the barbers in the shop, turned to me and said, "I hate these Black Americans. They don't try like the Whites do. They don't eat our food; they don't learn our language. The Whites ride the tro-tros and are very friendly. [The Black Americans] are not like the Whites!" Although this comment drew agreement and disagreement as well as consternation from a few of the patrons, Eddie's comments revealed a particular understanding of this group of Peace Corps Whites. The comparison of this group with the Black Americans is significant indeed, as is the construction of this group of Whites as more willing to integrate into Ghanaian culture and society. As I demonstrate in chapter 6, Ghanaian engagements with the Black American (both as a trope and as a person) reveal a particular kind of racial consciousness that structures the notions Blackness (and Ghanaian-ness) in ways that are acutely different from how Whiteness is understood. And though the practice is contested, people will often use behaviors and qualities associated with Whiteness (and White people) to compare both Black American and Ghanaian ineptitude. Thus, even in the discussions with university students, there would often be agreement with sentiments such as this one from Kweku. One of the students argued: "The Whites, by and large, are for me straightforward people. They give their word, by and large, you can take it. This is contrary to Blacks from the diaspora. Blacks from the diaspora are coming with a huge complex. . . . But the Whites, . . . they don't expect too much from you. . . . But by and large . . . dealing with Whites is much easier, much, much easier." Kweku made this comment; yet, later on in the conversation, after his colleagues insistently disagreed with his view, he offered that Ghanaians have "complex" attitudes toward Whites: "People think that Whites are superior . . . and so their attitude to Whites, we can see it in the streets, [Ghanaians] are not confident in themselves."

Many students in the room did not agree with Kweku's assessment that Whites were straightforward or "easier to deal with." Others responded that the Whites acted the same way as Black Americans, arguing that it was not fair to castigate Black Americans as bad compared with Whites. One of the ways Kweku's argument was countered was in a different set of discussions with students who said that Whites were not trustworthy. A few students gave examples of Whites disparaging Ghanaians and Africans in general. Responding to Ama, who said she believed that Ghanaians thought "Whites are so important," Richard said, "But one thing I have to say about the Whites is that they are not friendly . . . when it comes to talk with Blacks. . . . They always pretend that everything is nice . . . but when you leave, they say all sorts of things." Another student added, "Most Whites that we work with think that Ghanaians are lazy. . . . I was working with a lot of Whites who said to me, 'Most Ghanaians are lazy, but you, you are the exception.' Most think we are lazy [and that] we are not time conscious." This comment drew the most animated and sustained discussion, with many people expressing indignation at the thought of Whites disparaging Ghanaians, but with many more others agreeing that Ghanaians are "indeed lazy." In conceding to the charge that Ghanaians were deemed lazy, a number of the students justified such perceived view of Ghanaians by stating that Whites "are coming from a different environment." A young woman, Aba, continued, "Here, we don't get the reward for work that [Whites] in their environments do." Through this discussion about Whites and White positionality, we get a glimpse of an aspect of Ghanaian racial self-understanding. We see here a particular tension that emerges in relating to—and being positioned against—Whiteness.

3.4 A group of young white people in Accra, July 2007. Photograph by the author.

3.5 Foreign and local spectators at the PANAFEST 2005 celebrations,
Cape Coast, July 2005. Photograph by the author.

Indeed, it is difficult to assert positive Blackness in a context where tropes and practices of Whiteness normalize status. At times it seemed as if the students struggled but ultimately felt compelled to accept the inevitability (or reality) of their positioning against powerful White others. And consequently, the students were explaining themselves as much as they were Whites. I argue, however, this was not just the case in understanding the development Whites: Ghanaian self-understanding also draws on the positions and practices of those considered Peace Corps Whites.

Although many Ghanaians perceive White students, researchers, and volunteers as more capable of adapting to Ghanaian life, it is often a particular type of life that attracts these groups—the "traditional" life, untouched by modernity and Western values. In my interactions with some of these visitors to Ghana, I have learned that certain Ghanaian practices are dismissed as too Western and inauthentic by foreigners (Whites as well as non-Whites) in the country. Thus, even though there are large numbers of Ghanaians who can afford *not* to ride tro-tros, or who would not eat from the average street vendor, or who frequent high-end places, travel, or dress in the latest fashions, these practices are usually not deemed "traditional" enough to have value for the visitor looking for "authentic" Africa. As I demonstrate in

3.6 Local spectators and groups of white students from international volunteer organizations stationed in the area at the PANAFEST 2005 celebrations, Cape Coast, July 2005. Photograph by the author.

chapter 6, the need to find the "traditional" continues to be articulated even by diaspora Blacks and in Africanist scholarship on the continent, a need that we can directly link to the cultural practice of nativization (as discussed in chapter 1).

This idea was brought into clear relief during the 2005 PANAFEST celebrations in Elmina and Cape Coast (see chapter 5 for a detailed discussion of this event), in which I had the opportunity to spend more than a week that year. I was astounded during my stay by the unusually large number of young Whites (who appeared to be students) all over town. These young people were highly conspicuous, primarily because Cape Coast and Elmina are very small towns where foreigners—particularly Whites—are easily detected. In my years of traveling to Ghana and visiting the towns of Cape Coast and Elmina, I had never seen such a scene; in particular, I had never seen so many young Whites in the area. I wondered if many had come to attend the PANAFEST activities, which would be highly unusual given what would be deemed the extremely "radical" Pan-Africanist rhetoric of state officials.

The White students were most visible at the grand durbar in Victoria Park in Cape Coast on the seventh day of PANAFEST celebrations. This durbar was billed as an assembly of "royals, dignitaries, artists, and guests." Indeed, a master drummer was scheduled to perform, and he drew the attention of most of the crowd. When he stood up to perform (after state representatives had given all the official speeches and presentations), a group of these young White folk immediately rushed to the front of the stage with cameras and tape recorders. Speaking to a few of them after the durbar, I found out that many had come not to attend PANAFEST ceremonies, but, in the words of a young woman, to "see traditional performances." When I asked if they knew what PANAFEST was, Jessica, a twenty-one-year-old volunteer from Canada said that "we were told by our hosts that there would be dancing and drumming here, and that this would be a good place to see some traditional practices." A number of the other volunteers—primarily from England, Canada, and the United States—also said that they were attending the event because they expected to see Ghanaian traditional performances. Like most of her peers at Cape Coast during the summer of 2005 and throughout Ghana, Jessica represents a new type of White visitor. These young people were participating in six-week volunteer tours in parts of Africa—usually as stopovers after undergraduate studies and as a way to achieve some kind of community service before beginning graduate school. Most of the young White people I spoke with during the durbar told me that they were stationed in villages near the Cape Coast and Elmina, and they usually came to town or traveled to Accra or Takoradi on the weekends to take "a break from village life." Thus, although they work in various villages, a tradition among these young people is the inevitable trips to town to "civilization," as some call it, away from the villages.

Crewe and Fernando also reference this when they demonstrate how race is deployed and Whiteness affirmed through the actions of U.S. Peace Corps and UK volunteers who "often integrate into the local communities, but make contact with other (mostly White) expatriates when they visit larger towns and cities" (2006, 49). Indeed, these young people flock to many of the popular spaces in Accra, spaces such as Paloma or Champs, where they can escape and find comforting moments in spaces that are similar to those found at home. What is significant here is that, although these young White volunteers work in close contact with Ghanaian communities—in the villages and rural areas—and have seemingly adapted to Ghanaian society, they too retreat to familiar and unwittingly racially segregated "Western" places. In this way, the distinction I have drawn between two perceivably distinct White groupings does not seem to hold up under closer scrutiny. Although it is important to understand this distinction, it is clear that, regardless of differences, the presence of both development Whites and Peace Corps Whites has similar effects on the discourse of race and notions of Whiteness in Ghana. It is true that the Peace Corps Whites seem much more integrated into Ghanaian society and social life. As students and volunteers, they are assumed to be, as the *Sunday Vision* cartoon intimated, more "human" and warm and comparably less threatening than the development Whites. I want to argue, nevertheless, that though this group of Whites seems unproblematically integrated into working-class and poor Ghanaian society, their economic and social status is never questioned because it is directly connected to their racial identity and positioning. In other words, being considered White, regardless of lifestyle and general appearance, not only determines status, but it also structures opportunity and access. These are assets—opportunity and access—that a Ghanaian, in most cases, and especially one in the class categories performed by these Whites, does not have.

The White "Peace Corps" type actually indexes White positionality more acutely than the "development" one, since it points to White power and positionality that is based not on *actual* (or displayed) wealth and prestige, but on imaginings of notions of Whiteness and expectations of those racialized as White. It is a positionality that demonstrates the privilege of Whiteness in Ghana in unparalleled ways. The young White volunteer in the country for six weeks becomes not only the "expert" and "helper," she also benefits from her ability to "go native" in ways that the UN or IMF worker cannot. For that ability, the Peace Corps White gains respect on two levels: she is viewed through the prism of philanthropy and altruism; and, by virtue of her entrenchment in the communities in which she works, she is believed not to carry the burden of prejudice and condescension that her forbearers are assumed to have demonstrated toward Africans. In this sense, and in light of notions of race and ideas of Whiteness that proliferate around the globe, the Ghanaian racial terrain provides powerful incentives for Whites to accept—and indeed thrive in—their positionality. The racial and social economy of Peace Corps volunteerism or perceived altruistic development aid notwithstanding, White Europeans and U.S. citizens in Ghana continue to enjoy a high status and positionality that is directly linked to their membership in a racial community. It is a status and position that is occupied by no other group in the country. U.S. White identity in particular has gained even more value since the latter part of the twentieth century, a feat that has been achieved through global domination and capitalist ideology (Ingram 2001, 61).

At the same time, I want to stress the point here that the complexities of Whiteness extend beyond White positionality. Indeed, my argument is that contemporary Ghanaian racial consciousness is informed by the mutual constitution of White positionality and ideologies of Whiteness. These depend on one another and are informed by a long history of local negotiations with global structures of power. In other words, White positionality in Ghana—high status linked to global economic positionality—is significant inasmuch as it is structured by the history of colonialism and contemporary (postcolonial/neocolonial) relations of power *and* by ideologies and meanings of Whiteness that make White power and privilege part of the natural order of things. The meanings (and wages) of Whiteness therefore make White positionality in Ghana even more powerful because, however unfair and unmerited, White positionality is hardly challenged in any sustained way. Such ideologies of Whiteness have been deployed on a global scale and are filtered through local discourses and practices in Ghana, often in both subtle and unsubtle ways.

## The Race for Whiteness

In the second chapter of *Ghana's Concert Party Theatre*,[14] "Rereading Blackface in West Africa," Catherine Cole made the rare admission of the contradictions inherent in her positionality as a White researcher in mid-1990s

Ghana. As she sought to discover the origins of the Blackface (minstrel) character in Ghana's concert parties, she revealed that she had "difficulty framing questions about race that were meaningful to Ghanaians," but believed that this was "due to a lack of vocabulary . . . and not an absence of racial issues in Ghanaian life." Cole argued that her family's "Whiteness matter[ed]" in nearly every aspect of their life in Ghana, as they received preferential treatment, unquestioned access to various facilities, and "outpourings of hospitality . . . in a way that was *much* less frequently extended to African American researchers [they] knew" (italics in the original). While it is highly unfortunate that Cole did not take this opportunity to explore these issues more systematically (particularly in a book about a concert party replete with stereotypical racial imagery), her admission is significant in that it offers an intimate and personal, albeit brief, insight into the "ideology of white supremacy" in contemporary Ghana. Cole did not have the "vocabulary" to confront those who sincerely told her family that "You whites are wonderful" or "I know I can trust you because you are white" (2001a, 30). Yet, in light of the analysis in this chapter (and in the book more generally), this set of experiences appears almost banal. It is a wonder that most contemporary ethnographic studies of postcolonial Africa rarely mention race, much less Whiteness!

I have attempted in this chapter to establish Whiteness as an important site of racialization in Ghana and as a way to demonstrate the global significance of race and White supremacy. Of course my work does not characterize White racial positionality as unrestrained power and privilege. To be sure, negotiations of identity in this contemporary urban and postcolonial space rest on a complicated set of historical realities, assumptions, and relationships that work, often, to structure a hierarchy of positions that is by no means completely rigid. White positionality in Ghana often does not go unchallenged. Nevertheless, the very rights, advantages, and special treatment enjoyed by a relatively small group of people as a result of wealth or social status derived seemingly from membership in a particular minority race is significant inasmuch as it occurs in modern-day Ghana. Ghana is considered an African country with no clear-cut history of de jure apartheid or White-settler politics and ultimately no overt anti-Black racism. At the same time, the country is well known and admired for its extensive history of Pan-Africanist politics and activism (see chapter 4). The assumption, at least for many anthropologists, is that issues of White privileged positionality—indeed, issues of race—cannot, and should not, be considered issues at all. Yet, this is not the reality on the ground.

In his work on global White supremacy, Charles Mills argues that so-called Third World nations are part of a global racialized economy "dominated by white capital and white lending institutions . . . [and] by the cultural products of the white West" (1998, 102). My research seeks to uncover the not-so-hidden transcripts of race and processes of racialization that color daily life in this urban, postcolonial setting, transcripts that are indexed to a broader transnational template about difference, power, and status. Along the road of racial discovery in urban Ghana, I have encountered a number of competing racial projects that both challenge and reaffirm the global racial hierarchy with Whiteness as power position. These racial projects (four of which are the focus of this book), though always contradictory, point to a concrete set of practices and lived experiences. My focus in this particular chapter has been on how Ghanaian engagement with Whiteness (and Whites) and discourses of race, racial difference, and privilege occurs within a broader set of processes whereby local relationships continue to be structured by current global configurations of identity, economics, and politics. These current relationships, I maintain, are continuing the legacy of a very recent history of colonial/imperial domination. As Whiteness is being more firmly entrenched into the global economic and cultural order, and as it is becoming seemingly inseparable from power, race—understood both in its broad and specific sense—matters, in Ghana and elsewhere.

In this book, I am particularly interested in naming and exposing the often invisible power and naturalization of White positionality (even though White people are very much visible). As Cole revealed to us, examples abound in which Whites are served first, placed at the fronts of queues, and treated with more respect than myself and other Blacks. Whites enjoy a normative power that points to the country's intimate relationship with global practices of race. In other words, to speak of White privilege—particularly in a predominantly Black society such as Ghana—is to speak of race and racial domination in global terms. It is to both recognize and engage the connections between Western global capitalism and Western cultural and racial domination. Today's common sense about Whiteness (and therefore race) in Ghana reflects a history of negotiation with racialized cultural and political domination that continues to influence understandings of self and identity. Linked to the discourses around Whiteness, for example, are the explicit and complicated local practices around notions of aesthetics, particularly as they relate to light-skin-color valorization. These dynamics are structured through the work that Whiteness—among other things—has done in normalizing its power. Thus, the complex phenomenon of skin bleaching (to which we turn in the next chapter) and the desire for lighter skin in a self-consciously Black society point to another way that notions of race get deployed in contemporary Ghana. Significantly, they also point to the interlinked transnational notions of Blackness, in which the intricate negotiations around color-cum-race in Ghana are reflected in most, if not all, societies of Africa and the African diaspora.

# FOUR

# The Fact of Lightness: Skin Bleaching and the Colored Codes of Racial Aesthetics

For several years, some laboratories have been trying to discover a serum for "denegrification"; these laboratories, with all the seriousness in the world, have rinsed their test tubes, checked their scales, and begun research that might make it possible for the miserable Negroes to whiten themselves and thus throw off the burden of that corporeal malediction.

—Frantz Fanon, *Black Skin, White Masks*

Many blacks, in short, simply want to be beautiful and successful. But because no black can be white, it follows that there must be some other, achievable point of being beautiful and successful that is aimed at in such activity.

—Lewis Gordon, *Her Majesty's Other Children*

The body beautiful has been the white body.

—Charles Mills, *Blackness Visible*

"If you have soft light skin, then you use only the Maxi Light. But when you have, let's say, tough, black skin, then you will have to mix; you will have to maybe add the Lemonvate to the Maxi Light," Emma told me. I was sitting in Emma's living room, in one of the many small apartments surrounding the large courtyard of a very popular restaurant in a central neighborhood in Accra. It was a hot Wednesday afternoon, and I was speaking with Emma and her friend Sarah about skin bleaching. My friend Sam, who has known Emma for many years and who first introduced me to her, was with me. Sam and I had been led into Emma's small living room to wait for her by one of her friends and coworkers. When she came in, Emma's face was lightly covered with a white cream that made it look like it was painted.

4.1 Skin-bleaching products owned by a woman in Accra, June 2006.
Photograph by the author.

(Emma later told me that the cream was there to help clear up the pimples on her face). Emma was a woman of small stature who appeared to be in her early thirties. On average, Emma's complexion was not extremely dark; she was certainly a shade of dark brown, but not as dark as many other people. In fact, she would even be considered fair (light skinned) in Ghana. This point would come up later as we discussed the various ways to successfully bleach.

When we turned to the topic at hand, I asked Emma how long she had been bleaching. Emma shyly told me that she has been doing so off and on for about ten years. She quickly smiled and looked down upon seeing Sam's cheerless facial response and the surprised look on my face. As our conversation picked up, I asked Emma to explain the bleaching process. When she was about to begin, Sam stopped her and asked if she could bring out some samples of the products she was using. Emma stepped out of the living room and through the curtain that led to her bedroom; a few minutes later, she came out with her supply—an arsenal of small and large bottles and tubes containing creams and lotions. There was Sonet: Popular Facial Cream, which featured "before" and "after" pictures of an East Asian woman; the woman had a considerably lighter complexion in the "after" representation. Then there was Skin Light, which included a description in French that read "La Creme Eclaircissante Traitante" (the Brightening Treatment Cream). Packaged like prescription medicine and sold in a green-and-yellow tube was the Lemonvate Cream. Emma's collection also contained the Maxi Light cream, as well as a large lotion bottle with a faded top label reading "Body Clear," with "Skin-Whitening Lotion" written below. I was struck by how straightforward the names of these products were in their marketing of cosmetic—and, indeed, corrective—whiteness.

At one point during our conversation, I stopped and frankly asked Emma why she bleached. She seemed taken aback by the question. I am not sure whether this was because such a question had never been asked of her, but Emma chuckled gently and nervously and paused to consider her response: "As a woman," she began after a few moments, "when you are slightly light skinned, anything [color] you put on shows." Here Emma was articulating a seemingly common belief that people with lighter skin are able to wear clothing with a broader range of color, since the contrast with the skin is considered not as great as it would be if a person were dark. This is based on the assumption that especially dark skin absorbs color and does not show off colored clothing very well. Emma continued, "[Also] I am already light, so I want to be lighter."

"If you are already light, why do you want to be lighter?" I asked. "Why not want to be darker instead, or stay the color you are?" At this point, Sam jumped in and responded for Emma: "Light means beauty." He paused briefly, and Emma added, "You become prettier when you are lighter."

Using the phenomenon of skin bleaching as a springboard, this chapter explores the dynamics and politics of light-skin-color valorization as an important site of racialization in Ghana. I argue that skin-bleaching practices occur in direct relation, and in response, to White and light-skin-color privilege in Ghana that, in turn, actually reveals common ideas about the global nature of race. My research over the years in urban Ghana reveals that the roots of the skin-bleaching phenomenon lie in the country's complex historical relationship to race—but, here, explicitly the relationship of race to color—and its articulations with gender, socioeconomic status, class, aesthetics, and culture. Because skin bleaching is not exclusive to Ghana or postcolonial Africa, however, I also contend that the practice actually reveals common ideas about the *transnational* significance of race.

In recent years, the practice of skin bleaching in Africa and among populations of African descent throughout the diaspora has gained international attention. Journalistic as well as scholarly coverage of the phenomenon has generally focused on two key issues: the medical problems associated with bleaching, and the psychosocial and cultural implications of the desire for lighter or white skin. In the process, black bodies, noticeably deformed by toxic bleaching products, are often exhibited to demonstrate the severity of the problem, to highlight the need to regulate a popular-cosmetics market, and to convey outrage over the desire for lighter skin color. With headlines such as "Africans Look for Beauty in Western Mirror" (Schuler 1999) or "Fade to White: Skin Bleaching and the Rejection of Blackness" (Chisholm 2002), the skin-bleaching phenomenon in contemporary Africa is associated with the racialized aesthetic mores that attach value to Whiteness. On one level, this popular depiction is important, as it recognizes bleaching practices within the terrain of local ideologies of race. At the same time, however, there is a way in which the intense focus on the popularity of the phenomenon among Africans (and other racially non-White communities) may work to depict the desire for Whiteness as not only irrational, but also unique to this group. Similar to the valorization of Whiteness discussed in the previous chapter, skin bleaching has to be considered within global structures of difference and power, what Michel-Rolph Trouillot refers to as the "worldwide hierarchy of races, religions, and cultures" (1994, 146). Thus, rather than pathologize those who bleach, the point is to examine the broader contours of the social and cultural field—of history, memory, and habitus—within which the benefits of skin lightening are established for such individuals (Bourdieu 1977).

The ethnographically informed discussion in this chapter develops two-fold. First, I explore the actual skin-bleaching process within the historical context of its transnational expansion. This connects skin bleaching to racial ideologies that developed with European expansion into the New World, ultimately shaping the logic of Whiteness that underpinned the rise of the cosmetics industry. Second, I focus on the materiality of the interplay of race and color, by which lightness is the key marker of distinction from Whiteness as well as from Blackness. Here, I suggest that where attaining corporeal Whiteness is impossible for those racially Black (and dark), the desire for lightness is less about becoming White and more about becoming *less* Black in order to gain "certain aeasthetic and political-economic resources that pertain to being white" (Gordon 1997, 59). The interrelatedness of the materiality of Whiteness and lightness is therefore undeniable. I ground this part of the discussion within the Ghanaian social and cultural field, in which racial aesthetics, while undoubtedly local, are shaped by and respond to transnational racial regimes. I want to add that while skin-bleaching practices tend to maintain a coherent logic around the superiority

4.2 Billboard in the Asylum Down neighborhood,
Accra, July 2005. Photograph by the author.

of Whiteness, I hope that this discussion also demonstrates the complex local nuances that underscore such logic within the broad terrain of Ghanaian
racial formation.

## Exorcising the "Corporal Malediction"

If you were to pass by the intersection leading to the Asylum Down neighborhood in Accra, Ghana, in the fall of 2005, or if you were to walk by
Papaye, a popular restaurant in the center of the cosmopolitan Osu neighborhood as recently as the summer of 2006, you would surely not miss
the large billboard advertising BODY/WHITE. BODY/WHITE is the brand
name for a line of beauty products hailing, as we are told by the advertisement, from Paris, France. On the billboard advertisements, the individual products featured are: the Gel Eclaircissant (described on the bottle
as the "original bleaching treatment"); the Savon Eclaircissant (the "body-
brightening soap"); and the Gel Creme (described both as "formulae con-
centrée" and "eclaircissant intense"). Most arresting, however, is the image
used to market the product. Positioned on the left side of the advertisement
is the larger-than-life image of a well-coiffed, scantily clad, and presumably attractive and modern woman looking seductively into the camera and
holding a bottle of the BODY/WHITE Gel Eclaircissant. The woman has
an extremely light complexion—she is, in fact, almost "body/white"—with
long, straight black hair and bluish-gray eyes. Significantly, this woman
does not look racially White; her other features—a relatively broad nose
and thicker lips—work to mark her as undeniably non-White. It is as if the

intention of the advertisement is that she be perceived as racially non-White but capable of lightening her skin color.

Encountering this billboard around town, I could not help but think of both the irony and significance of its message. How can an advertisement for skin whitening have such a bold and seemingly unapologetic presence in urban Ghana? How can a product announcing its ability to transform the black bodies of Ghanaians into white ones—a transformation with clear sociopolitical as well as cultural significance—be advertised in a proud Black postcolonial African nation with an established history of Pan-Africanism? What does it mean for a black body to be "cleared" of its blackness, to become "body white"? What is the value of whiteness that it can purportedly be bought and sold? More importantly, what is at stake when transnational pharmaceutical and cosmetics corporations develop products that claim to bleach out and "whiten" dark skin?

After we took turns looking over the various labels on the bottles and tubes, I asked Emma to explain how she uses all of the products, and how often. "You have to mix some of them [the creams] together," she began. "For example, you have to squeeze the Lemonvate into the Maxi Light." I asked why. She continued, "This is what will make the layer [of skin] peel off easier. See, you don't know which will be okay [work better] for you, so you have to put different things [creams] together." By this time, I was thoroughly confused; I could not figure out if Emma was actually using all the products she had brought out, and I was curious to find out. I asked Emma to describe again her bleaching ritual in detail. Emma said that she began her morning shower with a bleaching soap, either a concoction she made herself by mixing "black soap" (a locally made soap) with some other (unspecified) ingredients or Robert's Soap, a well-known skin-bleaching soap. Then she combined equal parts of the Maxi Light and Lemonvate creams and rubbed the mixture all over her body. Emma said that she did not use the Body Clear lotion as often as before, however. I asked her why that was the case. Emma said that though the Body Clear lotion works well and can lighten the skin considerably, it was more risky for her to use now because she works near fire and heat. Using this lotion under such conditions may have the adverse effect of causing hyperpigmentation as well as other side effects. Later on in the conversation, I asked Emma how she knew which creams or soaps to buy and how to mix them together to get the desired results. She answered that she received advice from friends who also bleach; they told her which products to purchase and which worked well together. Upon hearing this, Sam jumped in to clarify: "You see, you have to keep trying; you have to put it all together, mix them in different ways, to see which will work better for your skin. It's all trial and error."

Skin bleaching is a practice by which women and men use various chemical and cosmetics products—in the form of creams, pills, soaps, and lotions—to attempt to lighten or whiten the color of the skin. These products most often contain either or both hydroquinone and mercury. Hydroquinone is a powerful, toxic substance originally used in photo processing, the manufacture of rubber, and hair dyes. Mercury is a heavy metal that exists in different chemical forms; skin-bleaching products often contain ammoniated mercury that is normally used as an ointment to treat impetigo, psoriasis, and other skin disorders. The more popular of the two chemicals is hydroquinone, although the widespread use of mercury in cosmetic products is growing. Topical hydroquinone has been around for a long time and remains a common ingredient in cosmetic products. It has generally been used to lighten areas of darkened skin such as freckles, age spots, and cholasma. Hydroquinone works by destroying or inhibiting melanin-producing cells and encouraging the removal of the top layer of skin, resulting in less pigmentation and ultimately the lightening of the skin's color. Mercury-based bleaching chemicals work in the same way to limit the production of melanin. Although mercury and hydroquinone are the most popular active ingredients in skin-bleaching products, they often contain other chemicals, such as various steroids. There are now also what scientists are calling second-generation skin-bleaching products, which claim to provide the same results as hydroquinone, without its harsh side effects. One of the more popular of these is kojic acid, which is marketed as an alternative to hydroquinone because while it also prevents the production of melanin, it is much less irritating.

The actual process of chemically bleaching one's skin is expensive, labor intensive, often impractical, and dangerous. The products that saturate Ghana's market are barely affordable, especially for the poor and working class, who often resort to cheaper products in the informal market or to household products such as laundry bleach, certain shampoos, and even ground bits of glass. Middle and upper classes buy the imported and expensive bleaching products, such as Vantex Skin Bleaching Creme from Fashion Fair Cosmetics, the largest US-based Black-owned cosmetic company in the world. In addition to the expense is the actual intensive process of bleaching. Emma's daily ritual, with baths with bleaching soaps followed by the application of a number of creams multiple times throughout the day, demonstrates this. Also, to be effective, skin-bleaching products have to be used consistently and over long periods of time. This affects both cost and increased medical risk. As Sarah pointed out to me, once a person begins bleaching extensively, she or he has to work diligently to maintain the process. Yet, when used in heavy concentrations, these products can cause extreme skin irritation and sometimes the development of ochrosis, a blue-black discoloration of the skin. The other active chemical ingredients found in bleaching products—mercury and corticosteroids—can also have extremely adverse effects. Because of the tendency of mercury to enter the body through pores in the skin, mercury poisoning is the leading problem associated with mercury-based skin-bleaching products. Other effects of these chemicals are speech and hearing impediments and kidney disease, as well as eczema and fungal and bacterial infections. As several Ghanaian doctors and dermatologists told me, the most dangerous hazard is that the destruction of melanin-producing cells reduces the skin's ability to protect itself against the hazards of sunlight and ultraviolet rays. Furthermore, some of these products work by actually thinning the skin, making it weak and sometimes spongy.

Manufacturers of products containing hydroquinone and mercury often warn consumers to stay out of the sun since the exposure will not only make the chemical less effective, but it can also cause the adverse reaction of hyperpigmentation and calloused skin. Because of this important precaution, Ghana's hot climate makes it extremely easy to detect a "bleacher," particularly those who are poor or working class. For example, in Makola, the large outdoor market in central Accra, those who bleach are easily recognizable by their wide-brimmed hats, long skirts or pants, thick woolen socks, and long-sleeved shirts underneath their dresses. This bundling is designed either to cover up the damage done to the skin by bleaching or to protect the skin from the hot sun once one has begun bleaching. As impractical as this may seem, it appears to be common practice among a segment of the bleaching population in Ghana.

There are social hazards involved with bleaching as well. Obvious bleachers are often openly ridiculed. Poor women, in particular, are castigated as either brainwashed or too illiterate to know better. Skin bleaching in Ghana is also primarily attributed to prostitutes, who often admit to bleaching for the purpose of attracting more clients. However, it is an open secret that many of the upper and middle classes—particularly professional women—bleach, a fact that allows for private ridicule and consternation. A most disturbing social hazard is the popular claim that bleached skin often emits a rancid, rotten odor over time. In fact, this was actually the most common complaint I heard from various people. In discussing the potential problems of bleaching, Emma admitted that she understood the risks that bleachers were taking. Focusing particularly on those she considered heavy bleachers, she said that when the person stopped bleaching, "you will see spots all over their body." "Then," she said, "there is the scent, the body odor, the not-so-nice smell coming from the creams and soaps that they use." A young woman, a producer at the local television station who conducted intensive research on the skin-bleaching phenomenon for a television documentary on the subject, also told me that it was the "bleaching smell" of one of her mother's friends that got her interested in understanding the phenomenon. "You know they have a smell, don't you?" she once asked me. Without waiting for a response, she continued, "The smell is so strong that it makes you want to throw up. I can't stand it!"

Cosmetic skin bleaching occurs worldwide.[1] The phenomenon is also prevalent in South Asia, and it is common particularly among various immigrant and communities of color in Europe and the United States (Rondilla and Spickard 2007; Glenn 2009; Miller 2006). It is an especially well-known and much-discussed issue in Jamaica, a place recognized as suffering from an epidemic of skin bleaching (Charles 2003; Kovaleski 1999; BBC News 2007). Until recently, hydroquinone was an accepted ingredient in many cosmetic products and in Western societies as well, as long as such products contained no more than 2 percent of the chemical. For example, anti-aging creams and ointments for skin spots and other discolorations all contained, and many still do contain, hydroquinone. These guidelines, however, have not been strictly enforced, particularly in non-Western countries where the unrestricted access of multinational corporations to local markets has enabled the introduction of bleaching products with as much as 30 percent hydroquinone, a deadly percentage. On the African continent in particular, medical problems associated with skin bleaching have forced governments to aggressively combat the practice through antibleaching campaigns. South Africa and Cameroon, for example, have moved to ban all products containing hydroquinone and have sought to educate their citizens about the adverse effects of bleaching. Products containing hydroquinone have also been banned in Australia, in Japan, and by the European Union. In August 2006, the U.S. Food and Drug Administration proposed a ban on products with hydroquinone, citing the chemical's potential to cause cancer and other adverse effects (Food and Drug Administration 2006). Despite such widespread efforts, many countries continue to lose the battle not only to the large and profitable informal market of skin-bleaching products, but also and especially to manufacturers and the multinational pharmaceutical and cosmetics companies whose marketing strategies tap into local (and transnational) ideologies of race, difference, and aesthetics.

If the practice is not unique to Ghana or postcolonial Africa, how then do we examine the widespread and continued proliferation of skin bleaching? In a provocative article, Amina Mire (2005) places part of the blame on the skin-whitening industry, which, she argues, reinforces and consolidates the global ideology of White supremacy. For Mire, the promotion of skin-bleaching products by major pharmaceutical and cosmetics companies fits within the "continuum of the western practice of global racism" (Mire 2005). This perspective reveals that African-descended (and other non-White) populations are only participating in an already existing set of discourses and practices about race—and particularly Whiteness—that extends beyond their individual, local communities. In this way, Mire forces us to move away from the tendency to pathologize women of color in particular for their seemingly unique and "dubious desire for unattainable corporeal Whiteness" (4) and instead to recognize the broader (global) context of the practice.

Thus, to understand the sociocultural politics of contemporary bleaching in Ghana, we have to grapple with the ways that global racial meanings, with ideologies of Whiteness as power, "constitute broad sociopolitical realms with control over the most intimate details of daily life" in various localities (Burke 1996, 159). In the first epigraph to this chapter, Franz Fanon satirically references laboratories set up to discover ways of effecting a chemical "denigrification" for "Negroes to whiten themselves and thus throw off the burden of that 'corporal malediction.'" But this process is more than skin deep: "Below the corporeal schema I had sketched a historico-racial schema. The elements that I used had been provided for me not by 'residual sensations and perceptions primarily of a tactile, vestibular, kinesthetic, visual character,' but by the other, the white man, who had woven me out of a thousand details, anecdotes, stories" (1967, 111). The desire to "de-blacken" thus emerges from the histories of the constructions of Blackness through racial science and what Fanon calls "historicity." This racial historicity also spawns various registers of Whiteness and its own regimes for chemical maintenance.

Contemporary skin-bleaching practices (in Ghana and elsewhere) can be traced to the modern development of the commercial cosmetics industry. According to Richard Dyer, much of the history of Western makeup is actually "a history of whitening the face" (1997, 49). Modern cosmetic and chemical skin whitening dates back to ancient Greek use of white lead (ceruse) on the skin that, because it was found to be poisonous, was replaced by rice powder in the nineteenth century. Kathy Peiss (1998) also details how the expansion of the White European and American cosmetics industry was, from the beginning, tied to ideologies of race. White women, with their consciousness and self-image structured by the discourses and practices that reinforced notions of White beauty, worked hard to achieve what they believed would make them beautiful—milky complexions. In the United States and in various parts of Europe and the Americas, White women developed their own concoctions, mixing various organic and chemical products to both conceal blemishes and enhance their light complexions. In fact, before the rise of the commercial cosmetics industry, White women were painting or whitening their skin with toxic paints, lotions, and other substances. Although these practices often caused major disfiguration and sickness, bleaching, lightening, and whitening the skin remained a key aspect of cosmetics preparation for these women. As the cosmetics industry became further established in the late nineteenth and early twentieth centuries, White women had a common goal in their pursuit of beauty: "They desired a lighter complexion" (8–9). To these women and society at large, a lighter complexion projected ideal White and genteel beauty, and it marked distinctions between and within social classes, all the while reinforcing "a noxious racial aesthetic" (31).

Indeed, the development of the cosmetics and skin-bleaching industry was based on a set of accumulated knowledge about race and aesthetics on a global scale, and it was linked directly to various ideologies of difference that emerged with European expansion. It was not hyperbole when a Ghanaian man insisted that "skin bleaching has been going on for a long time. . . . [I]t began when we had the British ruling over us" (Chisholm 2002). Official and popular eighteenth- and nineteenth-century beliefs about race imputed intelligence and beauty to racial classification, and "travelers, missionaries, anthropologists, and scientists viewed beauty as a function of race" (Peiss 1998, 31; see also Dyer 1997). Even as some espoused relativism, ideas about race and beauty always proclaimed the superiority of White racial beauty and aesthetics, and they were usually asserted in relation to people of color around the world. With the entrenchment of global White rule, particularly Anglo Saxon supremacy, Whiteness—specifically, white skin—represented virtue and civilization, further justifying European expansion (Dyer 1997).

Ironically, white skin, in the strict, physical sense, is elusive even for those who are White. In addition to the use of chemicals, there were a number of ways in which those racialized as White actively worked to appear whiter over the years. Dyer reveals, for example, that early painters and photographers of Europeans participated in the process of White-making, often rendering White people in pictures literally white (1997, 48). This whitening also had an explicit gendered dimension: White women, as the site of ultimate aesthetically desirable Whiteness, were always portrayed as lighter than their male counterparts. Whiteness, it seems, needed to be continually defined and policed in the context of European expansion and rule over racially non-White subjects. It is significant, then, that whiteness was constructed against non-Whiteness, which was often defined as much through habits, culture, status, and behavior as through skin color. In the rendering of Whiteness through its visible properties, white skin, specifically the white face, not only asserted cultural refinement and class privilege, but it also established and reinforced a distinct racial privilege.

Significantly, advertising for whitening products targeting White women in later periods offered fewer explicit claims about the actual process of chemically altering the skin. By the mid-twentieth century, cosmetics geared toward White women instead promoted products as "natural" solutions to conceal blemishes, bleach out freckles, and generally "clear" the skin of un-natural dark spots (Peiss 1998), a trend that has carried over to contemporary practices in the White cosmetics industry. In this sense, the chemical process of whitening White women's skin had become so naturalized as to hide the reality that such products were actually covering, coloring, and ultimately altering the skin. White women's cosmetic products, therefore, were presented as beauty enhancement (ibid.).

The story was different for Black women, however. In contrast to the practice of advertising the enhancement of White women's "natural" beauty, chemical whitening products, especially in the early twentieth century, were presented as "cures for 'disabling' African features" (Peiss 1998, 43). And although there were overlaps in how cosmetics were marketed to White and Black women, there is something significant about the difference between "enhancing" one's natural beauty and "transforming" one's features to achieve beauty. In that difference, we see a particular articulation of racial ideology—the ways in which Blackness can be continuously debased and devalued. Whitening creams—because they were originally made for White women—were no doubt bound to have a different effect on Black women. Because "really white Whiteness is unattainable" (Dyer 1997, 78) for both White and Black peoples, and because Blacks were deemed the most racially distinct from Whites, Black racial identity was presented as requiring drastic transformation. With that dynamic, a particular irony came into play. As Dyer correctly argues, Blacks, both then and now, who attempt to bleach are often openly ridiculed—both within and outside of the community—for aspiring to become and ultimately failing in becoming White. They are ridiculed for not knowing that no matter how much they try, they cannot really become White. Yet, what is often lost in this derision is that the desire for, and the various attempts to attain, real Whiteness is virtually universal. Within the context of global White supremacy, Whiteness/lightness—in terms of its symbolism, corporeal representation, and material benefits—is desired by most, including those who already have membership within racial Whiteness. Indeed, the anthropologist Melville Herskovits was probably accurate when, in discovering colorism in the U.S. Black community in the early twentieth century, he asked, "Why should there not be this selection [of White racial aesthetics] if Negroes respond to the same kind of cultural conditioning as Whites, particularly when we consider the prestige carried by that which is non-Negroid?" (Herskovits 1928).

## The Fact of Lightness; or, To "Simply Want to Be Beautiful and Successful"

After Emma told me that "you become prettier when you are lighter," I asked, "What makes lighter prettier?" Here, Emma did not have a clear response. She seemed to fumble for the right words. I repeated Sam's words to her in the form of a question: "So, lighter is prettier?" Emma nodded. Yet she seemed surprised by her own response. I continued, "When you bleach, do people tell you you're nicer [prettier] because you're lighter?" At this, Sam quickly told me that Emma was married. He then turned to Emma and asked if her husband approved of her bleaching. "My husband doesn't like it when I bleach so [too] much," Emma answered. "But a little bit is okay, right?" asked Sam. To this, Emma responded, "He likes it when I am light." Sam's interactions with Emma proved telling. It was clear that he was not only familiar with his friend's aesthetic preferences, but that he was also very aware of the discourses around skin color. In fact, my own conversations with Sam revealed a particular kind of (skin) color consciousness that was so naturalized as to go almost unnoticed. Although I have known him for more than a decade, it still surprised me whenever he would make often absentminded comments about skin color that revealed a particular view of light skin. One specific example includes a time when Sam was telling me about his youngest daughter, whom I had yet to meet. He began by describing how popular she is with the extended family because, as he said, "She is so pretty." Without prompting, he continued with, "She is fair, much lighter than me, you see? So everyone likes her." While I registered the sentiment, I didn't respond to the colorism underlying Sam's comments. I asked whom the baby took after the most in the family. He responded, "My mum. She is also very fair and pretty."

Contemporary discussions with Ghanaians about skin bleaching and the seeming desire for light skin often yield explanations for the phenomenon that range from a simple matter of aesthetic preference to charges of internalized racism. During a heated debate among a group of young people about skin bleaching one afternoon, Ama, a secondary school student, argued, "The women do it to gain more favor from their husbands." Joseph disagreed. "They do it because they hate Black. They want to be White," he said. Although some middle-class Ghanaians, such as these students, will dismiss skin bleaching as behavior found only in undereducated, lower-class communities, it is nevertheless common knowledge that the practice crosses class lines. In 2005 the director general of the Ghana Health Service, professor Agyeman Badu Akosa, published a news release stating, "An anti-bleaching campaign must be launched." For Professor Akosa, this was an urgent issue because bleaching saturated Ghanaian society:

> The size of the problem in Ghana is enormous and it cuts across age groups, sex and class or professional groupings. . . . Every identifiable group of persons are represented in the guilty group. Professional people including lawyers, doctors, nurses, teachers, etc., business persons, charismatic and non charismatic pastors or reverends, media people, traders, fishermen, chiefs and the worst offenders, queenmothers.[2] In the latter group particularly in the Ashanti Region of Ghana, if you are nominated and installed as a queenmother you must lighten your skin before the enstoolment. It brightens you up they say, in much the same way as putting on the light in a room. (2005)

But there is logic to this behavior among a large swath of the Ghanaian population. It is not lost on many people that there is a correlation between light skin color and prominent occupational positions; in fact, many people assume that a lighter-complexioned woman in a position of power has either bleached or is bleaching to achieve such status. Regardless of class status, what is significant is that such practices reflect common ideas about light-skin-color preference and the explicit and subtle ways they are articulated. During our conversation, Sarah, like Emma, also pointed out how "you become prettier when you are lighter." She said that bleaching made her "stand out." "People notice you," she continued, and "men think you are pretty."

Indeed, over the years of traveling to and living in Ghana, I have been repeatedly caught in conversations and situations that suggested an unabashed preference for light skin. Examples abound. During an interview about the relationship between gender, light-skin-color valorization, and skin bleaching one afternoon, a prominent Ghanaian lawyer and feminist activist unwittingly admitted to me, after she had denounced skin bleaching as "self-hatred," that "I don't know why, but people with lighter skin seem prettier to me—especially those mixed-race ones." My interlocutor's remarks also pointed to the fact that the discussion around beauty and lighter skin often included references, if at times indirect, to mixed-race individuals in Ghanaian societies (and outside). Here we see a direct extension of the interplay of the ideology and corporeality of Whiteness, both of which point to its materiality and power. I have often heard, in Ghana and elsewhere, the general convention that mixed-race babies are desirable by young women. This is usually followed by derisive (and sexist) claims that poor young women, in particular, seek out European tourists for procreation. Recently, myjoyonline.com, the website of the popular Joy FM radio station, published an article with the headline "People in Oil-Producing Towns Expect Mixed-Race Babies." While there were other "expectations" articulated—such as new roads, hospitals, fire service, and a police station—the main story was how the residents of Efaso "hope to raise mixed children who certainly will have a better life" (Daabu 2010). The idea that White parentage automatically links one to a better life speaks to the reality of the global privilege of Whiteness, real and imagined. But it also translates in a different register: the skin color of the mixed-race individual also becomes the site used to both establish a direct link to Whiteness (and all its accoutrements) and to determine one's place in a sociopolitical and cultural-aesthetic hierarchy. (And the fact that many leaders of independence married White women and returned with mixed-race children offers anecdotal evidence concerning persistence of Whiteness and mixed race as a marker of status in the postcolonial era [Appiah 1992]). Lewis Gordon has rightly noted that mixture among Blacks usually functions as an "organizing aesthetic" as well as a "tragic history": "On the aesthetic level, it signifies the divide between beauty and ugliness. On the social level, the divide is between just and unjust, virtuous and vicious; 'fair skin' is no accidental, alternative term for 'light skin'" (1997, 57).

That mixed race and light skin are interrelated here, in particular because they reflect a proximity to Whiteness, demonstrates clearly the multiple registers of racialization. Racial categorization and identity, however socially constructed, depends also on what Harry Hoetnik once referred to as the "somatic norm," (1967) an image formed during colonialism, when the color line came to be defined by the appearance of typical members of the (racially) intermediate class. The "somatic norm" image classified populations primarily based on skin-tone designations and other phenotypic requirements.[3] Indeed, though deployed in multiple ways with varying social and political effects, such designations and requirements are at the core of racial identity throughout the modern world. Thus, as the literature on race in Latin American, the United States, and South Africa has demonstrated, racialization has also worked through distinctive phenotypic variation—no matter the model determined by the individual social structure, such as the "one-drop rule" (Wade 1997). And though racial identity sometimes seems to trump phenotype (as is the case with the U.S. "one-drop rule," by which even those with a racially White phenotype are recognized as Black), there is nevertheless the correlation between race, phenotype, and socioeconomic, political, and even aesthetic and cultural privilege.

Yet, accumulated historical precedents and contemporary practices do reveal the significance of both intra- and interracial skin-color differentiation in the struggle over identity and meaning. As we saw in chapter 1, for example, the racial politics of the British colonial project in West Africa, and the Gold Coast in particular, necessitated the establishment of forms of racial apartheid, even as foreign rule depended on the aid of local actors. Linked to this is the history of prominent mixed-race families in the eighteenth and nineteenth centuries, who were distinguished from the local community through education, dress, cultural practices, and class status, and who articulated a distinctive racial identity based on ancestry and their positions in society. The European trade on the Gold Coast brought about the emergence of new economic and social classes. Connected with the rise of the middle class of African merchants and middlemen, in particular, was the emergence of a group of people then known as "mulattoes, sons and daughters of marriages between the white merchants and the local consorts" (Buah 1980, 75). Some of the more prominent of these groups, such as the Bannermans, the Reindorfs, the Van Dykes, the Bohams, the de Grafts, and the Grants, are still recognizable (ibid.; see also Gocking 1999). Primarily because of their connections to White European merchants, members of these groups were well educated and occupied influential positions in church, commerce, and state enterprises. And their wealth and influence enabled them to yield great power in the developing social and political life of the coast. Gocking refers to these families of Euro-Africans as making up the "better classes" and demonstrates how there was "considerable group endogamy," which worked not only to cement business and social relations, but also to establish the basis for group differentiation from the other local inhabitants. In this way, "intermarriage among the elite of the educated classes contributed to making this section of coastal society 'one large extended family of blood and affinal relations'" (Gocking 1999, 56).

This shared cultural experience created a particular part of racial identity making for this group. But the identification of its members was always subject to contestation, negotiation, and transformation, especially within local ethnic, cultural, and religious identifications. Nevertheless, the cultural and political presence of such communities reveals a unique history of the formation of racial consciousness in Ghana, particularly through the interplay of notions of race, color, class, and aesthetics (see especially Parker 1998; DeCorse 2001).

Significantly, in Ghana as elsewhere, the key is that racial lightness—because of its proximity to racial Whiteness, and in the context of global White supremacy—holds an overwhelming power position. The anthropological and sociological literature on White and light-skin-color privilege in various places throughout the world—from Latin America to Asia to the United States—clearly demonstrates this.[4] In the lesser-known studies about the skin-color differentiation of and among U.S. Black populations, we see the impact of skin color on specific resources such as wages and standards of living. One study reveals that "as skin shade lightens the wages for blacks rise" (Hamilton, Goldsmith, and Darity 2009). Hamilton and others found that "among Blacks in the U.S. *lightness*—possessing white characteristics as measured by skin shade—is rewarded in the labor market" (27). In recognizing that lighter skin gives individuals greater proximity to benefits associated with Whiteness, the scholars argue that, contrary to conventional understandings, effects and treatments of race in the United States may be more similar to those in Latin America, since phenotype rather than genotype governs treatment in the labor market. The literature on U.S. Black elites reveals a clear—and often ongoing—color hierarchy that has existed over time and that has such long historical effects that certain life chances, in terms of privilege or costs, can still be linked to skin color. In his study of the Black Americans at the turn of the twentieth century, Melville Herskovits discovered, for example, that "most well-to-do families in the communities in Harlem were known for mixed race heritage lighter skin; thus lighter, less Negroid individuals seem to have the favored position in the Negro community" (1928, 61). In addition, he recorded the specific practice of mate selection within the community, which was directly correlated with skin color. Here, the skin-color dynamics—and in particular light-skin-color valorization—within U.S. Black communities mirror directly their counterparts in Latin America, the Caribbean, and the African continent.

These dynamics work in similar ways in Ghana, from media affirmation of light skin as beautiful to everyday practices of light-skin valorization. One poignant example includes the common remark "I like your color" made to my friend Yvonne as we navigated our way through Accra city life during an extended stay in Ghana between 2000 and 2001. As we moved about town, shopping at the markets, attending popular events, and frequenting clubs and bars, reactions to Yvonne, particularly ongoing references to her skin color, which occurred much more often than references to mine (I am a dark-skinned Black woman), reflected a clear discourse of race as refracted through notions of color and gender. Yvonne was born in Brooklyn, New York, to Guyanese immigrant parents. And because of her light-brown complexion, she received a great deal of attention from men and women in Ghana. She would often complain to me of being overwhelmed by the constant refrain of "I like your color." At the same time, coming from Afro-Caribbean families, we both recognized that light-skin valorization was not unique to Ghana. Using the example of the politics of skin color in Haiti, Michel-Rolph Trouillot correctly argues that "if race matters, color matters with race" (1994, 170). Indeed, he continues, what is often described "in sibylline terms as the 'color question'" is actually etched within a framework of an international racial (and cultural) hierarchy that was formalized historically during European domination (148). In other words, color distinctions within non-White communities are not only based on racialized understandings of difference, but they also do not occur in a vacuum. As numerous contexts throughout the world demonstrate, one's proximity to Whiteness often determines life chances in any given society. If bleaching and attendant light-skin-color valorization occur in contemporary urban Ghana, this practice has to be contextualized within localized articulations of the country's history of racialized Western influence, which dates back to the early sixteenth century. Social evaluations of physical features—of color and other physical characteristics—continue to be influenced by this explicitly racial inheritance, as well as by contemporary practices that still link economic, political, and cultural superiority to Whiteness (and lightness as its surrogate). As a corollary to his point about race and color, Trouillot also reminds us that we cannot dismiss light-color privilege as just an avatar of Western prejudices. In local contexts, light-skin privilege is usually made complex and is at times challenged, even if partially, by certain local practices (as we will see in the discussion of the state's rearticulation of Pan-Africanism in the next chapter).

Of course, it is just as easy to find the real cultural value and material benefits attached to lighter skin in urban Ghana. To be sure, it is not just that lightness automatically means privilege; it is that it opens up the potential for both for attaining cultural capital and economic upward mobility. It is hardly disputed throughout Ghana, for example, that former president

4.3  Billboard at the Makola Market, Accra, July 2006. Photograph by the author.

Jerry John Rawlings's popularity—mostly with women—was based in part on his perceived attractiveness (which in turn was perceptibly linked to his biracial heritage).[5] During the 2000 election campaigns, a Ghanaian magazine, *Home Sweet Home*, published a report on an election poll that revealed why one candidate, Goosie Tanoh, may have fared better among women than the others: "Only 5 percent of the men were likely to vote for him against 40 percent of the women. This may be due to the 'color syndrome.' Several of our younger women indicated that Tanoh is a nice man with the 'right' complexion, something that helped Rawlings with the vote of younger women" (2000, 21). Similar examples abound. Thus, we see in Ghana that phenotype is salient even as people take pride in their racial identities and the country's racial homogeneity. And much like the skin-color dynamics and politics of the Caribbean and North, South, and Central Americas, we see in Ghana the daily and consistent reinforcement of the significance of color/race as it articulates with aesthetics, gender, and class. Within U.S. Black communities, for example, racial dynamics operate such that there is often the conflation of beauty and light skin (Hall 2005; Hunter 2007). More importantly, many studies have demonstrated the correlation between educational and occupation attainment whereby "lighter skin Blacks complete more years of schooling, have more prestigious jobs, and earn more than dark skin Blacks" (Thompson and Keith 2001). Where light skin color is directly linked to social and economic privilege, in addition to aesthetic privilege, it should come as no surprise that, in desiring lighter skin, "many Blacks simply want to be beautiful and successful" (Gordon 1997, 59). And while light-skin privilege and pigmentocracy are often variously contested, we see their constant reinforcement in a multitude of ways throughout the African diaspora.

The same can be said of light-skin-color valorization in Ghana. In a country where the great majority of people have dark skin, light-skinned women are featured on a large number of billboards and other picture advertisements—especially those marketing beauty products—throughout Accra and other cities. Many of these images are of African Americans that, ironically, reflect the U.S. Black community's own pigmentocracy (Hall 1995; Hunter 2002, 2007; Golden 2004). In a fall 2000 advertising campaign by Carsons Company West African, for example, Ghanaians were bombarded with huge billboards advertising hair-straightening products that used various images of very light-skinned African Americans (particularly women). Other signage featured biracial African American actress Halle Barry, advertising the South African–owned DSTV cable television network, and Janet Jackson, advertising Pepsi Cola. We see then how skin-color dynamics—like other processes—contribute to the ongoing construction of Ghanaian racial formation, and we better understand skin-bleaching practices within this context.

As I was leaving a busy shopping area of Accra late one morning in the summer of 2006, I received a phone call from one of my new acquaintances—a Haitian American woman who had just moved to the city with her Ghanaian husband. She was a fellow academic, and we had been talking a few days earlier about my research on racialization processes and her own on Muslim women in Ghana. When I answered, she said urgently, "Grab your camera and come to the Muslim Girls School in Osu. There is something you should see." When I arrived at the school's small campus, I walked around the back to the girls' bathroom. There, pasted on the brick wall across from the bathroom door, was what she was excited about: it was a large, aging poster with a picture of a young dark-skinned Black woman with a caption that read, "Black Is Beautiful. Do Not Destroy Your Beauty through Bleaching." The poster, issued by Ghana's Food and Drug Board, was obviously old—it was in black-and-white, looked weathered, and was rather frayed.

4.4 Poster at the Muslim Girls School, Osu, Accra, June 2006. Photograph by the author.

For me, the poster recalled this issue as a longstanding one in the community; but its message also seemed consciously affirmative instead of condemnatory. "Black Is Beautiful" summons the Black Power slogans in the diaspora from the 1960s and 1970s and makes a point that counters the light-skin valorization implicated in the skin-bleaching process. Here, Black

skin (and presumably dark Black skin) is the racial and color aesthetic promoted; yet, as skin bleaching and attendant skin-color valorization rages
on, it continues to be difficult to envisage the benefits associated with Blackness. Herskovits concluded his observation on Black-skin-color differentiation in the United States by stating:

> I have no doubt at all, however, that the non-negroid-appearing Negro has
> an advantageous position in the Negro community for social and historical
> reasons. It manifests itself strikingly in many ways. . . . This is not due to any
> inherent faculty conferred by the larger percentage of White blood. It is rather
> the result of a general reaction to dominant patterns of behavior, induced by
> the fact that the Negroes live in a White civilization, and that unconsciously
> they feel that the easiest road to cultural salvation lies in adhering as closely
> as possible to these dominant cultural patterns. (1928, 60–62)

The lasting power of light-skin-color valorization, as indexed by the skin-
bleaching phenomenon, comes directly from accumulated precedents of racialization process within the context of global White supremacy. Common
ideas about race—specifically the privileges associated with Whiteness (or
proximity to Whiteness)—continue to be revealed and reinforced through
such practices. At the same time, however, it clear that such a racial project
is not uncontested. Skin bleaching and light-skin-color valorization may be
prominent, but they are also matched, and challenged, by other processes.
It is the contestation of these various racial projects that creates the sociocultural and political field of Ghanaian racial formation. Thus, while the tropes
of Whiteness and skin-bleaching processes certainly affirm the ideology of
White supremacy, other projects, such as the Ghanaian state's own racecraft,
work to challenge this very ideology. It is to that project that I now turn.

# FIVE

# Slavery and Pan-Africanist Triumph: Heritage Tourism as State Racecraft

I wish to emphasize that PANAFEST is a Pan-African event. It is organized for Africans, peoples of African descent and all those who are committed to the ideals of Pan-Africanism as well as to the well-being of Africans on the continent and the diaspora.

—2005 PANAFEST souvenir brochure

Emancipation Day is an annual event in Ghana, the Black Star of Africa and the gateway to the Homeland of people of African descent in the Diaspora. . . . Ghana's claim to the position of gateway to the Homeland is well grounded in the fact that it was a major exit point for slaves on the West Coast.

—Ghana Tourist Board website[1]

The official wreath-laying ceremony that launched the 2005 PANAFEST/ Emancipation Day celebrations began with the usual pomp and pageantry, including drumming and dancing performances by commissioned arts groups at three event locations, and it ended with the somber laying of five wreaths (representing the various official groups in attendance) at the Kwame Nkrumah Memorial Park. Unlike the two ceremonies earlier in the day at the W. E. B. DuBois Memorial Center for Pan-African Culture and the George Padmore Institute, this was the main event. Like the majority of participants and spectators, I arrived before the official commemoration activities began, while event organizers were awaiting the arrival of the Accra-based Diplomatic Corps, state officials, and other invited guests. The Nkrumah Memorial Park is located on High Street, a central commercial area in Accra that houses the headquarters of major national and international banks and other businesses, as well as government offices, including

5.1 Kwame Nkrumah Mausoleum, Accra, July 2005. Photograph by the author.

the Accra Metropolitan Authority and the Parliament House. High Street is a bustling, high-traffic area, heavy with pedestrians and street peddlers. The sheer volume of cars on the narrow two-lane road usually forces drivers to a slow crawl. Yet, even while it is located within this commercial area bustling with energy and activity, the Nkrumah Memorial Park has an almost inconspicuous presence. Inside its white-trimmed cement walls and surrounded by its lush and expansive grounds, it is easy to forget the hustle and bustle just outside. The soft breeze from the Atlantic Ocean, the quiet serenity of the mausoleum where Nkrumah's body is entombed, and the pond anchoring the larger-than-life bronze statue of Nkrumah filled with bronze figurines of kneeling musicians playing instruments of cascading waterfalls all work to create this tranquil resting place of the country's first president.

As I joined the group of participants and visitors strolling through the well-manicured grounds while waiting for the final wreath-laying ceremony to begin, I could hear reggae music cycling through a number of well-known Bob Marley songs over the public-address system. After a short while, the music was replaced by a recording of Nkrumah's famous independence speech, a signal that the ceremony was about to begin. As people began to walk over to take their seats among the rows of white folding chairs arranged to the right of Nkrumah's statue and the mausoleum, Nkrumah's voice resonated even more loudly over the speakers. We could all clearly hear the end of the speech as we reached our seats, with Nkrumah famously proclaiming, "Ghana, your beloved country, is free forever!" to recorded thunderous applause. By this time, the number of official representatives had dramatically increased. The program indicated that other official participants, namely members of the Diplomatic Corps and ambassadors from South Africa, England, the United States, and Cuba, would soon be arriving. However, because the ceremony had begun earlier than planned, the Cuban ambassador was the only diplomatic representative to actively participate. Many of the other diplomats, such as the ambassadors from Togo and South Africa, arrived only at the end of the ceremony, when the crowd was dissipating.

After welcoming comments by the director of the Nkrumah Park, the representative from the Ghana Caribbean Association, and the representative from the Ministry of Tourism, the keynote speaker, Freddie Blay, took to the podium to give his address. In 2005, Blay was the first deputy speaker of Parliament and the highest-ranking member of Ghana's government representatives to attend that year's wreath-laying ceremony.[2] In his impassioned speech, Blay brought together the prevailing themes covered by the other speakers, as well as the broader state objectives of PANAFEST/Emancipation Day celebrations. He focused specifically on the goals of African emancipation, renewal, and development, suggesting that such goals would only be achieved by formally reconciling Ghana's history of slavery with Africa's contemporary economic predicament. He further stressed the need to employ this history in concretizing linkages between diaspora and African Blacks for the benefit of the "continental and diaspora African." An excerpt of his remarks reflects this focus:

> Emancipation Day should be a universal event because Africa endured a trauma unprecedented in the annals of history. . . . We carry the marks and scars of slavery and its later |result| of discrimination. . . . Slavery affected economic growth and social growth. . . . We salute the survival of the African—both on the Continent and in the Diaspora. . . . What we need is the unity of resolve and a purpose. . . . I therefore challenge this generation of Africans, whether on the homeland or in the Diaspora, to rise up to the challenge and prove the resilience of the African spirit and the resourcefulness of the African mind.[3]

For Blay, as for official state discourse, "emancipation" is tragedy recalled as both triumph and opportunity (Richards 2003, 17). Specifically, the brutalities of slavery and attendant racial terror demand not only recognition of African (and global Black) survival, but also an extension of that survival into a renewal of the "African spirit." In this moment, and for Blay, African spiritual renewal is understood to be self-determination and redemption through the hope of economic development.

What seems most significant in this speech and, indeed, throughout the discourses surrounding PANAFEST/Emancipation Day celebrations is the reframing by state officials and institutions of a national narrative that anchors the transnational and global history of the transatlantic slave trade at the center of local geography and imagination. That Ghana is the first continental African country to officially celebrate and commemorate Emancipation Day and to explicitly and actively claim the legacy of slavery as central to historical and contemporary national identification is remarkable.[4] As scholars have pointed out, "slavery is not integral to how most Ghanaians define themselves" (Richards 2005, 626; Holsey 2008). Indeed, the Ghanaian state's actions highlight the normally ambivalent place of the transatlantic slave trade in continental African imagination and historiography. For, though many African nations have begun to recognize the transatlantic slave trade as part of a past legacy, rarely has this recognition been translated beyond historical museums and memorials, or into active engagement with contemporary national identity formation. Neither has recognition been so variously, if not clearly, expressed of how this slavery legacy has structured a shared heritage of continental and diaspora Blacks. I want to suggest here, therefore, that by actively locating Ghanaians squarely within the legacies of slavery, in relation to and mutually constitutive of the experiences of those in the diaspora, state discourses and practices are also recasting Ghana's *racial* history. But what does it mean to understand this type of deployment, this national project, of race at this moment, and particularly in terms of its relationship to contemporary concerns of economic development?

This chapter examines the Ghanaian state's official activities surrounding heritage tourism in order to describe the complex dynamics and politics of contemporary state racecraft.[5] Focusing on the deployment of Pan-Africanist ideology and the history of the slave trade highlighted in the official promotion and celebration of PANAFEST/Emancipation Day, I demonstrate how the Ghanaian state enacts a particular racial project that uses the global circulation of the discourse of slavery to recall the country's racialized heritage in the service of economic development.[6] State-sponsored rituals of slavery reenactments and triumphant discourses of emancipation and Pan-Africanism work to create a counterpoint to local economic uncertainty. But in the process, state functions deploy a specifically *diaspora* narrative of slavery that gives primacy to New World experiences while subsuming continental African ones. And as a result, these functions diminish both the significance of slavery and the important legacy of colonialism in contemporary Ghana. I argue, however, that the adoption of the diaspora narrative of slavery reveals both the contradictions and creativity in the fashioning of a contemporary national identity. By hosting these internationalist Pan-African events, the Ghanaian state is drawing on its position in the global political economy, its own history, and diaspora linkages to begin mapping new or alternative geographies of transnational racial belonging.

The examination of contemporary Ghanaian state racecraft necessarily involves engagement with the relationships among the political economy of development, nation building, the politics of culture, and racial and historical consciousness. The state's deployment of Pan-Africanist history and politics occurs within the context of the liberalization of the global political economy and the attendant restructuring of Ghana's economic policies from the early 1980s. The potential economic benefits of heritage tourism—and the late entry of African nations into this arena of wealth generation—are also important factors to consider in this analysis. Since the concern with "development" is a key feature of postcolonial Africa's reality, we can also read the Ghanaian government's deployment of Pan-Africanism as one of the ways in which it is working to address its economic marginalization in an unequal and extremely racialized global political terrain. Indeed, the Pan-African movement itself was, and continues to be, "structured by the history of global racial inequality" (Pierre and Shipley 2003). And the current global political economy, in the meantime, has reinscribed "racial and cultural hierarchies within and between nations, communities, and regions, [affecting] processes of modernization, nationalism, and state formation" (Thomas 2005, 15). Ghana's (and Africa's) positioning within this (re)sedimentation of the global hierarchy of peoples, cultures, and nations (Trouillot 1994) links its historical and contemporary past to its present. The assertion of a Pan-African ideal (Anyidoho 1992) and of African racial recuperation and self-determination, therefore, also opens up a space for agency and the articulation of a positive and triumphant, if circumscribed, national identity.

This chapter has two sections. In the first, I examine the development of PANAFEST and Emancipation Day both as national holidays and within the context of renewed Pan-Africanist sentiment effected by the state at the height of compulsory dealings with international financial and political agents. I then present an ethnography of the 2005 PANAFEST/Emancipation Day celebrations, focusing on two state-directed events: the Reverential

Night and the Emancipation Day Durbar. This ethnography charts the role of slavery and race through two areas: a national historical narrative of a redemptive Pan-Africanism and the claim to racial and cultural kinship with diaspora Blacks. How is this state-sponsored Pan-Africanism different from earlier forms, what does it mean for transatlantic Black dialogue, and in what ways does it impact the Ghanaian social and political fields? The chapter ends with a discussion of the paradoxes as well as the opportunities that official Pan-Africanism proffer.

## Heritage Tourism: Culture, Politics, Economics

The July 22 wreath-laying ceremony was only the first of a number of events planned over the nine days of celebrations for PANAFEST/Emancipation Day 2005. The primary sites of the celebrations were twin cities, Elmina and Cape Coast, where the two largest former slave-trading forts in the country are located. The wreath laying was the official opening ceremony, and it occurred in Accra, the site of the memorials to Ghana's "Fathers of Pan-Africanism"—W. E. B. DuBois, Kwame Nkrumah, and George Padmore. Over the next eight days at Cape Coast and Elmina, the celebrations included a carnival day; an Akwaaba ceremony (or return journey for those from the diaspora); Rita Marley's[7] birthday celebration; a colloquium focusing on women and youth; a grand durbar of chiefs, queenmothers, and elders; a rites-of-passage/naming ceremony (for the "brothers and sisters from the diaspora"); and a "Reverential Night" scheduled late in the evening on July 31 with an emancipation ceremony at midnight (August 1), which led to the climax and final ceremony, a grand durbar at Assin Manso, the current site of a national museum commemorating slavery.

The Pan-African Historical Festival (PANAFEST) is a "cultural event dedicated to [the] enhancement of the ideals of Pan-Africanism and the development of the African continent" (PANAFEST 2005, 7). The PANAFEST movement emerged in the 1980s when Ghanaian dramatist and Pan-Africanist Dr. Efua Sutherland proposed a "Pan African Historical Theatre Festival."[8] Dr. Sutherland conceived the celebration as a way to reinvigorate Ghana's Pan-Africanist history through a showcasing of African-inspired cultural production. She sought to create a movement that would uplift and reunite African and diaspora peoples through the arts (36). Indeed, Dr. Sutherland belonged to "an extensive global network of friends"[9] and attached great significance to connections between Africa and the diaspora. Along with a group of other intellectuals and artists, she was critical in establishing the W. E. B. DuBois Memorial Center for Pan-African Culture in

Ghana as well as in advocating the promotion of continent's rich cultural legacies.

Dr. Sutherland's proposal for a Pan-African cultural celebration was formally adopted by the Ghanaian state (then under the leadership of Flt. Lt. Jerry J. Rawlings) in 1992. Sponsored by the Ghanaian government under the auspices of the Organization of African Unity (OAU), the first PANAFEST occurred during the second week of October and was celebrated across three cities—Cape Coast, Elmina, and Accra—with the theme "The Re-Emergence of African Civilization." Since then, PANAFEST has been celebrated biennially in Ghana, bringing together hundreds of artists, musicians, theater groups, dancers, and intellectuals from all over the African continent and the diaspora to perform, exchange ideas, and "strengthen the bonds of brotherhood [sic] between Africans and black people in the diaspora" (Daily Graphic, August 3, 1999). In 1997, for example, 1,400 participants from twenty-seven countries, most prominently the United States, Nigeria, the United Kingdom, and Jamaica, attended under the theme "Uniting the African Family for Development." In 1999, the year that the Ghanaian government did not fully sponsor the event, there were reportedly five thousand participants from more than forty countries.[10] Over the years, PANAFEST celebrations have offered a stock set of events that include a combination of cultural performances, concerts, academic colloquia, and conferences on local social issues, all of which have elicited participation from various state organizations, institutions, and individuals. PANAFEST therefore represents the link between expressive culture and intellectualism as a basis for promoting mutual political progress and what its organizers see as the positive attributes of "African civilization" around the globe. Indeed, the main theme of the festival—"The Re-Emergence of African Civilization"—remains the same over time, while its subtheme changes every two years to address current issues.

Emancipation Day, a "day for remembering the horrors of the slave trade and slavery and honoring those who worked to overcome the challenges of that condition" (Obetsebi-Lamptey 2005, 5–6), was initially celebrated independent of PANAFEST. It was established as a state holiday in 1997 by former President Rawlings upon his return from an official visit to Jamaica's own celebration of Emancipation Day.[11] Ghana's first celebration of Emancipation Day occurred in late July 1998. As a nine-day event under the primary theme "Our Heritage, Our Strength," it brought a large number of people from the United States, Europe, and the Caribbean to Accra (Ghana Forum 1998). Whereas PANAFEST was understood as a platform for deploying arts and culture in the spirit of Pan-Africanism and for national and continental development, Emancipation Day focused primarily on the legacy of the slave trade and slavery. Its annual celebrations included various events, such as nationally televised dramatic programs that foregrounded the reenactment of the horrors of the slave trade—from the marching of shackled enslaved Africans through public streets to artistic representations of life under the system of slavery. The most defining event in the early celebrations of Emancipation Day was the repatriation of the remains of two former enslaved Africans—"Carson" from the United States and "Crystal" from Jamaica—to the "Monument of Return," to "immortalize the emancipation struggles of all African peoples" (Carson 1999).[12] This Monument of Return is located inside the newly constructed slavery museum at Asin Manso, a town near Cape Coast, and it is built around what is known as the "Slave River," where captured Africans purportedly took their last baths before being taken to Elmina or Cape Coast Castle-Dungeons for shipment to the Americas (ibid.).

Though its programs had a different focus, state officials and other organizers believed that Emancipation Day sufficiently articulated a similar Pan-Africanist message to that of PANAFEST celebrations. In particular, the events' two primary themes—"Re-Emergence of African Civilization" and "Our Heritage, Our Strength"—clearly reflected the ideal of African survival and renewal. At the same time, state officials recognized the potential of the internationalist characteristics of these celebrations to boost the heritage-tourism industry. In 2001, PANAFEST and Emancipation Day celebrations were combined into one major Pan-African cultural and political event under the auspices of the Ministry of Tourism.[13] When government officials argued that the state could no longer afford to support the events, a PANAFEST Foundation was created and given the mandate to raise private and corporate money to sustain the festival. Since 1999, therefore, the PANAFEST Foundation has depended on a worldwide network of supporters and volunteers to access primarily private funds and has generated financing from a number of multinational corporations and other international organizations. The shift in this funding has impacted programming strategies and priorities, particularly in terms of the dependence on outside organizational and financial aid and participation.

Of course, all this has occurred within the context of the growing relevance of tourism as a potential foreign-exchange earner for the nation. The linking of heritage tourism with development certainly is not unique to Ghana; indeed, it reflects a global trend in which "culture" has become the most important aspect of tourism. Whereas cultural tourism has been a staple of the economic-development strategies, not to mention national identity formation, of Western nations, it is a relatively recent development in the global south. Various internationalist organizations such as the World Tourism Organization, the United Nations Sustainable Development Commission, and the United Nations Educational, Scientific, and Cultural Organization (UNESCO) have shaped heritage tourism in Africa. These groups have worked to help foster the link between tourism and economic development. Most important has been UNESCO and its "World Heritage" initiatives that have, in the past two decades, sought to balance out its European-heavy heritage sites with those from the rest of the world. As a result, struggling African nations have worked with these organizations, taking a cue from their "developed" counterparts in the global north, to harness natural resources and package events and experiences to attract foreign tourists and attendant foreign exchange.[14] The PANAFEST/Emancipation Day celebrations came to fit neatly into this new vision. They allowed the Ghanaian state to exploit the country's abundant points of interest, such as the former slave trading forts,[15] as well as its well-known history of Pan-Africanism for economic progress. With the guidance, economic aid, and technical assistance from various private corporations, European nations, and other institutions such as the Smithsonian, the U.S. Agency for International Development, Shell Oil, and the U.S. Midwest Universities Consortium for International Activities, the Ghanaian government has been able to restore and construct various heritage sites to market itself internationally and, simultaneously, to refashion its national identity (Richards 2005; see also Holsey 2004; Singleton 1999; Ghana Tourist Board website).

Along with these concrete steps toward enhancing its heritage-tourism potential, the Ghanaian government has restructured some of its cabinet positions to promote its tourism-based development programs. In 2002, for example, the Ministry of Tourism became the Ministry of Tourism and Modernization of the Capital City. The ministry would transform once again in 2005 to become the Ministry of Tourism and Diasporan Relations.[16] The various incarnations of this ministry are noteworthy because they point to the state's developing consciousness of the increasing link between tourism, economic development, and the important role played by the diaspora in both. Indeed, once "tourism" and "diasporan relations" were combined, the mandate became clear. By summer 2005, officials in the new ministry were preparing to launch another program, the Joseph Project,[17] to supplement the PANAFEST/Emancipation Day festivities, as well as to coincide with Ghana's fiftieth-anniversary celebrations planned for 2007. The Joseph Project seemed to be an effort by that administration to puts its own stamp on a long-established state project of deploying Pan-Africanism and the politics of diaspora kinship to harness resources for development. On one level, this is a political move through which that government could benefit from pursuing the project of a previous administration without actually giving it credit. At the same time, enhancing PANAFEST/Emancipation Day celebrations with the Joseph Project also demonstrates the continued significance of such Pan-Africanist rhetoric and programs for national cultural identity and consciousness—a significance that extends beyond the ruling administration.

To be sure, it was never completely clear how much the state—or at least the 2005 government—was *ideologically* committed to the tenets of Pan-Africanism and its message of global Black emancipation. Many older Ghanaian scholars and activists have condemned the activities of the NPP government as self-serving rather than as authentically trying to harness Pan-Africanism. Kwesi Armah, a Ghanaian intellectual attending the 2005 Emancipation Day celebrations in Elmina, complained bitterly that the celebrations were substandard.[18] During our discussion, he surmised that the government was only giving lip service to the history of Pan-Africanism. To him, the government did not fully support the programs primarily because the NPP has historically been known as ideologically opposed to the ideals of Pan-Africanism. "These people in government, the party in charge, they were the anti-Nkrumahists," he told me emphatically, continuing, "How could they now claim to be Pan-Africanists?" Indeed, in its debut, PANAFEST ideologues (who were usually leftist academics, some of whom were advisors to the state) often imagined that economic and political development of Africa could come when the "African family" was "reunited" and spiritually regenerated enough to begin (re)building the foundation of a "rebirth of African civilization." For example, early PANAFEST organizers listed as their main objectives establishing truth about the history of Africa through arts and culture; promoting unity between continental Africans and those in the diaspora; defining Africa's contribution to world civilization; and promoting Africa's economic and political development.[19] These goals were not so different from earlier invocations of African self-determination in various other Pan-African cultural festivals throughout the continent and in the diaspora. For example, celebrations such as the 1966 Festival of Negro Arts in Dakar (Senegal) and the 1977 FESTAC (World Black and African Festival of Arts and Culture) in Lagos also had a similar vision for uplifting and reuniting African peoples through the arts.

It is also significant that the "rebirth" of the state's Pan-Africanist ideals occurred within the context of political upheaval, the shift to a neoliberal economic agenda, and the concomitant growth of the global heritage-tourism industry. Indeed, with these celebrations, we see a distinct conversation about, on the one hand, Ghana's (and Africa's) economic marginalization and political instability and, on the other, Black African peoples' comparable positions to Black peoples elsewhere. The 2005 NPP government inherited the cultural celebrations of PANAFEST/Emancipation Day amid worsening economic conditions, but also after Ghana's decidedly liberal shift in the economic arena in the 1980s and in the political arena in the early 1990s. These festivals and the official deployment of Ghana's Pan-Africanist legacy were initially launched with the support of the Provisional National Defense Council (PNDC), the military government under the leadership of Jerry John Rawlings. Arriving on the national scene through a set of coup d'états in 1979 and 1981, the Rawlings government was quickly forced to turn to international financial organizations, the World Bank and the International Monetary Fund, for help in reviving a comatose economy. Years of political turmoil and economic crises—from a series of military coups dating back to the overthrow of Nkrumah to the drop in world cocoa prices as well as massive drought and forest fires in 1983—compelled the PNDC to pursue a neoliberal or free market agenda (Boafo-Arthur 2007).[20] In exchange for aid packages, the Rawlings government accepted the recommendations of these international financial organizations, which included the disengagement of the government from its active role in the economy, the privatization of state enterprises, the devaluation of the currency, and the rebuilding of industrial infrastructure through (foreign) assistance programs. By the early 1990s, this economic restructuring yielded several results: it fundamentally changed the government's social, political, and economic orientation; it shifted the burden of economic growth to the private sector; and it further increased national debt and dependency on foreign aid and investment.

A most prominent, albeit indirect, effect of the liberalization of the Ghanaian economy was the growth of the national tourism industry. Tourism had the potential to attract foreign exchange to the country, effectively helping to diversify Ghana's primarily agricultural-based economic market. In 1993, the Rawlings government, with the assistance of the World Tourism Organization, established the Ministry of Tourism and prepared a fifteen-year tourism-development plan for the period 1996–2010 (Teye 1999). For a state, the economic benefits of tourism are twofold. First, tourism promotes economic growth because it generates foreign exchange and increases government revenue. Second, at the microlevel, it creates jobs and helps facilitate income and revenue distribution (ibid.). The state's investment in tourism has yielded very positive results: depending on the source, tourism is currently the fourth-largest foreign-exchange earner in the economy (following the trade in cocoa and minerals such as gold and bauxite), with earnings of 1.6 billion dollars in 2009 (Ghana Business News 2009).[21]

The liberalizing shift of Ghana's economics and politics pursued first and most aggressively by the Rawlings administration directly linked the rhetoric of Pan-Africanism and the history of Ghana's cultural nationalism to economic development. Rawlings's role in this cannot be overstated. Initially surrounded by radical leftist advisors, Rawlings was able to articulate an ideology of socialist economic principles and support internal social democratic forces even as he pursued an "antithetical economic and political agenda" (Boafo-Arthur 2007, 6)[22] This "unnatural equation" (ibid.) was a direct result of the contradictions inherent in the government's adoption of neoliberal economic policies while it rhetorically presented itself as ideologically Marxist-Leninist and economically socialist. As Kwame Boafo-Arthur has argued, Rawlings's despotic tendencies certainly enabled the successful implementation of antipeople economic policies without much solid resistance (1999). At the same time, those who criticized the Rawlings government for the continued economic downturn in the country were directly met with Pan-African rhetoric. In effect, Rawlings deflected blame for his administration's role in perpetuating Ghana's economic malaise by focusing on a reverential past and calling for African self-determination as well as an end to the continent's "neocolonial" mentality. Pan-Africanism was thus used in a dual strategy. On the one hand, amid worsening economic conditions, it helped state officials explain the country's relative powerlessness in terms of both its position in the global political economy and the people's "neocolonial" mentality. On the other hand, the focus on Ghana's history of Pan-Africanism and the development of heritage tourism were practical ways to generate income for the nation and counter economic regression.

From the early 1990s, the Rawlings government directly appropriated the country's historical legacy of Pan-Africanism. This took on many forms: the establishment of public memorials and research centers in honor of Ghana's "illustrious sons,"[23] W. E. B. DuBois, George Padmore, and Kwame Nkrumah; the support of foreign research scholars; the development of private-investment incentives for foreign business; the promotion of repatriation and tourism among diaspora peoples; the development of international cultural festivals; and the restoration of former slave-trading castles (Pierre and Shipley 2003, 2007). It is out of these initiatives that we see the emergence of PANAFEST and, later, Emancipation Day celebrations. The

2005 government under the leadership of president John A. Kufuor and the NPP had no choice but to continue with these programs, in part because it was in ideological agreement with the economic policies of the previous administration. The NPP was also riding the contemporary wave of international support for both its economic policies and its promotion of local World Heritage sites. Although historically an ideological opponent to Nkrumah's Pan-Africanist and cultural nationalist agenda, the Kufuor government aggressively deployed the rhetoric of Pan-Africanism, particularly the motto of African self-determination, and used it as an aspect of its economic-development strategy. These cultural festivals were important for the government for two other reasons. First, they fit neatly into the economic agenda, and state officials have recognized tourism as an important foreign-exchange earner. Second, the country's fiftieth independence anniversary was around the corner, and the NPP had to come to terms with the growing resurgence of the local and continental popularity of Nkrumah and his Pan-Africanist legacy.

It is often easy for some in intellectual and political circles to dismiss the Ghanaian state's actions as either self-serving, politically and culturally trivial, or misguided (Hasty 2002; see also Bruner 1996; Hartman 2002). While I acknowledge the numerous contradictions that inhere in the state's deployment of Ghana's Pan-Africanist history, I want to move beyond discussions of intentionality to argue instead that the state's actions can also be read as reflecting, at least in part, the country's marginalized position within the global political economy. The deployment of Pan-Africanist rhetoric and the organization of attendant activities not only promise economic development, but may also offer a way to foster national integrity and self-worth. We need only point to interlinked economic strategies, particularly the neoliberal economic policies employed by the state, as it combats its persistent economic and political marginalization. Even if it is not a clearly calculated (or articulated) strategy, the state's actions nevertheless have potentially powerful consequences. Indeed, even as reactions to the state's deployment of Pan-Africanist rhetoric have been multiple, complex, ironic, and especially contradictory, PANAFEST/Emancipation Day, as well as the continued memorialization of DuBois, Nkrumah, and Padmore and dialogue about African and diaspora racial kinship, continue to give concreteness to Pan-Africanism—the various relationships and politics it generates and the sociopolitical cultural field it informs. In particular, these festivals have opened up the space not only for broad dialogue about tourism, but also for expanding the terrain for the development of racial consciousness, the reconstruction of lost histories, and, ultimately, the formation of new political subjectivities. The recasting of the history of the slave trade and slavery clearly reflects this.

## Revisiting, Enacting, and Narrating Slavery

To attract tourists, Ghanaians must remember a history they learned to forget.

—Sandra Richards, "What Is to Be Remembered?"

By Sunday, July 31, I had been in Cape Coast and Elmina for five days, participating in a number of Panafest/Emancipation Day activities in the two towns. I had attended the various daytime activities, such as the official opening ceremony of PANAFEST 2005, which was one of the many grand durbars of international dignitaries, local artists, and government officials that occurred in the courtyard of Cape Coast Castle-Dungeon.[24] I had also attended the grand durbar of chiefs, queenmothers and elders, at which various state officials, including Ghanaian vice president Alhaji Aliu Mahama, were in attendance. In addition, I spent most evenings at the PANAFEST Village, where Elmina's large Adisadel Park had been turned into a mega entertainment and commercial center. Within the inner walls of the enclosed PANAFEST Village were numerous booths and vendors, and at the front center of the park was a very large and tall stage for the various performances by artists from throughout Africa and the diaspora that would occur during the week of celebrations. Over the several nights I was at the village, there were many cultural performances, including those by Nigerian dancing troupes, Jamaican jazz musicians, local hiplife artists, a junior high school girl choir from Barbados, and a fashion show of local designers. Although the fee to enter the park was exorbitant by local standards, the village grounds were filled every night with primarily young Ghanaians and other visitors. Overall, the twin cities of Elmina and Cape Coast were extremely lively during the week, with tourists, Peace Corps volunteers from nearby towns, and local officials and government dignitaries filling the streets and commercial areas during the day.

On the schedule of events for PANAFEST/Emancipation Day 2005, the "Reverential Night" was described as a "solemn ceremony on the event of Emancipation Day [that] will feature an evening commemorating our ancestors and end with a midnight proclamation of Emancipation Day." The Reverential Night had actually begun with a candlelight procession through the principal streets of Cape Coast to the large Cape Coast Castle-Dungeon courtyard. As I entered that evening, the courtyard was both festive and

5.2 Reverential Night ceremony in the courtyard of
Cape Coast Castle, July 31, 2005. Photograph by the author.

solemn. On the one hand, the cobble-stoned courtyard was filled with
hundreds of white plastic folding chairs lined up in rows leading from a
performance stage to the arched entrance. There were floodlights and speakers set up in various corners of the venue, and organizers and performers
moved around quickly as they made final preparations for the big event.
At the same time, however, the courtyard still had its usual appearance: it
was surrounded by the various dark arched openings leading to the dungeons. The dark dungeon openings stood out starkly against the "offensive
Whiteness" (Richards 2005, 623) of the whitewashed castle walls and the
newly placed bright lights and white chairs. Furthermore, standing in the
courtyard, visitors could see the very visible sign marking the "Door of No
Return" and, beyond it, hear the roar of the Atlantic Ocean—both powerful
significations of the slave trade.

As we waited for the Reverential Night ceremonies to begin, I reluctantly
agreed to join some friends in a nighttime tour of the dungeons. Although
I had visited and toured the Cape Coast and Elmina slave-trading forts on
numerous occasions, it was the first time I had been there at night. As soon
as I followed my friends through the dungeon doors, I could feel a transformation, both in the atmosphere and in my mood. Inside the first dungeon, a single low-intensity light bulb had been haphazardly hung from

the ceiling, perhaps to accommodate nighttime visitors who would hardly be able to walk through the dungeon's natural darkness. This solitary light source in fact worked to enhance the eeriness of the scene: people inside the dungeon transformed into moving shadows, while the various dark corners and spaces of the room became more pronounced. Even with this small light bulb, it was dark enough for it to feel as though the dungeon fully enveloped us. My friends must have felt the same apprehension and dread as we immediately sought each other. Together, we tried to make our way through the various tunnels connecting the dungeons, walking on an unstable ground that at times sloped steeply and at other times had jagged slants. In one dungeon, we saw a shrine that, judging by its lit candles and fresh flowers, seemed to have been recently visited. Within the dark walls, we could hear not only our own shrill echoes but also those of the many people walking through, as well as children screaming in what seemed like both fear and delight. At that moment, I *felt* slavery. *We* felt slavery. In her discussion of tourism to Elmina and Cape Coast Castles, Sandra Richards explains that visitors are usually forced to reenact aspects of African captives' experiences, imagining the actions that transpired when "burdened by the oppressive presence of the confining castle-dungeons" (2005, 623). Indeed, it seemed that the *affect* of the dungeons was just as important as the ceremonies enacted and speeches given to recast and remember slavery. Some believe affect is determined by prior cognitive processes through which the identification and meaning of an event or setting influences emotive responses (Brewin 1989). While the reaction of the various audience members to both the ceremony and the dungeons is difficult to discern, it is clear that the environment of the dungeons, coupled with recognition of their particular—indeed peculiar—history, certainly may have informed the perceptions around and responses to the state's management of the narrative of slavery at that moment. At the very least, the Cape Coast Castle-Dungeon, as site, signaled the convergence of social, cultural, and political forces in concretizing this narrative.

By the time we walked out of the dungeons, the courtyard was almost filled to capacity with people. There were few empty chairs, and those not fortunate enough to have found seats simply stood around and behind the chairs, filling up most of the empty space of the courtyard. Others who wanted a better view of the stage lined the stairs surrounding the courtyard that led to the second level of the castle-dungeon. The audience itself seemed like a mix of government officials, local royalty (chiefs and queenmothers), foreign dignitaries, various performers, and tourists, as well as people from the surrounding towns. Government officials and other invited guests and performers aside, it was not clear what motivated audience presence at this event. The few people from the surrounding towns that I interacted with expressed only curiosity about this major production, with little or no reference to the actual agenda of organizers. Nevertheless, the courtyard was full as the ceremony began. The Reverential Night was scheduled to begin at 8 p.m., with a number of speeches and performances scheduled up until midnight, when an official proclamation of Emancipation would be read to end the evening. After moving around the castle-dungeon courtyard trying to get the best possible view, my friends and I finally managed to find a few empty seats in the front near the stage in unoccupied reserved seating.

At the start of the evening's ceremony, two young male actors, dressed only in loose, sack-colored shorts were marched up the aisles of the courtyard to the stage in what was an obvious performance about captivity and enslavement. Each was taken by their respective captors to either corner of stage and forcibly seated on the ground. The men were in shackles: each had an iron collar around his neck and a shackle on each wrist, with the two wristbands connected by a chain. Throughout the performance, the men acted distraught and looked as if they were crying silently. Yet, other than this grand entrance and even as they remained at the far corners of the stage, the men were given no more attention, nor were they mentioned in the nearly four-hour program.[25] During the ceremony, however, they performed their enslaved status. At times either or both of the men would raise their shackled arms in the air, seeming to pray; at other times, their facial expressions would shift wildly from terror to despair to resignation, and they would hang down their heads. Though they did not generate much attention, the fact that these two men remained in the shadows of the stage during the ceremony seemed to affect the general tone of the event. From their locations on the stage, the men appeared almost ghostly, and one wonders if this effect was the intention of the organizers. At the same time, I wondered how many in the audience actually saw the men's entire performance, and whether it fulfilled the objectives of the reenactment. It was not until the minister of tourism and diasporan relations, Jake Obetsebi-Lamptey, took the stage to proclaim emancipation that the two actors became much more visible: suddenly, they stood under the spotlight, triumphantly raising their arms in the air to reveal that their shackles had been broken.

The Reverential Night was not the only time slavery was reenacted during these PANAFEST/Emancipation Day celebrations. A more prominent slavery performance came the following morning, on August 1, at the grand durbar celebrating the official observance of Emancipation Day. This durbar was held in a large open field in the nearby town of Assin Manso, the site of a new slavery memorial to the Slave River. In keeping with conventions of cultural tourism and Ghanaian festivals in general, the grand durbar was another opportunity to display the pomp and pageantry of Ghanaian royalty. It began with the elaborate procession of local royal leaders, some riding in palanquins and all generously adorned with gold. In keeping with the other durbars of PANAFEST/Emancipation Day activities, members of royalty rarely participated in the speech making, a fact that confirmed their symbolic role. In any event, none of the speeches during this grand durbar strayed far from the themes of the celebrations: all condemned the slave trade out of Ghana and the country's contemporary neocolonial predicament, even as they also emphasized the spirit of African survival and renewal. The durbar also had the usual variety of performances of drumming, dancing, and reenactments, including another reenactment of the slave trade.

Although I was seated in a front-row seat at the durbar, it was difficult to keep track of the various events and to hear many of the performances occurring in the center of the open field, away from the stage and microphones. As usual, the layout of the grand durbar was such that the audience was seated under tents that formed a large open square, with the dignitaries and other important guests seated on a raised platform at the center of one of its sides. The podium and microphone were located on this platform. The positioning of the seating meant that people in the audience could see one another, and the various theatrical events all occurred in the vast open space inside the square. However, it was difficult for the audience to follow the events because those performing within the square of tents in the large field did not have access to the public-address system, which was on the raised platform and reserved for the dignitaries. Thus, I had not heard the announcement for the slave-trade reenactment. Soon after a dance performance by a cultural troupe, two young men approached the center of the durbar field. They were dressed in black trousers and black jackets, they carried rifles, and they were dragging behind them three women who were chained together and who appeared to be prisoners. These young women were disheveled; they were dressed in ragged shorts and shirts. Not only were they tied together at the waist by a long chain, their hands were also tied behind their backs. Once they were in the center of the field, the guards forced the women to sit on the ground; the guards then briskly walked away and returned with two more female captives.

As this was occurring in one part of the field, four other men appeared from the other side of the field. They headed away from the captives and toward seats that had been placed behind a standing microphone. The men's

5.3 Foreign and local spectators at the Emancipation Day grand durbar, Assin Manso, August 1, 2005. Photograph by the author.

ASSIN MANSO

GARDEN OF REVERENCE, SITE OF SLAVE MARKET, LAST BATH AND GRAVE YARD

FOR FURTHER ENQUIRIES CONTACT:
GHANA TOURIST BOARD
CENTRAL REGIONAL OFFICE
P.O. BOX CT 847
CAPE COAST
TEL: (042)-32062 FAX: (042)-36622
Website: www.ghanatourism.gov.gh

5.4 Marker for the Garden of Reverence, slave market, last bath, and graveyard, Assin Manso, August 1, 2005. Photograph by the author.

5.5 Ancestral graveyard within the grounds of the slavery museum
at Assin Manso, August 1, 2005. Photograph by the author.

attire distinguished their differing positions. Two of them wore large mul-
ticolored smocks representative of the clothing styles of groups living in
northern Ghana, and they were carrying rifles. Another man wore a popular
Ghanaian-style print shirt, and he seemed to represent a local urban en-
trepreneur. The last man wore a suit and tie and very deliberately carried a
suitcase. As the four men sat in the middle of the field and began to speak
to one another, I focused my attention on the interaction.[26] A few minutes
into the conversation, I realized that this was a reenactment of the sale of
African captives. The conversation was multilingual with one man translating between those dressed as northerners and the man in a suit and tie, with
the man in the suit and tie seeming to understand only English. It soon became clear that the men were negotiating the sale of the three young women
who had been brought into the open field in chains. At one point, the four
men went over to the shackled women and conducted what seemed like a
deliberate visual inspection of them, checking the women's arms, necks,
and teeth. I then realized that the man in the suit and tie carrying a brief-
case was performing the role of a White European. Perhaps the organizers
felt the audience would have made this recognition quickly, given that this
Black Ghanaian man performed all the markers of Whiteness—clothing,
mannerism, and his deliberate diction when speaking English (see chap-

ter 3). Nevertheless, I wondered if this recognition had really dawned on most of the audience and, more importantly, if the man's performed racial difference mattered at all.

The performance lasted no more than fifteen minutes and concluded with the four men wrapping up their negotiations with the "White" merchant and transferring the young women captives to him. The entire group exited the performance stage with the women being pulled along wailing loudly and struggling with the merchant who was leading them away, presumably to be sold into slavery. Significantly, the performance was not followed by any commentary either by the organizers or the many invited speakers. In fact, the audience was treated to more dancing and drumming by the commissioned cultural troupes immediately after the reenactment. This was followed by the various speeches—mostly by the same people who had spoken the evening before and throughout the week, including Obetsebi-Lamptey and African American scholar and activist Leonard Jeffries.[27] And although the main theses of African survival and renewal were reiterated, these speeches seemed distant from the actual reenactment of slavery. As the durbar was drawing to a close, audience members were asked to proceed across the street to the large slavery museum for the final ceremony of Emancipation Day—the pouring of libation at the mouth of the Nnonko Nsuo, the Slave River.

How do we read the public, state-sponsored reenactments of this particular narrative of slavery history? Why does the celebration of emancipation necessitate these various reenactments of the slave trade? What are these reenactments meant to demonstrate? What meanings do they produce? What feelings do they evoke? Among the various other performances and activities during PANAFEST/Emancipation Day, how do such reenactments render the memory of slavery concrete and contemporary? At the same time, what kind of work are they doing for both the state's own conception of itself and its ongoing construction of national identity and meaning? I suggest here that, within the context of a celebration of African emancipation and Pan-African cooperation, these reenactments create the space for the state's concrete production of social meanings about history, politics, and race. Specifically, the performances work to construct a particular narrative of slavery that reclaims racial affiliation through the convergence of continental African and diaspora experience around this historical phenomenon. For this to occur, however, the narrative that is told has had to shift Ghana's history of slavery toward the Atlantic in ways that actually give primacy to a distinctly *diaspora* experience, one that begins at the moment of capture and shipment and ends away from the African mainland.

To better understand this particular construction of meaning around slavery, we must first examine the ways that slavery is presented in these reenactments. At both the Reverential Night and Emancipation Day durbar, the most poignant visible symbol of slavery is the bound African captive. This powerful image, represented through both male and female bodies, sets up the narrative of slavery with a variety of components. First, African victims take center stage—even though the events take place within the castle-dungeon or at the site of the Slave River, these captives are the most visible representation; they are shackled and bound and treated as chattel. This image is made even more palpable at the durbar, where the captives are not only publicly displayed and examined, but where they also become the objects of a clear financial transaction. Although there are other events that are occurring in tandem with the spectacle of the African captives—for example, the ongoing speeches and performances at the Reverential Night and the microphoned interactions among the businessmen at the durbar— audience members clearly see their victimization. The visual effect of their subordination is deliberate. However, another component of these reenactments is the way that the locality of the captive's victimization is quickly, and paradoxically, pushed to the background of the experience of captivity. In other words, the victim's actual experience of enslavement is not reenacted; rather, the reenactment begins and ends at capture (except during the Reverential Night, where, as we will see below, capture quickly shifts to emancipation). Audience members, therefore, are not made directly aware of what happens after the event of capture. Moreover, the actual process of enslavement is presented as though it does not occur on Ghanaian soil but, instead, rather far away from the local scene. Ironically, for the audience, it is the *consequence* of capture (presumably the experience of enslavement in the New World) that is expressly highlighted, even though this aspect of the experience is not actually performed. What happens to those left behind, and to the homeland of the captive, remains elusive. Consequently, the staging of these reenactments allows the construction of a narrative that, however unwittingly, reduces the significance of the aftermath of slavery on the local scene (in Ghana and on the African continent).

Yet, the state's effort to promote heritage tourism focuses on a narrative of slavery that, in this context, is most readily translatable. Where there is not yet an available local discussion of slavery that addresses local/national experiences, concerns, and legacies, the Ghanaian state taps into already established discourses, images, and ideas about the transatlantic slave trade. Indeed, because of its economic and political positioning, the Ghanaian state's projects around heritage tourism have only been successful to the extent that the country has received considerable international monetary and technical assistance. Ghana was one of the first countries on the African continent, for example, to be tapped by the United Nations Slave Route Project. This UNESCO project, officially launched in 1994, has endeavored to make the history of the slave trade a "matter of concern to modern society" (UNESCO 2006, 2) through an elaborate set of objectives that includes education and cultural programs.

The Slave Route Project is international in scope, partnering with a number of national governments and multinational corporations. Some of the programs initiated by the project include: the establishment of scientific research, training, and education on the slave trade; the selection of places of memory to construct archives and memorials; public-awareness campaigns; the establishment of slavery museums in key locations throughout the world; the successful sponsoring of legislation in the UN that called for recognition of the slave trade as a "crime against humanity"; and the development of teaching materials to disseminate in various national contexts. Because of its many material relics of the slave trade, Ghana was identified early on as a key site for mapping the routes of the slave trade. Thus the development over the past decade of Ghana's many heritage-tourism sites—such as the museum at Assin Manso, as well as the archiving of documents relating to the slave trade—is directly linked to this broader transnational UNESCO program. The country has received financial, educational, and technical assistance to participate in this global effort to acknowledge and commemorate the slave trade. It is within this context that we have to place the state's deployment of the history of slavery. If we are to consider the UNESCO Slave Route Project, the narrative of slavery that emerges is one in which the ultimate focus is, first, on tracing the routes of captives from the continent to the New World and, second, on the experiences of enslavement in the diaspora. There is a way in which this serves to present slavery not only as the property of those captives taken away from the continent (the diaspora Blacks) but, more importantly, as Laura Chrisman has observed, slavery here "is consistently accorded a primacy which colonialism is not" (2003, 80). In other words, there is the "systematic isolation" (85) of the phenomenon of slavery from the broader historical context of the development of racial capitalism, even though Black Atlantic subjectivity and identity is shaped as much by colonialism on the African continent as it is by transatlantic slavery. As we will see in chapter 7, this systematic historical isolation (of slavery from colonialism) is not unique to UNESCO or to the Ghanaian state's heritage-tourism endeavors; it is the conventional trend in narratives of slavery that seems to recognize neither the necessity of

combining racial slavery and racial colonialism nor the mutually constitutive nature of the experiences of their victim-subjects (Chrisman 2003).

Ironically, an effect of this adoption of the diaspora narrative of slavery—even as the state appears, paradoxically, to claim at least part of it as its
own—is the silencing of certain aspects of the history of slavery that results
in the implication of Ghanaian people both as perpetrator and victim. Although African victims are prominent in the two Emancipation Day slavery
reenactments, accomplices and perpetrators are only subtly invoked, if they
are invoked at all (Richards 2005, 627). This is hardly surprising since, as
Richards notes, this is the usual way that the state as well as local communities
have managed the memory of slavery. In the scene with the African captives
on stage during the Reverential Night, audience members do not see *how* the
captives were captured, *who* captured them, or *why* they were captured. Of
course, the absence of a clear explanation for these very basic details can perhaps be explained by the organizers' presumption that they are well known
by the audience. But, because public discussion of slavery—particularly the
transatlantic slave trade—in Ghana is relatively new (Perbi 2000; Holsey
2008; Richards 2005), it becomes important to ask to *which* set of audience
members the reenactments are geared. The reenactment at the Emancipation Day durbar was more explicit in demonstrating both perpetrators and
victims; here Africans were on both sides of the equation, while the lone
European was presented as perpetrator-benefactor. The reenactment at the
durbar, particularly followed as it was by the solemn pouring of libations at
the Slave River, seemed to present a more direct discussion of the dynamics
of the slave trade. At the same time, Ghana's concrete link to this history
beyond the sites and routes—the castle-dungeons and the Slave River—remains elusive. Because the reenactments and general state discourse do not
concretely make this connection, the local population remains strangers to
this history. Moreover, their education on the phenomenon, a crucial part
of national historical legacy, both removes them from the position of key
agents and shifts the focus to the diaspora.

In effect, the various activities that structure state discourse around the
deployment of this legacy continue to work to put the experience of racial
slavery in the local consciousness, even as it problematically reinforces the
slavery-as-diaspora-experience narrative. Following the objectives set forth
by the UNESCO Slave Route Projects, and in the effort to increase the country's heritage-tourism potential among diaspora Blacks, state officials and
organizers of these Pan-Africanist celebrations have begun to "educate" the
Ghanaian audience about both the history of slavery and the experiences
of diaspora Blacks. This initiative comes partly within the state's heritage-

tourism agenda, through which officials have recognized the need for ongoing training and preparation of local vendors, tour operators, businesses. One aspect of this education effort is the preparation of the local population to better interact with (and, importantly, to not offend) Black diaspora visitors in Ghana.

In a lengthy discussion with me during the summer of 2006, Jake Obetsebi-Lamptey, minister of tourism and diasporan relations, enthusiastically rearticulated the state's commitment to reclaiming its legacy of both the slave trade and Pan-Africanism. Without prompting and with the earnest excitement of one who has only recently uncovered his own cultural heritage, Obetsebi-Lamptey began our conversation by recounting the history and horrors of the slave trade and its devastation for both continental and diaspora populations. He continued by railing against colonialism and enduring racial discrimination, stressing (perhaps for my benefit) that "we need reparations from the Europeans who enslaved and colonized us." Yet almost immediately, he followed that statement with: "But we [Africans and diaspora Blacks] cannot get it without unity." "So, what we want to see," he continued, "is Africans coming together."

To Obetsebi-Lamptey, however, one of the main impediments to Africans coming together is the lack of mutual identification on both sides of the Atlantic: "Africans and African Americans don't know enough about each other." Because of this, he proudly stated that his ministry has begun to focus on educating the Ghanaian public about the history of New World slavery. The hope is that the average Ghanaian will not only develop a better appreciation of diaspora Black history and experience, but will be better able to interact with diaspora tourists in Ghana. To set this agenda in motion, Obetsebi-Lamptey told me of his ministry's new Akwaaba Onyemi (Welcome Brother/Sister) program,[28] a set of education projects aimed at promoting the racial kinship of diaspora Blacks and Ghanaians. One of the first events for this new project was the state-sponsored national broadcasting of *Roots*, the popular epic-drama that follows several generations of an enslaved family from capture in West Africa in the 1700s to emancipation during the U.S. Civil War. Broadcasted in the United States in the late 1970s, *Roots* had a great impact on national consciousness, serving as a catalyst for discussions of race and the legacy of slavery.[29] It also sparked off intensive interest in genealogical research by African Americans, bringing continental Africa to the forefront of the group's consciousness. Though there are no official records detailing local response to the movie, Obetsebi-Lamptey said that the broadcasting of *Roots* was highly successful; at the very least, he argued, it was the first time that many people in Ghana came to see what life under slavery entailed for those in the diaspora. Indeed, Obetsebi-Lamptey felt that the response was positive enough to merit similar broadcasts. At this point in our conversation, he gestured animatedly to a shelf next to his desk where there was a copy of the four-part Public Broadcasting Service series *Africans in America: American's Journey through Slavery*. "We will broadcast this next," he said.

In a context such as Ghana, where slavery is not a regular topic for discussion at any level, it becomes important to recognize the potential significance of reenactments and the national broadcasting of films and educational programs on slavery. What is also significant is the kind of history of slavery that is deployed. As with the reenactments during PANAFEST/Emancipation Day celebrations, the experiences that are prioritized are those of slavery-descended Blacks. The documentary *Africans in America*, for example, is purposely chosen to reveal the diaspora experience to Ghanaians, a fact that, though laudable in intent, in effect diminishes the complexity of the *Ghanaian* relationship to this same historical event. The result is that slavery remains distant both historically and experientially from Ghana and Ghanaians; it remains primarily a fleeting, past, and partial history, and, more importantly, it becomes an event that has more significance for New World Blacks. Moreover, those in the diaspora are presented as the triumphant survivors of this history, a view that taps directly into the state's desire to also use this triumph as an example of (continental) African survival and spiritual renewal.

With the theme "Our Heritage, Our Strength: Honoring Our African Heroes," the goal of Emancipation Day was to focus on the strength and resilience of the African, particularly the "role of people of African descent in the struggle for and emancipation of the black man [*sic*] from the evils of the slave trade and slavery" (Obetsebi-Lamptey 2005, 6).[30] This meant, at the very least, some attention to the "evils of the slave trade," which was provided, as I've shown above, through the two reenactments depicting the capture and sale of Africans. However, during the Reverential Night celebrations, as well as throughout the entire PANAFEST/Emancipation Day activities, the historical event of slavery seemed to also compete with the rhetoric of triumph and awakening. Upon the very stage on which the actors portraying enslaved Africans sat during the Reverential Night, there were various other props that articulated related yet distinct narratives. For example, directly behind the standing microphone at center of the stage was a large poster exhibition of the "African Heroes of the Emancipation." This exhibition reflected the event's subtheme and was replicated in the official brochure for Emancipation Day. The large black felt posterboard was decorated with the official PANAFEST/Emancipation Day banner and draped with material in the three colors of the Ghanaian flag. The "African Heroes of Emancipation" were highlighted on this board, along with pictures and biographies. The represented heroes included: Frederick Douglas, W. E. B. DuBois, Anna Julia Cooper, Harriet Tubman, Nathaniel Turner, Sojourner Truth, William Wells Brown, Francis Harper, George E. Ferguson, Toussaint L'Ouverture, and Nanny of the Maroons. What was significant here was the fact that U.S.-born Black heroes were overrepresented in this depiction, with those from the Caribbean given secondary status, and Ghanaians represented only by George Ferguson.[31] In any case, how do we analyze this dearth of Ghanaian representation among the heroes of emancipation? It may be that there are indeed no prominent Ghanaian figures in this particular understanding of emancipation particularly since it is a celebration that focuses on the emancipation of diaspora Blacks from slavery in the New World. All the same, this move actually points to the divergent ways that various groups on both sides of the Atlantic experienced the legacy of the slave trade. In the particular rendering of the slavery and emancipation narrative at PANAFEST/Emancipation Day celebrations, Ghanaians cannot have a legacy of emancipation since such is presumably reserved for diaspora Blacks who actually experienced the travails of slavery.

Nevertheless, in celebrating the triumph of "African Heroes" and claiming it as part of national history and memory, the state further consolidates Ghanaian-diaspora historical and racial kinship. It is a kinship that allows the construction of the state narrative of triumph and spiritual renewal. Those in the diaspora, particularly U.S. Blacks, have survived a brutal history and have essentially succeeded. As "brothers and sisters" of the continent, they therefore have the responsibility to aid in the "emancipation" of the African continent from economic and political marginalization. In a sense, those in the diaspora have more possibilities to become heroes because, according to the narrative, not only were they the ones to physically suffer the fate of enslavement, but they also emerged victorious, with access to vast resources and power. They are indeed what Obetsebi-Lamptey calls "modern-day Josephs." The embrace of this racial kinship, even though it positions Ghanaians as the "sisters and brothers" in need, works to link Ghanaians directly to the real and presumed wealth of diaspora Blacks. In light of Ghana's contemporary economic realities, this link allows Ghana to share in the triumph of Black diaspora emancipation.

It is important to note that this is a significant shift in the ways that Pan-Africanism has been deployed. As state officials often remind us during these events, newly independent Ghana was the "beacon of hope for the

Black race" (Mahama 2001). Ghana's independence was hailed triumphant over colonial rule and the presumed demise of imperialism. Nkrumah's Pan-Africanism led the way to global Black emancipation and unity. But the ideological template for this Pan-Africanism was not necessarily fueled by discourses of slavery and emancipation; racial colonialism was the culprit and Ghanaians and Africans were victors. This is not to say that the state did not tap into its diaspora links for economic development, or that the new Ghanaian state did not recognize the clear connections of colonialism to the plight of Blacks in the diaspora (as I mentioned in chapter 2). But the point is to demonstrate that this current deployment of Pan-Africanism emerges out of the particular contemporary circumstances of both Ghana and diaspora Blacks as well as the continually shifting but significant globalized racial hierarchies. Nevertheless, the adoption of diaspora narratives of suffering and ultimate triumph underscores the contradictions in this new Pan-Africanist moment: in important ways, it minimizes the historical and contemporary racialized structure in Ghanaian societies and, perhaps inadvertently, reduces diaspora experience solely to vindication.

## Neoliberal Pan-Africanism and Ghanaian Racial Formation

The first event of the 2005 PANAFEST/Emancipation Day occurred at the DuBois Memorial Centre in the quiet Cantonments neighborhood in Accra. On that morning, officials, tourists, and local participants gathered to commemorate DuBois's contributions to Pan-Africanism and to Ghana. The various official statements at the event revealed a combination of Nkrumah's cultural nationalism and call for continental emancipation, DuBois's appeal for intellectual and political Pan-Africanism, and Padmore's call for Ghana to challenge its position within the global political economy. The larger theme, however, was the relationship between Africans and diaspora Blacks, particularly as it concerns the history of Pan-Africanism and the role of heritage tourism as one of Ghana's strategies for economic development. The director of the Ghana Tourist Board, Bridgette Katchku, reminded the audience that "[g]overnment and the people of Ghana have a strong belief in Emancipation. That's why we encourage [our] sons and daughters [in the diaspora] to return. . . . We believe we are the same people even if [some of us] are far away."

Four years earlier, Ghana had been designated by the World Bank as a Highly Indebted Poor Country (HIPC). Even as some Ghanaians satirically and sarcastically joked, "We are hipic now!" the implications of this designation did not escape them. In accepting the HIPC designation, state officials confirmed the depth of Ghana's poverty and its marginalized position within global political and economic hierarchies. It also reminded many that Ghana, like most African nations, is ruled in significant part "by transnational organizations that are not in themselves governments but work together with powerful First World states within a global system of nation-states" (Ferguson 2005, 100). This is a process akin to "re-colonization" (ibid.), and it reflects the reality that these impoverished nations are not truly sovereign or independent. As Ferguson (who echoes radical scholars such as Walter Rodney) recognizes, the international order is actually just a "constellation of states" that "segments off the exploited . . . regions within discrete national compartments with 'their own problems,' thereby masking the relations that link the rich and poor regions behind the false fronts of sovereignty and independence that have never existed" (65). Yet, PANAFEST/Emancipation Day celebrations, as well as other cultural programs in the name of national economic development, are promoted at the same time that the global neoliberal economic restructuring makes it clear that the African "elites" in charge of these postcolonial states in fact have little control of their economies (Ferguson 2005).

How can there be rhetoric of African triumph and redemption in this difficult context? I believe that this has occurred by the restructuring of the narrative of Ghanaian national identity in ways that both depoliticize the historical exploitation it has experienced by the imperial West and force African self-critique. Indeed, the development of heritage tourism within the context of a neoliberal economic order that presents a narrative of slavery that is decoupled from racial colonialization and that is without European perpetrators in fact works to neutralize the impact of the country's colonial history, silencing the effects of exploitation. At the same time it decouples White Western power and African subordination, shifting responsibility to Africans, thereby reifying the racial and cultural differences that undergird traditional understandings of Africa's economic and political predicaments. As we saw above, the concrete history and relation of Western colonial exploitation is completely removed from heritage-tourism activities and from reenactments of the slave trade. Instead, participants in these celebrations are offered African victims and Black diaspora "Josephs."

In spite of these contradictions, I also see the potential for creativity and the possibility for transformation. As the state continues to host and sponsor these contemporary international Pan-Africanist events, it not only reaffirms its particularly raced existence, it articulates an ideal of internationalist citizenship while at the same time creating the space for the crafting of new racial subjectivities. Though the state acts primarily on a political level, I suggest here that its activities have potentially broad reach, informing practical relations and transforming the local cultural terrain. It is true that the terms of engagement with the Black diaspora continue to shift. For some, nevertheless, the memory of the slave trade emerging from such heritage-tourism activities may offer an avenue for the continuation of a transnational discussion among Ghanaians and other members of the Black Atlantic (Gaines 2006). In this discussion, as well as in the actions that enable interaction and discussion, we also find the space for ongoing negotiations of racial and political subjectivity. It is to these negotiations that I now turn. The next chapter offers an ethnography that focuses on the Ghanaian local terrain and examines the racial project created through Ghanaian-diaspora interactions.

# SIX

# "Are You a Black American?": Race and the Politics of African-Diaspora Interactions

Ghana was unrivaled among African nations in its willingness to provide sanctuary to black . . . radicals from the United States, the Caribbean, Africa, and Europe
unable to function politically in their countries of origin. For many of these expatriates, this willingness made Ghana a destination of radical hope.

—Kevin Gaines, *American Africans in Ghana*

I looked at the guides in their basketball vests and Nike sneakers. America for
them meant Kobe and Shaq and Michael Jordan. Across them stood the tourists.
In their eyes Africa was a land of enduring wisdoms. They were its lost kings and its
Nubian princesses. Both groups saw in the other a reflection of their own dreams.
Africa and America converged . . . each searching the other's eyes.

—Ekow Eshun, *Black Gold of the Sun*

The dialogue between Africans and African Americans has not always produced
the harmony and unity dreamed of by Pan-Africanists, but it has produced significant transformations of political identity, religious practice, and culture generally
in both Africa and its diaspora.

—J. L. Matory, "Afro-Atlantic Culture"

"So, you're one of those Blacks from the diaspora."

It was early August 2000, and Lynette, an African American graduate student from the United States, was in Ghana for the first time. She had come
to attend the annual conference convened by the members of the Black association of her discipline. I was her unofficial tour guide in Accra: I was the
one who encouraged her to make the trip and offered to host her while in
the country. On this day, I had taken Lynette to meet some of my graduate

student friends at the University of Ghana, Legon, with the hope that this familiar environment would acclimate her more quickly.

"You are one of those Blacks from the diaspora," Kofi repeated definitively.

"Um, yes, I guess so," Lynette responded.

Kofi stared at her and smiled, saying almost triumphantly, "So, you are one of the lucky ones."

Both Lynette and I were surprised. We had not expected this welcome. *I* had not expected this welcome. I was surprised—shocked, even—that one of my friends would have such a view of the African diasporic experience. And, frankly, I was embarrassed that Lynette was subjected to this rather jarring welcome. To my chagrin, Lynette did not have an immediate reaction. She stood there, spellbound, I assumed, by the weight of the observation. I, on the other hand, attempted to address the issue directly. "What do you mean by 'lucky'?" I asked, trying to maintain an even tone.

"Well," Kofi responded, "I mean that your ancestors were lucky to have escaped the poverty and hopelessness that we are now living in Africa."

"Lucky?" I asked with incredulity in my voice.

"Yes," Kofi answered firmly. "Look how well you all are doing over there; look how far you have gotten."

My first explicit education in the politics of Pan-Africanism and transnational Black social and cultural cooperation occurred in Accra around 1995. I was in the country for a yearlong stay when I met a group of young Ghanaian men and women who identified themselves as members of the All-African Peoples Revolutionary Party (A-APRP).[1] They invited me to participate in their weekly reading-group meeting, which also doubled as a planning meeting for their weekly cultural programs for high school students. When I arrived one Sunday afternoon to attend my first reading-group meeting, the discussion had already begun on W. E. B. DuBois's book *Africa and the World*. Members of the group warmly greeted me as I took a seat in the corner to listen in. This was my first introduction to DuBois's book and the first time I came to know his work beyond a U.S. context. The discussion was lively and not only covered the contents of the book, but also the historical and political context of its production. It also appeared to be an attempt to come to terms with what members believed to be DuBois's "colonialist" representation of Africa while trying to extract some Pan-Africanist ideological wisdom. By the end of the discussion, group members had decided that a better follow-up book on the A-APRP list would be Walter Rodney's *How Europe Underdeveloped Africa* (1980).

I learned a lot from these reading-group meetings. I was introduced to a number of key Pan-Africanist texts; watched and discussed films such as Sam Greenlee's underground classic *The Spook Who Sat by the Door*,[2] about a Black CIA agent who uses his training to lead a guerrilla insurrection in Chicago; and participated in ongoing ideological debates on the nature of a global Black cultural, economic, and political cooperation. Before my encounter with its Ghana chapter, I did not know much about the A-APRP. I soon learned that it was a party established to "combat the forces oppressing Africans worldwide" in a struggle for equality while uniting them through a revolutionary Pan-Africanism.[3] Originally called for by Ghana's first president, Kwame Nkrumah, in his *Handbook of Revolutionary Warfare*, A-APRP came into existence through the efforts of Kwame Touré, the U.S. civil rights and Black Power movement activist formerly known as Stokely Carmichael. Under Touré's direction and leadership, the party expanded throughout the African continent and the African diaspora. Ghana's A-APRP chapter, it was explained to me, was devoted to the teachings of Nkrumah, Sekou Touré, and Kwame Touré, and it worked toward African unity (as defined by Pan-Africanism) while advocating an ideology of "Nkrumahism-Touréism."[4] Ghanaian party members, similar to other members, also sought to maintain a balanced lifestyle of work and study. The reading group fulfilled this requirement, and it also helped members achieve an active Pan-Africanist education, which stresses raising one's political consciousness. During my stay in Ghana that year and afterward, I became extremely involved in all of the events of the group. The most exciting for me were the weekly Saturday morning cultural activities organized for secondary school students at the W. E. B. DuBois Memorial Centre. Members of the party would gather at Kwaku's house on Friday evenings to prepare for Saturday's event. I relished these Friday evenings. Kwaku would spend all day cooking food and snacks for the children, and we would join him later in the day, preparing the meals for distribution, while working on the next day's program. My relationship with the Ghanaian chapter of A-APRP would have a profound effect on my understanding of the complexity of Ghanaian identity formation, particularly in relationship to a transnational Black diaspora politics.

This chapter extends the discussion of racecraft in Ghana. Its primary goal is to examine the cultural and political terrain of contemporary urban Ghanaian interactions with people of African descent from the diaspora. I highlight this complex and dynamic terrain to call attention to the fact that such interactions are mediated by historical relations and a set of global social, economic, and political forces that have structured particularly racialized understandings of identity for populations of African descent on both sides of the Atlantic. The ethnographic moments described above reveal these understandings; they demonstrate accumulated historical (and indeed global) precedents of race and power wherein racialized meanings structure the sociopolitical realm and details of daily life. Thus, even as the encounter between Kwaku, a Ghanaian, and Lynette, an African American, signals understandably disparate interpretations of African and diaspora histories, it nevertheless represents a particular recognition that links through the historical arc of slavery and colonialism—and the overlapping history of Blacks from the diaspora and those left behind on the continent. In the second ethnographic moment we see an explicit project of racecraft among this group of young Ghanaians; it is one that advocates a project of global Black or Pan-African cooperation. The central argument in the chapter is that Ghanaian and African diasporic interactions occur within mutual processes of discourses, practices, and (mis)recognitions that are informed both by African diasporic racial consciousness and identity and by Ghanaian racialized consciousness and agency. As I have done throughout the book thus far, I focus particularly on this Ghanaian racialized consciousness and demonstrate that it is actively constructed and negotiated in part through encounters with Blacks from the diaspora. Over the years, these encounters have fostered a familiarity and identification of Ghanaians with people of African descent that is reflected in a variety of ways, one of which is the development and deployment of a peculiar trope of "the Black American." I contend that this trope, concocted within the crucible of transnational racialization processes, already exists in the terrain of Ghanaian-diasporic interactions and, as such, plays an important role in establishing and framing terms of engagement for diaspora Blacks with Ghana.

This chapter has the additional aim of shifting the focus of the current lively and often contentious debate on African American and African relations, while simultaneously challenging the basic premises and assumptions underlying this debate.[5] The proliferation, in recent years, of scholarly and journalistic discussions about diaspora "heritage tourism" to Ghana has been astounding. While I recognize the long historical discourse of the African American relationship to Africa as one of "homeland" and visits by African Americans to Africa as "pilgrimages," I believe that this narrow focus obscures not only the range and history of African-diasporic interactions, but it also reduces them to a very local, and often parochial, discussion of "Ghanaians versus African Americans," removed from the broader terrain of national and transnational structure and politics and particular relations of power. Rather than center my analysis on "pilgrims" or "heritage tourists" (see Bruner 1996; Ebron 1999; Hasty 2002), I use ethnographic detail to broaden the scope of analysis. I do so in three specific ways. First, I move beyond the tourists at the former slave castle-dungeons—and the attendant discourse of slavery—while not denying their significance. As will become clear, my research in Ghana most explicitly belies the idea that the heritage tourism of a certain group of African Americans (namely, the "Afrocentric") is the only source of Ghanaian-diasporic interaction. Second, moving beyond the slave castles also allows the space to draw attention to a distinctive Afro-diasporic network of young professional and cosmopolitan Ghanaians and diaspora Blacks whose complex and mutually constitutive experiences are, more often than not, elided in anthropological discussions of postcolonial Africa.[6] Linked to this (and third), I demonstrate that the complex burdens of race, Blackness, and even slavery are not those of diaspora Blacks alone to bear. What I mean here is this: Ghanaian identity formations, on the ground, at least, may not yield the same engagement with slavery (and its attendant histories and processes) as those of some diaspora Blacks, yet this does not mean this major historical event is any less significant for the Ghanaian population. This chapter thus echoes the major thesis of this book that Ghana and Ghanaian identity formation must be understood within broader processes of racialization that often render analogous if dialectical the identity formations of Ghanaians and those of African descent in and from the diaspora. Specifically, the encounter with diaspora Blacks shows the ways in which local meanings of the racialized (Black) Ghanaian self is, and has always been, constructed through a complex set of overlapping histories that are set within transnational understandings of race and Blackness. An important aspect of this is the ways that such local meanings are shaped through the interplay of Black people's active agency with a European-dominated Atlantic political and economic complex (Matory 1999).

The discussion in this chapter is framed by three ethnographic moments. All focus on Ghanaian-diasporic interactions as a way of mapping a conceptual and theoretical space to engage Ghanaian racialized consciousness. I begin with a discussion of my experience of touring the Elmina Castle-Dungeon with a church group from Washington, DC, and I use this description as a springboard to examine both the representation and the history of diaspora Blacks in Ghana. From there I explore the trope of the Black American in the context of the experiences of a group of Black academics who held their annual conference in Ghana in the summer of 2000. Finally, I present a completely alternative view of contemporary African-diasporic interaction through a discussion of First Fridays Accra. Similar to the local and global forces that affect Ghanaian state politics regarding heritage-tourism events (see chapter 5), the First Fridays phenomenon in Accra offers a glimpse of the broad terrain upon which such interactions occur. Overall, these examples should provide us with a template for a contextualized and situated analysis of Ghanaian racial formation that can serve as the basis for a critical revision of the ways we engage postcolonial Africa.

## The Return of the Black Diaspora: Tourists? Pilgrims? Cultural Imperialists? Racists?

As I was attending the 2005 PANAFEST/Emancipation Day celebrations in Cape Coast and Elmina, I decided that it would prove informative to take an official tour of Elmina Castle-Dungeon while it was full of tourists and other visitors. Around midday on my fourth day in town, I jumped into a taxi for the short ride along the Atlantic coast from Cape Coast to Elmina. When I arrived at the castle, the forecourt and grounds were sparse, a striking contrast from the busy scene just a few days earlier, when there was a grand durbar for the PANAFEST official welcome ceremony. I crossed over the wooden bridge leading to the main entrance into the castle. At the front desk, I asked for Ato, a Ghanaian friend who worked as a tour guide. Ato had been working at Elmina for years, and his tours had the reputation of being comprehensive and historically sound. In addition, Ato was known not to soften or change his narrative of the history of the trade at Elmina in the presence of Whites (unlike, apparently, some other guides). He had also recently published a book on the castle and the history of the slave trade at Elmina.[7] Taking the tour with him was therefore a treat.

Ato suggested that I join his afternoon tour. Once the group convened, we embarked on the relatively long tour around the castle. No matter how many times one does it, taking a tour of Elmina is never easy. Most people visiting Elmina will be affected by the dark and dank dungeons, which, at the height of the slave trade, housed hundreds of enslaved Africans who, waiting sometimes several months to be transported west, wallowed in the dark, breathing and living in their sweat, tears, and excrement. From these dungeons, the enslaved who survived this "storage" period would be led through the "Door of No Return" to the waiting slave ships. As visitors are led toward the large courtyard that housed the female dungeons, the tour guide usually points to a trap door through which the desired African females were sent to serve European traders and administrators. In the many tours I have taken of the castle, this part, along with the view of the Door of No Return, usually elicits the most reactions from tourists. People are often shocked to learn about the sexual exploitation of African women, who were humiliated as well as assaulted. Yet as mothers of children born through this exploitation, they would at times, ironically, become conduits of European power on the coast.

As the tour proceeded, I began to get to know the members of my group. They were a group of mostly middle-aged people of African descent who were members of a Christian church in Washington, DC. They had come to Ghana on a visit arranged by their minister, who was also participating in the tour with us. We were quiet, however, throughout most of the tour, with the occasional soft bursts of surprise, murmurs, or short comments about the darkness, the smell, and the smallness of the dungeons. As we were finishing the rounds, we were led to the last set of dungeons, the ones containing the Door of No Return. To reach this door, we entered through one of the larger male dungeons, then had to carefully walk down a steep slope at the end of which we had to step up, single file, through a small door. Ato led us to this smaller door and stood at the edge holding out his hands to help each of us climb up and through the door. Once through the door, we found ourselves in a very small room facing the Door of No Return, a narrow opening blocked by a heavy iron-barred door through which we could steal glimpses of the Atlantic Ocean. Even though we numbered only eight people, the room felt small and crowded.

With his back to the Door of No Return, Ato continued his narrative, giving a description of the door's original purpose, pointing out that during the days of the slave trade, the ocean reached the castle, and small boats would be at the door waiting to take their cargo to the larger ships out at sea. At the end of his detailed description, Ato asked that we take a moment of silence in memory of those who had passed through the door. After this somber moment, members of the group I was with conducted their own ceremony. The minister took out a small bottle of red wine and began a prayer on behalf of all who perished during the slave trade. He then asked members of the group to silently reflect on others who have passed before us and, if we felt so inclined, to call out their names. One by one, members of the group called out the names of loved ones. At the call of each name, the minister poured libation—a small amount of red wine—on the dungeon ground as the church members responded with *Ashe*.[8] Once all the names had been called and the libation poured, the minister said a final prayer, and we all proceeded to the next part of the tour. I was surprised by this set of events. In my many tours of Elmina Castle-Dungeon, I had never seen a group interrupt a tour and insert its own ceremony. Later, referring to this particular experience, I asked Ato how often such impromptu ceremonies occurred during his tours. He said that, though they were rare, this was not his first experience with this kind of behavior from a group. "Some people tend to take ownership of the castles," he said, and many feel they have the right to conduct their own ceremonies. I was even more surprised by the obvious Afrocentric elements of the ceremony from a Christian church group. The pouring of libation to honor the dead, the Yoruba symbolism, and the Ashe all seemed to jar with what would be deemed conventional Christian traditions.

By the end of the tour, I felt a certain closeness to the members of the group. On some level, this was not unusual. As a Black woman living in the United States, my position within the history and narratives of slavery both inside and outside of the continent is assumed. It was also obvious that members of the group felt comfortable with me in their midst, probably because I was of African descent (Ato contends that the dynamics of tour groups differ according to the racial makeup of the groups), and I did not seem to be uncomfortable during their ceremony at the Door of No Return. When Ato was finished, I chatted with the church members on the top balcony of the castle, just outside the former quarters of the European administrator. It is then that I found out that a few of the members were not strictly African American, but were Caribbean immigrants living in Washington, DC. Most surprising to me was the fact that the minister of this church group was born in Ghana. He had lived in the United States for more than twenty years and had been leading his church members on these tours for a number of years. This fact in itself, and particularly in combination with the group's Afrocentric ceremony, contradicted most representations of the heritage tourist in Ghana as singularly African American. My conversations with the minister after the tour and my conversations with members of the church group were instructive. They unsettled the rigid distinctions between what is African American and what is Ghanaian. Recognizing and acknowledging the diversity of even the most self-evident groupings—particularly of people of African descent—at the castles and throughout Ghana should also help challenge conventional representations of heritage tourism as a site where culturally essentialist (read Afrocentric) U.S.-born Blacks hold hegemonic power. My experience with the church group made evident the historical reality that the construction and deployment of what is Africa and African has been an ongoing active project for Black populations on both sides of the Atlantic.

In the scholarly attention given to the Black diaspora presence in Ghana, contemporary sojourners are described variously as visitors, pilgrims, repatriates, and, above all, wealthy tourists (and agents of U.S. capitalism) who have the freedom to travel for pleasure (Ebron 2002 Hasty 2002; Holsey 2004). Scholars present travel to Ghana by visitors and tourists as being about much more than leisure. Indeed, many Black diaspora visitors journey to Africa for cultural and spiritual renewal—to claim a lost past while simultaneously experiencing, to use Sandra Richards' phrase, "racial dignity at its source" (2005)—for repatriation, or for business and other professional ventures. Nevertheless, the general tendency is to focus on the heritage tourist in Ghana and, within that focus, there are two popular approaches: on the one hand, there are those who attempt to explore the effects of U.S. Black heritage tourism on local communities, highlighting cultural and political dissonance between Africans and diaspora Blacks; on the other, there is the tendency to explore solely diaspora Black subjective confrontation with the physical memories of the transatlantic slave trade.

Casting the Ghanaian state as the main regulator of global flows into the country, Jennifer Hasty argues that it attempts to further its hegemonic rule by exploiting African American needs for spiritual and cultural identification with Africa, particularly the group's "trans-Africanist" logic (2002). This trans-Africanist logic—the Black diaspora's assertion of cultural and racial unity with continental Africans—is, according to Hasty, based primarily on "political agendas predicated on essentialist antinomies" that have no direct connection to the local practicalities of Ghanaians (ibid.). Diaspora Black engagement with Ghanaian society, therefore, is considered superficial at best. Moreover, for Hasty and some other scholars, local politics are rendered distinct and distant from the transnational and global experiences that are engaged by the collaborative activities of state and diaspora Black tourists. Local inhabitants in this scenario are depicted as little more than pawns in a great game of Pan-African politics orchestrated by the state and diaspora Blacks. Ultimately, for Hasty, diaspora presence and "pilgrimage" is seen as harmful for Ghanaians because it "threatens to destabilize the routine production of national locality, predicated on historical, regional, ethnic, and political hierarchies" (ibid., 63). In a similar vein, Edward Bruner forecasts that diaspora Blacks' call for the memorialization of slavery could lead to an unwelcome racial conflict in Ghana. He asserts that "the attention of diaspora Blacks to the dungeons and the slave experience has the potential consequence of introducing into Ghanaian society . . . possibly a heightened awareness of black-white opposition" (1996, 298). How is it that recognition of the slave trade could lead to the *introduction* of Black-White racial conflict in postcolonial Ghana? Although neither Hasty nor Bruner directly state them, it is clear that there are specific assumptions about slavery and race being made. To interpret the discussions around slavery and racial commonality both as exclusive to diaspora Blacks and as potentially harmful insertions into Ghanaian society is to make a clear statement about particular understandings of local history, politics, and culture. In this case, and for Bruner especially, the idea that slavery would bring heightened awareness of Black-White opposition speaks specifically to race; not only does it assume that race is not an aspect of Ghanaian identity formation, but it also depicts diaspora Black tourists as the only source of racial consciousness for the country. Hasty's analysis is similar to Bruner's even if it does not directly refer to racialization because it argues that "the diasporan preoccupation with slavery dredges up historical, ethnic, regional, and transnational hostilities that may destabilize the political order" (2002, 63). Such interpretations bring up important questions: Under what circumstances can a discussion of slavery create so much hostility? Why do a Black diaspora presence and a "preoccupation with slavery" present such powerful potential for political destabilization on the local level and transnationally? Why is not the same charge made, for example, of the presence of European and U.S. business interests, or of Ghana's contemporary marginalized position within the cultural and political hierarchies of Western hegemony? I contend that the answers to these questions lie in the particular framing of diaspora presence in Ghana, where local practices and activities are presumed by some researchers to be unaffected by racialization processes. Yet, it is precisely because racialization processes continue to undergird Ghanaian national and political identity and activity—and because certain scholars are, however unwittingly, aware of this fact—that one might worry that a discussion of race and slavery could unsettle local politics.

The second prominent approach to heritage tourism in Ghana examines diaspora Black identity formation in relation to the historical experience of slavery. Saidiya Hartman (2002) explores how the encounter with slavery memorials works to produce a particular Black diaspora identity as "a collective memory of the past" structured by "loss" and "grief" (758). She argues that this "ideological construction" of slavery by diaspora Blacks is guided by nothing more than current political interests of "racial subjection, incarceration, and impoverishment" (765–66). Similar to Hasty and Bruner, Hartman is critical of the Ghanaian state because it exploits the grief of diaspora tourists for economic gain. Moreover, Hartman's concern is not only with the diaspora "politics of memory," (773) but particularly with the African American cultural and racial essentialism that shapes the ongoing search for origins. In Hartman's rendering, the local scene seems to work only as a prop for the diaspora search for identity; we do not learn much of Ghanaian experience and engagement with slavery beyond local inhabitants' assumed cynical misunderstanding of diaspora culture and identity. Sandra Richards's examination of African American heritage tourists' experience in Ghana extends to a critical and thoughtful engagement with local responses to slavery reenactments and performances at the slave castle-dungeons. Richards argues that Ghanaians and diaspora Blacks remember and forget the transatlantic slave trade in differing ways, rendering heritage memorials as sites of contradiction and dissimilarity. Indeed, because "slavery is not integral to how most Ghanaians see themselves," the people have to "remember a history they learned to forget" (2005, 626). Unlike other scholars of heritage tourism, Richards offers a rich analysis that integrates the machinations of the Ghanaian states, transnational economic and political investments, local Ghanaian interpretations of heritage-tourism events, and African American tourist negotiations of the psychological trauma of dealing with the physical representations of the slave trade.

Regardless of approach, however, the scholarship on Ghanaian-diasporic interactions works from a similar set of assumptions. In addition to the predominant focus on heritage-tourism sites, there are two other theoretical and epistemological convergences. First, as I discussed in the introduction to this book, there is the epistemological convergence on the treatment of slavery. The experience of slavery takes analytical precedence over that of colonialism, whether as a key trope of racial terror or in constituting modern Blackness (Chrisman 1997). As we saw in the previous chapter, there is also the focus on the diaspora narrative of slavery—as opposed to Ghana's own complex history of slavery—as the key site for investigating Ghanaian-diasporic encounters. Second, there is theoretical convergence on the deployment of race. Here, race and processes of racialization are often assumed to be significant only for Black U.S. subjects and mostly in self-consciously multiracial societies with clear histories of racial conflict. This assumption comes through clearly in the analyses of African American heritage tourists in which slavery and race are seemingly designated issues of concern only for diaspora Blacks. Postcolonial Ghana, with its mostly Black population, is presented as distant from the direct legacies of slavery, as well as from global processes of racialization. Moreover, the assumption is that such issues come into play only through the presence of diaspora Black heritage tourists in Ghana. Of course, it is not that awareness of racialization in contemporary West Africa is lacking; it is rather that such processes are not adequately analyzed in this or other contexts where they matter. When we consider that Black diaspora heritage visitors, for example, do not make up the bulk of Ghana's tourists, or that this group's travel to Ghana is also more than matched by travel to Ghana by other continental

Africans, Chinese and Indian nationals, White foreign-business executives and investors, aid-agency workers, and academics, the singular focus on heritage tourism itself belies the reality that there is a broad range of relationships and structures that work to anchor the transnational history of the transatlantic slave trade and race at the center of local geography and imagination.

Diaspora Blacks have traveled back to Africa since the beginning of the slave trade. They have returned as individuals, as organized groups, and as volunteers; they have been visitors, tourists, repatriates, and settlers; they have been politically and culturally diverse; and they have returned for many reasons, not least to escape the brutality of life under the grip of racialized terror in the Americas. Ghana has been a popular destination since political independence. The contemporary presence of diaspora Blacks dates back to the mid-1950s, as Ghana's independence and the Pan-Africanist vision of its first president, Kwame Nkrumah, reverberated throughout Africa and the diaspora. According to Kevin Gaines, Nkrumah's Ghana was "unrivaled among African nations in its willingness to provide sanctuary to Black (and non-Black) radicals from the United States, the Caribbean, Africa, and Europe unable to function politically in their countries of origin" (2006, 10). A number of diaspora Blacks became Nkrumah's key advisers and administrators and were joined by a sizable African American and West Indian community of artists and professionals who settled in Ghana (Gaines 2006; Walters 1993; Angelou 1986). By the mid-1960s, however, this community's strength and visibility waned as Nkrumah was deposed in a coup (Pierre and Shipley 2007). Although diaspora Blacks continued traveling to Ghana between the mid-1960s and early 1980s, it was not until the late 1980s— with the self-styled "populist" government of Jerry J. Rawlings—that the Ghanaian state would explicitly build upon the cultural nationalism of the Nkrumah era to advocate a renewed form of Pan-Africanism. There are indeed more diaspora Black tourists in Ghana today. It is the result of various circumstances, not least of which include the changing economic status for some Blacks in the diaspora and the worldwide attraction to tourism. Yet, this contemporary tourism is not the only source of diaspora travel to Ghana, nor should it be considered the primary site through which we explore diasporic-Ghanaian interaction.

What has remained clear over the long history of interaction is the powerful role of European-dominated Atlantic politics in establishing the conditions for African-diaspora dialogue. Diaspora Black and Ghanaian contact and interaction therefore occur within a broad cultural terrain on which active Black agency emerges through and against the constraints of global power dynamics. Consider, for example, that during Ghana's first ten years of independence (1957–67), the United States, as Penny Von Eschen has noted, "intervened culturally and politically to influence the terms of solidarities among Black Americans and Africans" (1997, 128). As communist nations seized on turbulent race relations in the United States to challenge its influence in Africa, the U.S. Information Agency (USIA) in Ghana, with the support of the State Department's Cultural Affairs, Psychological Warfare and Propaganda Board, embarked on a project to counter the country's poor image abroad. Ghana became the first Cold War battleground in Africa as the United States sparred with the Soviet Union and China for political influence. "Race relations" was the site of this sparring, and communist nations quickly seized on the subordinated positions of Black Americans as a tool to weaken U.S. influence on the African continent. In response, government agencies launched a major cultural offensive in Ghana that sought to highlight African American progress in the United States. The effort included numerous exhibits and conferences, distribution of pamphlets on African Americans, and sponsorship of lectures and performances by African Americans. In 1957, for example, USIA staff in Ghana "used photographs supplied from Washington to produce a picture exhibit entitled *Africans in the United States*, and displayed them in the window space of its central Accra office (Heger 1999, 6). This exhibit was wildly popular with Ghanaians, particularly the youth. And the campaign was so successful that it became the mode for U.S. cultural propaganda in other African nations (Von Eschen 1997). How are we to analyze the implications of such programs that mediate Ghanaian–African American relations through the international politics of the Cold War? One way is to recognize that the long history of interaction between Ghanaians and diaspora Blacks is not only facilitated by the active negotiation of people of African descent on both sides of the Atlantic, but also structured by global social, economic, and political processes that continue to inform racialized understandings of identity for these populations.

Another example of these interrelated global processes of racialization emerges in the history of the "blackface" feature in Ghana's concert party theater. Catherine Cole (2001a) traces the use of minstrel images in Ghana to theatrical conventions in colonial Africa. These conventions were transported from the United States, which, by the early 1900s, had a long tradition of minstrel performances. By the late 1920s minstrel performances had moved from New York vaudeville houses to Hollywood, through films such as Al Jolson's *Mammy*, which re-created in film the classic nineteenth-century minstrel show (Cole 1996). These films were distributed throughout the world, and particularly in remote colonial outposts. Such minstrel films were primarily for the White colonial class, but Africans would later see them. Ironically, however, Jolson's movies attracted Africans who often copied the fashions and dance steps believed to be authentically Black American (ibid.). In this, and in the future development of the Ghanaian concert party, we see the ways that ideologies of race and Blackness—in the figure of the blackface minstrel—traveled. As Cole tells us, these travels—similar to raw materials, commodities, and Africans—linked nations, colonies, and empires. The concert party found "fertile soil in the ideology of white supremacy that shaped relations between white and nonwhite populations" (195). I would also add that such representations shaped the perceptions and relations of African Black and diaspora Black populations; along with British colonial policy of allowing racial affiliation that was no threat to empire while actively curtailing such affiliation when it stood against colonial rule, it enabled the dissemination of particular images of Blackness and notions of racial consciousness. In this way, it becomes clear, as Cole demonstrates, that Ghanaian racialized consciousness is "neither a presentist projection nor an imposition of Black nationalist or Pan-Africanist desire: It was a historical fact of Ghana's past" (2001, 38). Acknowledging the historical reality of the development of this racialized consciousness helps reveal how the mutual constitution of local agency and global racial processes work to mediate on-the-ground relationships between diaspora Blacks and Ghanaians. At the same time, such racialized consciousness is also constantly being reconstructed as Ghanaians meet and interact over time with, among other groups, diaspora Blacks in various contexts. It is through this extensive exposure and contact, with the resultant familiarity—all occurring with a broader racialized terrain—that we can begin to explore Ghanaian imaginings of self and of those from the diaspora.

Given Ghana's long familiarity with diaspora Blacks, particularly African Americans, we need to recognize that diaspora Black visitors to Ghana encounter a social and cultural field that is already filled with images of transnational Blackness, particularly conceptions of Black American-ness, that have been constructed over time. Besides the obvious association of African Americans with wealth and power—a direct consequence of their U.S. citizenship—familiarity with this group also has fostered a combination of Ghanaian identification with, resentment of, and respect for, but also indignation toward Black Americans, all indicative of a certain fascination. Ghanaians, particularly those in major cities, are quite familiar with African Americans or, at least, the image of African Americans. I believe that the image of diaspora Blacks comes as much from the caricature of what it means to be African American as it does from actual knowledge of and interactions with this group. As Randal Jelks has observed of contemporary Ghana: "Accra . . . is awash with African American culture. . . . Ghanaians have no clue to the realities of ordinary lives of Black Americans, but they intently watch Eddie Murphy, the Wayans Brothers, and Chris Rock in movies. They see Janet Jackson and Halle Berry posted on billboard advertisements. Barbershops have painted signs depicting the hairstyles of Denzel Washington and P. Diddy" (2001). Indeed, as it is in many places outside of the United States, African American popular culture is ubiquitous in Ghana. Its influence and particular significance is important to note in order to understand how such knowledge informs on-the-ground interactions between the two groups—from blackface minstrelsy films shown publicly by colonial authorities to Pan-African politics to state-sponsored cultural programs to the famous 1971 Soul to Soul concert that brought numerous African American musicians to Ghana. And it continues through recent visits by high-profile popular African diasporic figures such as Jay-Z, Will Smith, and Omarion, as well as the residencies of Stevie Wonder and Rita Marley. In the contemporary moment, this knowledge is reflected in the most ordinary ways. For example, Joy 99.7 FM, the most popular radio station in Accra (and with sister stations in three other major cities) ironically celebrates Black History Month in February. One aspect of this celebration is the discussion of little-known African American historical facts; another is the commemoration of successful African Americans. In February 2002, for example, Condoleezza Rice and Colin Powell were celebrated. In addition to local radio programming, we find coverage of particular African Americans in the local print media. For example, Ghanaian newspapers seem to focus on international tennis or boxing matches in which there are Black (diasporic) competitors such as Venus Williams, Serena Williams, or Mike Tyson. And of course the 2008 election of Barack Obama and the January 2010 earthquake in Haiti bring to the fore the sense of connection and familiarity with diaspora populations.

This extensive exposure and contact and its resultant familiarity with African American politics and culture are also important to consider when examining the local terrain upon which diaspora Blacks interact with Ghanaians. Specifically, this long history of contact helps to frame contemporary "Afro-Atlantic dialogues" (Matory 1999) within processes of global racial formation. I hasten to add that these encounters—and the seeming ubiquity of African American presence and influence in Ghana—are not devoid of power differentials. Nor do they represent "unity" or "harmony." Rather, this interaction—this live "Afro-Atlantic dialogue"—has produced "a set of new, hybrid discourses of self-expression and identity" (37). It reflects the little-acknowledged agency on the part of both diasporans and Ghanaians in the making of African and African diaspora culture and identity.

## "Are You a Black American?"

The Ghana Airways flight into Accra was late, as usual. It was 8 a.m. in early August 2000, and the flight was originally scheduled to land at 6:30 a.m. I waited for Lynette in almost uncontrollable anticipation. I had arrived at the airport at 6:00 a.m. with my friend Paul and was anxiously pacing back and forth, all the while excited that Lynette would finally be able to visit Ghana. Lynette's opportunity to visit Ghana did not come easily. After she found out that this particular academic association was to have its conference in Accra, she worked on a plan to save enough money to purchase the expensive airline ticket. Even after she began saving, she was not sure she would be able to make the trip after all, since she still had to pay for accommodations and conference fees. It was only after she found out that I would be in Ghana at the same time conducting fieldwork and could therefore help accommodate her that she decided to make the trip.

While waiting for Lynette on this early morning, I began to take stock of my surroundings. There was indeed great anticipation in the air. Members of the University of Ghana School of Performing Arts music-and-dance troupe had set up near the main entrance. They were dressed in "traditional" folkloric dance costumes, and they were arranging instruments and various props in preparation for greeting the conference participants, who would be landing at any moment. Adding to the excitement of the moment was a group of college and high school students moving about with an official hurry. They were all dressed in blue jeans and matching bright yellow T-shirts; the T-shirts were printed with the logo of the U.S. academic association, the Adinkra *sankofa* symbol, on the front and the word "PROTOCOL" in large capital letters on the back. The tour company in charge of local preparations for the convention had hired these young people as guides. They walked around busily, with cell phones and notepads, making the necessary preparations. Across the street from the airport were six large tour buses. They were parked, their engines idling, waiting to take the visitors to their respective hotels. In addition, the airport grounds were filled with other people, many who lived close by and were curious about the commotion. The occasion was, of course, monumental. For, in just a few moments, the first batch of over five hundred diaspora Blacks—participants of the conference and members of their families—would descend upon Ghana. I later found out that the group had chartered (and filled up) three Ghana Airways planes to Accra, and all three flights were due in that day.

By the time the first plane finally landed, everything was in place for the big welcome. The music-and-dance troupe began its performance of drumming, dancing, and singing as the first of the many travel-weary passengers began trickling out of the airport doors. My friend, Nyame, a student at the University of Ghana, who was also one of the hired guides for the conference, stood by the door of the airport and gave the official welcome to the visitors. Referring to the Black academics and their families as "brothers and sisters," Nyame welcomed them back "home" after "years and generations of absence." He continued by saying that their "Ghanaian family" had been long awaiting their return. Throughout Nyame's welcome address, and as the passengers streamed out of the airport, the University of Ghana performance troupe continued its drumming and dancing. It was certainly a remarkable scene. I spotted Lynette, and we took her to one of the conference hotels to register for the convention. During the next ten days of the conference, my participation in a number of conference events and my general observations of the varied interactions between the African American academics and Ghanaians would prove invaluable to a textured understanding of not only the complex dynamics of such interactions, but also the mutually constitutive nature of African-diasporic identity formation.

From the start, the content of Nyame's welcome speech sparked my interest. In the many years of traveling to and living in Ghana, I had become familiar with this type of welcoming. That morning at the airport, though, it was obvious that Nyame's language was carefully chosen for the audience. Although I am not sure how much of the speech represented his own feelings or how much of it was suggested by the organizers, Nyame's words nevertheless expressed a familiarity with the diaspora Blacks. This familiarity came through in a number of complex and sometimes contradictory ways. I have met a wide variety of Ghanaians, some of whom felt enough of a personal connection to diaspora Blacks that they insisted they were long-lost "brothers," "sisters," or "cousins." There was also the specifically "racial recognition," a particular structure of feeling that occurred because diaspora Blacks *looked* and were recognized as Black and were therefore linked to Ghanaians. This was the dynamic at play when the USIA's propaganda about U.S. Blacks in Accra became extremely popular among Ghanaians or when Ghanaian newspapers were fascinated by diaspora Blacks during the heyday of colonial rule. African American "advancement" in the United States, the USIA officials noticed, captured particular attention. More recently, there has developed another type of familiarity with diaspora Blacks that is based on the assumed expectations of this group. One of these expectations is that those arriving in Ghana have particular feelings toward Africa in general, and that Ghana often works for them as a surrogate. In this context, and linked to various historical events and circumstances that bring Ghanaians into contact—direct and indirect—with diaspora Blacks, Nyame's language of kinship and family was not necessarily surprising.

I also had reason to believe in the sincerity (rather than just the mere functionality) of Nyame's speech. I knew him from his work in a different context. We were both part of an international African and diaspora youth organization, the African Futures Forum (AFF). I had met him during one of the recruitment meetings that I had helped to organize at the University of Ghana to set up the Accra chapter of the organization during the early part of summer 2000. This organization had been started by a group of young professionals of African descent living in Washington, DC, who had come together to create a "youth" solution to the global problems of Black people throughout Africa and the African diaspora. Members of the founding chapter in DC were primarily Black immigrants in the United States, and they hailed from a diverse group of countries including Eritrea, Ghana, Nigeria, South Africa, Uganda, Haiti, Jamaica, and Barbados; the other members were African Americans. My young Ghanaian and Somali friends had introduced me to the group while I was living and conducting fieldwork in Washington, DC. Since my trip to Ghana coincided with the trips of a couple of the Ghanaian members of the organization, we decided that summer 2000 would provide the perfect opportunity to create an AFF chapter there. Nyame had become an active member of the group, stressing his commitment to trans-African organizing and collaboration. In this—in his belief in trans-African collaboration and organizing—Nyame was not different from many young people I had encountered over my years of traveling to Ghana.

Once Lynette had checked in to the conference and made contact with some of her other friends from the States, I took her to the campus of the University of Ghana, Legon. Since Lynette could not afford to stay at the expensive conference hotel, I had arranged a room for her in one of the graduate student dormitories at the university. This is where she met Kofi, who told her that she was one of the "lucky ones" from the diaspora (as I recounted at the beginning of the chapter).

Though jarring to Lynette and me, and to the other Ghanaian students, Kofi's reaction to Lynette was also not surprising. It helps demonstrate one of the ways in which diaspora Blacks are understood in the Ghanaian context. Unlike the members of the A-APRP or other Ghanaian Pan-Africanists who have a distinct understanding of the detriment of the history of slavery for diaspora and African Blacks and who would not consider the plight of that group "lucky," Kofi clearly articulated, in profound terms, a particular view of diaspora Blacks. Indeed, as we saw in the previous chapter, the Ghanaian government's current Joseph Project affirms this view, however implicit, of diaspora Blacks as not only "lucky" to have been enslaved, but also as the economic and political beneficiaries of such history, and therefore as having a responsibility to their brethren in Africa. In one sense this view works on the assumption of, ironically, the positive consequences of slavery. In another sense such a view, as I argued in the previous chapter, reaffirms the notion of a slavery that is distinctly the property of diaspora Blacks.

The view that diaspora Blacks are "lucky," and as a result of this "luck" of a slavery past, are "rich," certainly affects the interaction of many Ghanaians with that group. It is part of the narrative constructed about diaspora Blacks that often determines the terms of interaction. Recognition of diaspora Blacks as "Josephs"—as those with political and especially economic capital—for example, can mean a number of things to Ghanaians. On the one hand, such recognition is an explicit acknowledgement of kinship (since Joseph was the favored *brother* sold into slavery), and it comes with recognition of the links between the historical experience of slavery and the formation of an African diaspora, with the resultant connection to the communities of such a diaspora. On the other hand, it can also mean a particular set of unique expectations of diaspora Blacks, expectations that members of this group should be much more culturally aware (along with disappointment when they are not) and, most importantly, that they should feel a responsibility for the economic wellbeing of their "brothers" and "sisters."

Of course Kofi did not want anything specific from Lynette; he seemed to be merely commenting on her presence at the university at that moment. And I am not even sure that his claim that Lynette was lucky was explicitly meant to be a critique of some sort. But I want to suggest that, whatever the intentions, such a claim does emerge from the complex landscape (in Accra and in Ghana more generally) in which the construction and understanding of diaspora Blacks—however varying and contradictory—are very much already part of the local consciousness. In this, the narrative of slavery—or, more importantly, the *redemptive* narrative of slavery (as it is sometimes understood)—works to explain the relative economic and presumed political position of African Americans who hold citizenship in the world's most powerful polity. It is certainly understandable, of course, that some diaspora Blacks are economically advantaged, as evidenced by their ability to freely travel to Ghana, stay in expensive hotels, and dispense foreign currencies. In the context of a stifling and oppressive existence within a racialized global capitalism, diaspora Blacks' relative wealth compared with that of those in postcolonial Africa is astounding. And it often makes sense that such wealth can be directly linked to the historical circumstances of diaspora Blacks; hence, the redemptive results of slavery. This idea is thrown into almost comic relief when Maya Angelou describes the incredulity that some Ghanaians expressed during her stay toward diasporans giving up life in the United States to repatriate Africa. It was as if, she writes, "after slavery White Americans gave their money to the Blacks and now all Blacks [are] rich" (1986, 64).

The presence of the large group of diaspora Blacks in Accra for an academic conference only accentuated this clear (mis)perception. As is common during most U.S. academic, professional, or business gatherings, conference participants were housed in the few expensive hotels in the city. The dynamics of such a normal conference gathering became magnified in small Ghana and in even smaller Accra. In 2000, there were only a few four-plus-star hotels in Accra. Accordingly, conference participants were housed in the two largest ones—Labadi Beach Hotel and the newly built La Palm Royal Beach Hotel—situated side by side along the most popular beach in Accra. Furthermore, because of their numbers and because most of the conference events were occurring at the University of Ghana School of Administration, participants had to be shuttled back and forth in groups in large buses. This circumstance not only heightened the visibility of the conference participants in Accra, it also gave diaspora Blacks a particular position and status during that time. To the few Ghanaians that closely interacted with them or the many that observed them from afar, all these circumstances proved that diaspora Blacks were extremely well off, if not wealthy. The interactions of the conference participants with vendors were most telling. Vendors at the main conference site (University of Ghana) and at the hotels sold their wares at highly inflated their prices. The conference participants, particularly Lynette's friends, were sometimes unaware, but often uncaring, of such price hikes. I was present for a number of exchanges between vendors and conference participants—at the conference sites, in hotel lobbies, or on the beach near the hotel. During one such interaction on the beach, a young Ghanaian man approached our group with a stack of woodcrafts and jewelry as we sat around one lazy afternoon during an escape from conference activities. Addressing us as "my brothers and sisters," he attempted to convince us to purchase his wears. Simon, one of Lynette's friends and a conference participant, began talking with the young man (whose name was Gameli) both about his products and his life (as a Ghanaian). I did not participate in the discussion or negotiations, but I intervened when I realized that the young man's prices were much more than exorbitant. Speaking to the young man, as is conventional in such situations, I told him to try to lower his prices a bit. The young man responded with, "But you are my sista. I [am] giving you a good price." I argued that the price was not good and, to drive the point home, I asked, "Why are you giving us *obruni* prices?" Here, my strategy was to use the common knowledge that prices for *obrunis* (mainly Whites) are usually double or triple those for Ghanaians and others who negotiate well; I wanted to create the space for him to recognize that I was familiar with the prices. Gameli was quick, and he smiled as he responded earnestly that his prices for the *obrunis* would be three times more than he is asking his "brother," Simon. At this point, Simon intervened and said that he would pay the asking price. I remained silent, but was uncomfortable. This had been happening around me all week with other conference participants not willing to negotiate for prices, as was customary. My concern at the time was how Simon and his colleagues' willingness to spend money so lavishly—at least in this context—further upheld the stereotype of the wealthy Black American. When Gameli walked away after making a great sale, I asked Simon why he chose not to negotiate for a better price. For Simon and the others, engagement with Ghanaians, particularly the vendors and conference staff, linked the acute need for connection with real concern about the economic plight of the average Ghanaian. Simon told me that he recognized that the prices were inflated and that he was being overcharged for various services and items. "But," he said, "I don't mind." He continued, "It's the least I can do since things are economically so bad here. Even if they do cheat me, it only adds up to a few dollars. At least I feel like I'm helping, even it's just a little bit." Indeed, Simon's response was echoed among the conference participants, who seemed to be simultaneously sad about the poverty they were witnessing and relieved that they could find a way, however limited, to help alleviate the misery. This was and is a constant expression that I experience in my conversations and interactions with various individuals and groups of diaspora Blacks.

Yet, even as diaspora Blacks make conscious efforts to find a connection with Ghanaians, they also, however unwittingly, reinforce the view of themselves as exceptionally wealthy. In this sense, the field of interaction gets constructed and reconstructed anew. As diaspora Blacks, by virtue of the nature and circumstance of their presence in Ghana as well as global processes and transnational circulations of Black American images, they are assumed to be wealthy, and they reinforce that view by their actions on the ground. In fact, and in hindsight, I believe that my attempted intervention in the dealings between vendors and conference participants was a selfish concern. As I would later complain to my Ghanaian friends after the conference, these participants were making things bad for us diaspora Blacks who were residing long term in Ghana, since they reaffirmed the view that *all* of us were wealthy.

I have often found that the construction of diaspora Blacks as wealthy, particularly through the reinscription of all diaspora Blacks as African American, is based on a particular understanding of the consequence of slavery, life outside of Africa, and the power of the trope of the Black American. For example, even my own background as a Haitian-born U.S. resident gets conflated with the trope of the Black American. When they learn about my Haitian background, many people I encounter in Ghana will quickly reference Haiti's ongoing "civil war" and "that priest" (former President Jean Bertrand Aristide), while saying things like, "Haitians look like Africans." At the same time, however, Haiti's status as the poorest country in the Western Hemisphere (a fact that is always foregrounded in any journalistic or academic coverage of the country) rarely gets acknowledged. I am seen as a wealthy Black from the diaspora, and therefore so are all Haitians—those living in Haiti and outside. In fact, I am sometimes asked about migration (and job) opportunities in Haiti—rather than in the United States! This (mis)identification is as complex as it is logical. After all, I *am* able to travel to Ghana and therefore much more mobile than the average Ghanaian; moreover, I have U.S. dollars at my disposal. To me, what makes this view of the wealth of diaspora Blacks significant is its often differential interpretation precisely because diaspora Blacks are distinct in the Ghanaian imagination. In other words, it is not just that Blacks from outside of Ghana are perceived as wealthy. That in itself would not make the interaction between Ghanaians and that group significant since all tourists to Ghana are perceived as wealthy. What is important here, therefore, is how this perception plays into the broader understanding and often tragic complexity of what it is to be a Black American in Ghana.

I want to suggest that the perception of diaspora wealth is a source of both resentment and deference toward diaspora Blacks. This comes into clear relief when compared with assumptions of the wealth of Whites and others visiting Ghana. As I suggested in chapter 3, while White wealth is assumed, the demands made on Whites do not seem to be so personal and distinct. But for diaspora Blacks, there is a clear sense in which, at the same time that their wealth is understandable, it is almost seen as "unnatural," if not unfair. This, I would argue, emerges in the often implicit expectations of diaspora Blacks, particularly in their responsibility toward Ghanaians. And here I contend that this responsibility is assumed *precisely* because of the presumed kinship with diaspora Blacks. During my stays in Ghana, I often heard the complaint that diaspora Blacks were not doing enough to help their "kin." These comments often came within discussions of, and Ghanaian response to, the presumed expectations of diaspora Blacks of Africa that the "motherland" *owed* them recognition and acceptance. In this complicated set of moral and economic exchange and obligations, it becomes clear that diaspora Black presence in Ghana is distinct from that of other groups.

Depending on the context, Lynette and her friends received differential and *deferential* treatment particularly because they were perceived as Black Americans. And being a Black American was distinct from being a White. Even when they were identified by the signifier *obruni*, as happened a few times during our movements around Accra and surrounding cities, it was clear that the *obruni* of the Black Americans was not the same as the *obruni* of the Whites. I often wondered about the conscious and strategic use of that term in relation to diaspora Blacks. Because *obruni* is also reserved for Ghanaians, especially those who have traveled abroad and have acquired the cultural, economic, and political capital of the West, to differentiate them from others who have not had such opportunity, it seems to me that a similar interpretation of Black Americans is occurring. As we saw in our discussion of the relationship between Whiteness and economic and political capital and clout in chapter 3, a Black *obruni* is so unusual as to merit specific attention. This is what I mean when I say that Black wealth, in this context, is "unnatural," whereas White wealth is so naturalized as to go unnoticed. Since Blacks are not usually the ones associated with wealth, a wealthy Black stands out—be she Ghanaian, another continental African, or a diaspora Black. And with this attention comes a measure of resentment.

In Ghana, as well as in other places on the African continent, the Caribbean, and the United States, I have frequently been fascinated by the acrimony and often unfair expectations exhibited by Black groups toward those Blacks with wealth or cultural and political capital, when the same does not happen among Whites. I want to suggest that within the context of global White supremacy, racial expectations (what Omi and Winant call "racial etiquette" [1994])—rules shaped by our perceptions of race and the "sedimented contextual knowledges" (Alcoff 1999, 18) based upon such perceptions—determine appropriate modes of conduct and (moral) values for particular groups. In this sense, it becomes easier to contextualize the particular mutually constitutive expectations that emerge in the interactions of different racialized-as-Black groups. As Linda Alcoff perceptively notes, our historically determined racialized identity—and in turn our racial sub-jectivity—"permeates our being in the world, our being-with others, and our consciousness of our self as a being-for others" (1999, 25). In other words, it is precisely the "sedimentation" of historical beliefs and practices that form their mutually constituted Black racial identities that in turn inform the structure of interaction (and the complex mix of identification and resentment). Importantly, comparing Ghanaian response to diaspora Blacks—in terms of expectations within an identification/resentment ma-trix—highlights, however implicitly, the structure of global White suprem-acy and the place of populations of African descent within it. In effect, it is necessary to link such Ghanaian–diaspora Black interactions to the differ-entiating processes of White supremacy in order to clearly demarcate how such interactions are always concocted within the crucible of global racial culture and politics.

Yet, even with the stifling presence of White supremacy (what Brackette Williams calls the "ghost of Anglo-European hegemony" [1991]), we see the often strategic agency exhibited by those who are most affected. As I have ar-gued, global White supremacy has structured, and continues to inform, mu-tual identification among Black populations. And Ghanaian perceptions of, identifications with, and constructions of a trope of diaspora Blacks clearly reflect this. In her study of colonial Ghanaian engagement with diaspora Blacks, Cole argued that Ghanaians "imagined themselves as members of an expanded transnational and transcultural black community . . . [particu-larly] through an active, performative process of consumption. Colonial Ghanaians not only watched Hollywood films and read newspaper articles about the Negro: They *performed* Negro identity and thus imagined new communities through their bodies" (2001, 37). Cole demonstrates, how-ever, that the identification with Blacks across the Atlantic often reaffirmed certain stereotypes of Blackness that entrenched the racist representations of people of African descent. In the 1930s some Ghanaian performers ap-propriated "Negro culture" in the form of blackface minstrelsy, adopting the types of performances provided by Hollywood. Ghanaians copied minstrel imagery, thus affiliating with African American culture *through* racist rep-resentations (Cole 2001). Although there was considerable debate during that time about the authenticity and appropriateness of such images, it was nevertheless clear that Ghanaians' racial affinity to African Americans drew them to such images. Such engagement with images of diaspora Blacks—particularly of African Americans—has a long history in Ghana. As Maya Angelou remarked about her negative interaction with a young Ghanaian woman in Accra soon after independence in the early 1960s, "Her Knowledge of my people could only have been garnered from hearsay, and the few old American movies which tacked on Black characters as awkwardly as the blinded attach paper tails to donkey caricatures" (1986, 34).

During my research in Ghana, I came to realize that the image of diaspora Blacks comes as much from the caricature of what it means to be African American (that is, African American as trope) as it does from actual knowledge of and interactions with said group. The appropriation and representation of stereotypical imagery of Black Americans was a constant topic of conversation among Lynette and her friends. Examples abound. There was the time when a group of young Ghanaian kids came up to them on the street with the greeting, "What's up, my nigga?" They were surprised and upset by this greeting since, as Simon responded to the young man, "We don't talk like that to each other, brother." Such moments caused the group much distress, and at times members expressed the desire to shift such perceptions. They sought to do so through various means, from acts of generosity toward Ghanaians to open arguments with Ghanaians against such stereotyping. That Ghanaian understanding of and interaction with diaspora Blacks is as fraught as it is complex is a reality. What is also clear is that, in a general sense, Ghanaian interactions with diaspora Blacks are perhaps more complicated than with Whites. As we saw in chapter 3, the unnamed privileged meanings of Whiteness (as well as the general position of Whites) allow it to remain out of the realm of the everyday—even in Ghana. Whiteness, though assumed as the power category both in Ghana and globally, remains problematically unpacked and uninterrogated. On the contrary, Ghanaian interaction with diaspora Blacks reveals particular sets of discourses and practices of race and identity formation that have, I believe, much to do with how the two groups are positioned within a global hierarchy of peoples and cultures (Trouillot 1994). Ultimately, this interaction shows the ways in which local meanings of the racialized (Black) Ghanaian self is, and has always been, constructed through a complex set of overlapping histories that are set within transnational understandings of race and Blackness.

A contemporary example of these overlapping histories and experiences of diaspora and African Blacks emerges when we explore yet another context of interaction: First Fridays Accra, a social networking event in contemporary Ghana that has origins among African American professionals in the northeastern United States. The social networking of young people of African descent at First Fridays Accra presents us with an alternative narrative, one that points to the broader dynamics of the local terrain and therefore offers the opportunity to develop a multifaceted argument regarding race and identity at the interface between the diaspora and Africa.

## In Accra, on First Friday

On an early Friday evening I enter the lobby of the Golden Tulip Hotel on my way to First Fridays Accra. The Golden Tulip is a four-star, first-class hotel known for its sophistication, particularly its beautiful decor featuring local artwork. The Golden Tulip is a social hub; middle-class local families splurge on a lazy Sunday afternoon by its pool, joining members of the expatriate community and other tourists; young partygoers meet up there for drinks before heading out to the nightclubs; business associates gather there for happy hour or late-night revelry. This hotel, then, is the perfect site for First Fridays Accra, an after-work networking and socializing affair. The hallway near the entrance to the event is lively, abuzz with conversations among young men and women either waiting for other friends to arrive or taking a break from the hectic scene inside. I greet a few friends, jot down my contact information, pay my entry fee to one of the three young Ghanaian women in business-casual clothes stationed at the welcoming table, pin the provided nametag to my dress, and enter.

Inside the large hall, a festive scene beckons. A crowd of people are milling around, talking. A band is stationed opposite the entrance, playing a lively combination of highlife, soul, and R&B. Tables set up around the room promote various businesses, from local restaurants to international banks. To the right of the band is a bar staffed with bartenders and stocked with bottles of wine and spirits. In addition, wait staff circulate around the room with trays of appetizers. I do not get far into the room before I begin meeting and interacting with people. The first person I encounter is a young Ghanaian Internet technology professional who introduces himself to me and strikes up a discussion about the event. During our conversation, an old friend, Kweku, greets me with a hug. I introduce Kweku to my new friend, and the three of us converse. Such is how the night proceeds—for me and, I am sure, for many other participants. I know many people in the room, and I meet and mingle with many others, collecting business cards while enjoying lively banter.

The success of First Fridays Accra entails a lot more than the interaction of middle-class and professional Ghanaians. I spend the evening surrounded by a lively group of young people primarily of African descent with personal biographies and professional trajectories that speak to, among other things, the modern and highly transnational place that is Accra. By the end of the evening, I have met diverse groups of Black people: Ghanaians native to Accra; those who immigrated from other parts of the country; Nigerians or Liberians who now live in Accra; Black South Africans visiting Ghana for the first time; Haitian and Haitian Americans who have moved permanently to Accra; second-generation Ghanaian Americans who are either visiting or have repatriated to their parents' home; Jamaican American and African American graduate students conducting research; and African American professionals who have either decided to set up businesses in Accra, are working for companies stationed in Accra, or are on short-term volunteer trips. Clearly, this First Fridays Accra event is where people from all over Africa and the African diaspora converge in the making of a modern Black cosmopolitanism in Ghana. This Black cosmopolitanism represents an important reality of postcolonial African societies that comes into play when we explore the issues central to this chapter: the dynamics and politics of the interaction of diaspora Blacks with contemporary Africa.

As the evening wears on, the hall in the Golden Tulip Hotel gets crowded. And hot. There are two sets of double doors on either side of the live band that open up to an outside balcony where overflow traffic is directed and where people can get fresh air. The large hall is too small, and the air-conditioning system is not working to its full capacity. I move in and out of the room, sometimes to the outdoor balcony, at other times to the entrance, where a small crowd has also gathered. The band continues its highlife and R&B rotation, and the waiters continue circling the room with appetizers. By this time, I've moved on from my conversation with Kweku and his friend, and I'm standing by the doors leading to the outdoor balcony. I am really standing there to be closer to the AC unit, one of four that has been placed around the room to compensate for the underperformance of the larger system. Two older Ghanaian men join me and begin engaging in a discussion about business in Ghana. One is a technology professional, the other, as he tells me, dabbles in real estate, among other things. We chat a bit about Ghana's booming real estate market as well as my profession as a university "prof." While speaking with these two men, my cell phone rings, and it is Reginald, a young African American in his early twenties who has just moved to Ghana. Reginald is a cousin of one of my colleagues. We had planned to meet up once I arrived in Ghana, and this seemed like the perfect venue. Reginald tells me that he has made it to the event. As I am heading toward the entrance to find Reginald, I run into another acquaintance, a Haitian American woman who has been living in Ghana for more than four years as the director of a U.S.-based international nonprofit, nongovernmental development organization. We quickly exchange greetings, and I rush off. At one point in the evening, I find myself in the company of three other Haitian Americans, one of whom, Joanne, is the co-organizer of First Fridays Accra. As we continue our nationalist assemblage, laughing at the improbability of our congregating—as people of Haitian descent—in Ghana, Joanne tells those surrounding us that this is "Haiti at its best."

First Fridays Accra has its origins in a similar event in the United States. First Fridays (U.S.) is a socializing venture initiated by and for young African American professionals who seek "to develop, foster and promote opportunities, which encourage and enhance personal and business-related interactions and unity among African American individuals, organizations, and businesses."[9] Touted as the "largest networking organization" in the United States, First Fridays events began in various cities in the 1980s as a record number of African Americans joined the corporate world.[10] It is now an established phenomenon, as First Fridays organizations operate in thirty cities across the United States.[11] First Fridays is part of a growing trend of networking organizations that bring together young people—particularly African Americans and other people of color who are often isolated in their respective professions—for mentorship and social networking. For young African Americans and other people of color who have to navigate the White-dominated U.S. professional world, these gatherings are especially significant; they provide support, community-building opportunities, and advocacy.

A four-member team of U.S.-educated young Black people who had relocated to Ghana in recent years established First Fridays Accra. In establishing First Fridays Accra, organizers wanted to tap into their extensive and overlapping networks of friends and colleagues in Ghana in order to create an avenue for dialogue and socialization. These overlapping social and political networks are a significant part of the success of First Fridays Accra. They provide access to a broad range of people in various sectors of Ghana's business and professional community. At the same time, these networks also reveal a particular social field in Ghana where pragmatic, amiable, and mutually beneficial African and African diasporic interaction is commonplace.

The four organizers' own personal and professional backgrounds give credence to this reality. Robert, for example, is a second-generation Ghanaian who was born and raised in New York City. As an undergraduate student at an Ivy League institution, Robert's social circle reflected that of many Black college students in predominantly White institutions, where minority status, a racially hostile campus environment, and general social marginalization almost force the explicit articulation of a Black community. Robert was deeply involved in this community, becoming president of his university's chapter of a Black Greek-letter fraternity. Thus, Robert's experiences as a young Black person in the United States included not only recognition of his Ghanaian heritage, but also immersion in African American culture. When Robert decided to move to Ghana a few years ago, this background placed him directly within a transnational circuit of friends and colleagues on both sides of the Black Atlantic. The second co-organizer is a young woman of similar age to Robert who was also born in New York City, but to Haitian-immigrant parents. Joanne decided that she was no longer willing to endure life in the United States and chose instead to live in Africa. Although she had no direct connection to Ghana, she moved to Accra a few years ago and brought along her son and her Haitian mother. Joanne attended the same undergraduate institution as Robert, yet the two did not meet until both were in Accra. The third co-organizer is a young man in his early thirties who was born in Nigeria but attended school and worked in the United States for almost a decade. The fourth is an African American woman who has lived in numerous international locations, including a number of other cities throughout the African continent. In my various conversations with these four young Black people, it was clear that their reasons for moving to Ghana were various and included personal and professional goals. What is also clear is that the decision to move to Ghana was not the nostalgia for a motherland, based on a slavery-induced longing for identity, that we see depicted so often in journalistic and scholarly coverage of diaspora Black returns. To be sure, all of the organizers expressed the desire to work and live in an African country in part because the environment provided a welcome anonymity for Blacks that is not available in the United States. Yet there seemed to be no illusions about uncomplicated claims of identity or expectations of being "welcomed home" as "brothers and sisters."

Notably, First Fridays Accra organizers had overlapping experiences of education, travel, cross-cultural contact, and, indeed, race and class formation, which would be true of all of the Ghanaian and non-Ghanaian participants at the events. Through First Fridays Accra, I was introduced to a social and professional milieu that I did not know existed in Ghana, even though I was familiar with the large Black expatriate community in the country. When I attended a First Fridays Accra event for the first time in 2006, I was also not prepared either for the national and cultural diversity of the participants or for the numerous reasons shaping Black continental and diasporic presence in Ghana. First Fridays Accra events boast—and would be deemed—an "elite" gathering of young professionals in Ghana. Yet, there is a way that this label belies the complex dynamics of such gatherings. These events attract primarily people of African descent from all over the world, Ghanaians as well as some long-time expatriates and short-term visitors and tourists. In addition to the business professionals and nonbusiness working-class individuals I have met at these events, I have also come across non-Ghanaian African undergraduate and graduate students, missionaries, and diplomats. This is not to say, of course, that these young people do not participate in other networks in Ghana or that First Fridays Accra does not appeal to other audiences.[12] What is remarkable about First Fridays events is that they are decidedly diasporic and cosmopolitan and that they represent the mundane reality of transnational Black interaction and identity formation. This is indeed the narrative of "routes" of the ongoing Afro-Atlantic dialogues that emerged with the transatlantic slave trade and attendant racialization of African peoples (Gilroy 1993).

From an event organized to support isolated African American business professionals in urban United States to one providing networking opportunities in urban Ghana, the trajectory of First Fridays is remarkable.[13] And First Fridays Accra, whose cosmopolitan participants also share experiences of cross-cultural contact and racial formation, presents us with an alternative view of contemporary African-diasporic interaction. Similar to the local and global forces that affect Ghanaian state politics around heritage-tourism events, the First Fridays phenomenon in Accra, at the very least, offers a glimpse of the broad terrain upon which such interactions occur.

As I attempt to map this complex terrain within which Ghanaians engage diaspora Blacks, I cannot help but wonder about the politics informing the clamor of interest around this particular relationship. Of course, there is the obvious ongoing discussion within African diaspora studies, in particular, about the significance of Africa (as trope and geopolitical space), Blackness, and race for communities of African descent in the New World. Yet, both Gaines (2006) and Matory (2005) have reminded us of the reality that diaspora Blacks were not, and are not, the only people traveling to and settling in Ghana, nor are they the only ones informing local politics of racial subjectivity. Gaines asserts that the "pilgrimage of radicals and progressives to Ghana was more than matched by the migration of foreign business executives and investors seeking to capitalize on the new nation's promises of development" (2006, 15). Similarly, Matory insists that "not only traveling black pilgrims, businesspeople, and writers, but traveling white writers and photographers, as well as their publications, have long been vehicles of transformative knowledge in the production of . . . 'black Atlantic' culture"

(2005, 40). What makes these travels to Ghana any less worthy of exploration? Or, better yet, why are they not included in discussions of Ghanaian-diasporic meetings in Ghana? Indeed, in 2006, the majority of tourists came from a number of other African countries, followed closely by those Europeans and United States citizens with business interests (Ghana Tourist Board 2008). Even the Ghanaian government's consideration of extending dual-citizenship status for those in the diaspora includes overseas Ghanaians. Thus, who makes up the bulk of Ghana's tourists? And what explains the disproportionate focus on diaspora Blacks?

The convergence of a series of events—which includes, but is not limited to, the Ghanaian state's neoliberal policies, African American continued interest in Africa, and, importantly, scholarly interest in African American interest in Africa—structures such "returns." These events, as well as historical relationships and global racial processes work to mediate on-the-ground relationships between African Americans and Ghanaians. The discussion in this chapter is in part an effort to challenge such narrow—and often cynical—response to contemporary African diasporic and Ghanaian interaction. Ghanaian relationship to populations of African descent from the diaspora is not new. It is not unidirectional. It is not only about heritage tourists. Instead, my work reveals the long history of interaction that was not only facilitated by the active and conscious negotiations of people of African descent—on both sides of the Atlantic—but was also shaped by global social, economic, and political processes that have worked to inform racialized understandings of identity for these populations. As such, my aim has been not to limit my focus on complex negotiations in the contemporary making of African diasporic and African relationships, but to reframe these negotiations both within a long historical durée of Afro-Atlantic dialogues and within processes of global racial formation. In this sense, even as African diasporic and African relationships are often fraught and contradictory, they nevertheless reflect a particular type of engagement that allows for a more dynamic configuration of both African and diasporic identity formation.

In the next chapter, I explicitly map the theoretical contours underlying the discussion of these interactions—and this book's thesis on the significance of the parallel racialization processes for diaspora and continental Blacks—through a discussion of the scholarly conventions in studies of global Black populations.

# SEVEN

# Race across the Atlantic . . . and Back: Theorizing Africa and/in the Diaspora

Double disposition in consciousness and cognition, that fracture in black ontology produced by Western Imperialism, is not the exclusive property of the diasporic branch of the black Atlantic: it is to be seen both here, in the Old World, and there, in the New.

—Kwaku Larbi Korang, *Writing Ghana, Imagining Africa*

In an essay entitled "Going to Meet America" (2008), the Nigerian scholar Pius Adesanmi reflects on his first encounter with Black poverty in the United States by remembering his first experience with "black textual cultures" in rural Nigeria. His father's home library, filled with books on West African, South African, and African American history and literature, covered three important themes: colonialism, apartheid, and slavery. The Black world he encountered in these texts was a seamless and borderless "world of ideological intermeshing," one in which the histories of slavery, colonialism, and apartheid together formed a unified narrative of identity. And while the texts acknowledged the distinct experiences of varied Black groupings, all members of this Black world had equal claim to this collective identity and history. The history and memory of slavery in the New World belonged as much to diaspora Blacks as it did to continental Blacks; the history and experience of European colonialism belonged as much to continental Blacks as it did to diaspora Blacks. Adesanmi described this as a "soporific" view of the Black world, one undercut by a certain set of realities in which national identities trump transnational connections, disciplinary exigencies in academia constrict interdisciplinary discussion, and global Black relations are fraught with tension. While there are certainly other factors to explain how this—or *any*—view of a seamless, borderless Black world may be untenable, Adesanmi's naming of this particular set of issues—that is, the politics of postcolonial nationalism, the imperatives of academic practice, and the dynamics of inter-Black relations—provides an important point of entry to explore the ways we have imagined and discussed Black identity formation in a global sense. For me, Adesanmi's observation highlights an intractable yet mostly imperceptible trend in contemporary scholarship on Black communities in Africa and the African diaspora—a clear divide between studies that deal with Africa and those that address race and transnational Blackness (Vinson 2006). Though principally a theoretical and conceptual trend, it has facilitated the construction of rigid ideological and political boundaries, introducing new configurations of Blackness that do not reflect enough of the complex realities of the communities on either side of the Atlantic.

My goal in this chapter is to bring together this book's major thesis on the fundamental significance of processes of racialization in the mutual constitution of Black continental and diasporic identities and my two primary disciplinary fields of engagement—African studies and African diaspora studies. Following Adesamni's lamentation and recognizing the fragmentation in the ways we conceptualize global Black studies, this chapter poses a number of questions: What are the ideological and conceptual precepts guiding contemporary research on Black identity formations? In what ways do the various and contentious meanings of "Africa" remain central to cultural and political debates about community and identity? Are our contemporary efforts to delineate the contours of global Blackness adequate? I explore the details of this struggle while provoking a rethinking of the ways we approach the shaping of Black identity formations. I focus on what I am calling the "problematic of race" in African studies and African diaspora studies, examining how its differing notions and deployments have worked to delimit the ways "Africa" and "Blackness" are conceptualized in the respective fields. I show how prominent strands of African studies have either taken race for granted or reinforced racializing tropes of Africa and, at the same time, have not acknowledged the continued significance of Africa's racialization to the articulation of modern processes, including the articulation of Blackness. I show how prominent sections of African *diaspora* studies have either taken Africa for granted or reinforced Africa's marginalization and, at the same time, have not acknowledged Africa's contemporary racialized existence in the ongoing construction of a modern Blackness. The fact that there hardly seems to be a theoretical dynamic that affords a "conceptual entrée" (Mills 1998) for issues of race in postcolonial Africa and that Africa is often a mere "baseline" (Matory 1999) consideration when it comes to discussions of diasporic (racial) identity formation is testament to both a particular historical amnesia and a certain poverty of theory; it is also, I believe, evidence of the ongoing inability to fully and concretely come to terms with the mutuality of African and diasporic sociohistorical experience.

The following discussion unfolds in three parts. First, I examine the institutional formation of African studies in the Cold War United States. Second, I look at the ways in which race and ethnicity have been considered within Africanist anthropology. Third, I examine how Africa has been marginalized within late twentieth-century African diaspora and Black Atlantic cultural theory. I begin the discussion with a brief exploration of the broad historical and political context that allowed for the development of the Africa-diaspora divide in current intellectual circles. I conclude the chapter by gesturing toward a theory of diaspora that offers a new way out of the ongoing ambivalent relationship among Africa, the diaspora, and race.

## Historicizing Black Studies

In the late 1970s, St. Clair Drake saw African diaspora studies as an intellectual by-product of the ideological and political split between what he deemed "continental" and "traditional" visions of Pan-Africanism. Diaspora studies was still an important aspect of "traditional Pan-African activity," but it was a particularly New World response to the emerging independent continental African politics (Drake 1982). For Drake, independence from colonialism shifted the priorities of Africans from transcontinental collaboration against racism and imperialism to nation building and continental cooperation. Consequently, the struggle against racial oppression was understood—by Drake and others—to be primarily an issue for diaspora Blacks. Drake made the case for U.S. Blacks in particular: "It was clear that an enslaved black majority within the most powerful capitalist nation on earth where racism was rampant within the working-class was not seeing the problems from the same perspective [as those] from sovereign states" (359). It is significant that Drake attributes this continental-diasporic divide partly to a shift in race thinking, placing African nationalist sentiment in contradistinction to Black (diaspora) racial cooperation and political organization. The assumption, of course, is that independence and political sovereignty ushered in an era for continental Africans in which issues of race and its connections with imperialism were no longer primary concerns.

There has been some debate about the validity of the claim of a shift in Pan-Africanism, particularly for scholars interested in mapping the histories of Black internationalism and of the African diaspora as an intellectual project. Approaches vary. Brent Edwards (2001) argues, for example, that the emergence African diaspora studies did not so much represent a shift in the content of studies of Black internationalism as it did a conceptual turn away from the increasing political baggage of the term "Pan-Africanism." Diaspora studies, in this sense, was a way to come to terms with continued Black internationalism in the face of acute backlash against Pan-Africanism as a *politicized* concept and movement. Nevertheless, there seems to be recognition, at least from 1945—during and after the fifth Pan-African Congress—that a general transfer of momentum from the diaspora to continental Africa had taken place. I suggest, however, that Drake's marking of this shift is important for broader and more substantial reasons beyond the self-conscious recasting of Pan-Africanism's history into "continental" and "diaspora" elements. Taking the year 1945 as a point of departure, then, we can see how drastic changes in global politics transformed Black international cooperation and scholarship. These global changes brought about not only the realignment of relationships among nations and the postwar restructuring of the global political and economic landscape, but they also helped determine the terms of intellectual engagement. And key to the new shaping of Black studies were new liberal definitions of race and the apolitical framing of Africa (Von Eschen 1997).

In the introduction to their compelling volume *Out of One, Many Africas* (1999), editors William G. Martin and Martin O. West frame the history of the study of global Black populations within three intellectual traditions: Africanist, Continental, and Transcontinental. The Africanist tradition, they argue, has held near-hegemonic status over the study of Africa since the last half of the twentieth century. Emerging in the 1950s in the context of U.S. ascendancy as a global superpower, this tradition of African studies was part of the dramatic development of "area studies" in universities that were powered by Cold War politics and generously funded by major foundations. With the backing of the U.S. government, the Africanist presence in the academy from the outset demanded "a strong policy orientation befitting its close association with the extension of U.S. power across the world" (22). More importantly, the Africanist tradition—its established paradigms, programs, and international networks—was built upon "intellectual, material, and racial pillars" of U.S. national politics. This meant in particular the "purposeful displacement of a competing and older tradition of black scholarship" (85; see also Amory 1997) and, along with that, the conceptual division of the study of Africa and the diaspora.[1] Elliot Skinner, for example, discusses how Black scholars of Africa in historically Black colleges and universities (HBCUs) were ignored by the newly minted White African studies establishment and were often denied foundation funding (1983, 17).[2] In fact, while the majority of Africanist scholars in prewar years were from the Black diaspora (especially the United States), "few could find research funds for research in Africa and few published" (Curtin quoted in Skinner 1983, 18). HBCUs were also excluded as foundations searched for potential sites to house Africa studies centers.

The Continental and Transcontinental traditions are clear examples of these differences, as West and Martin contend. The study of Africa by scholars based on the continent—the Continental tradition—is the most recent of the three traditions and is considered "largely a reaction to the intellectual hegemony of the Africanist enterprise and the hubris and racial arrogance of Africanist scholars" (Martin and West 1999, 15).[3] Unlike those within the Africanist tradition, this first generation of postcolonial African scholars often works without the benefit of state or foundational support; some such scholars are affiliated with a series of regional research institutions outside of the universities, while others are dependent on intermittent and short-term academic positions in Western nations. The regional research institutions,[4] moreover, are usually funded by Western donor organizations, a fact that often shapes scholarly output and generally limits its capacity for broad impact. The Continental tradition, therefore, does not have the power or global authority of its Africanist counterpart. Its research agenda is usually focused on establishing or promoting "indigenous" paradigms and intellectual networks, with specific reference to what are seen as the concrete problems and conditions of the continent (Martin and West 1999). While clearly an important endeavor for self-representation—especially as a response to western Africanist traditions and continued pathological representations of Africans—Continental scholars nevertheless followed a number of conceptual and epistemological paradigms similar to those followed by their Africanist counterparts. These included the treatment of the continent or some of its regions as isolates and, crucially, the maintenance of the Africa-diaspora conceptual divide (see Magubane 1971 for one of few exceptions). It is in this way—in the type of isolated continental focus and research subject matter—that the Continental tradition is both similar to the Africanist one and different from the Transcontinental one.

Unlike the Africanist tradition, the Transcontinental tradition did not develop within the context of specific nation-state geopolitics and did not achieve the high status and official sanction and sponsorship necessary for institutionalization. This tradition depended on a loose collection of mostly Black scholars and activists—based in North America, the Caribbean,

Europe, and Africa—who worked to dismantle the global power structures of Western empire. Although scholarship in this tradition is usually considered "vindicationist"[5]—an appropriate label given the historical and ongoing need to challenge Eurocentric dehumanization of Black peoples—this designation often obscures its other important epistemological claims about the role of scientific research in the pursuit of social justice and in challenging ideas about structural and institutional power. In this framing, the Transcontinental tradition differed considerably from the Africanist (and, to a lesser extent, the Continental) one, both in purpose and content. On the one hand, the Transcontinentalist concern with the effects of global structures on racialized (non-White) communities resulted in scholarly output that was inherently transnational (transcontinental) and that, methodologically, relied on the examination of broad cultural and political processes informing transatlantic connections among Black communities. On the other hand, the Africanist tradition's presumed concern with "scientific objectivity" in the post-1950s study of Africa was area and region specific and encouraged intense and focused specialization on "tribes" or "ethnics" within the continent, often at the expense of structural analysis linking the continent to the rest of the world and to global history.

Yet, to better understand the differences in the content and theory of Black studies, we should go back further in history. The post–World War II period becomes especially significant here because it signals a watershed moment in global politics and in knowledge production. As we have seen, the powerful position of the United States at this moment enabled the development of "area studies" that shifted the orientation of African studies, establishing paradigms that worked in the logic of empire: to contain or direct anticolonial movements and, later, to influence African independent states. This strategy followed the British school of African studies that was developed alongside that empire's colonial ventures; the primary concern of that school was to acquire knowledge about tribal or ethnic groups in the service of "pacification and creating divisions" (Campbell 1999). However, the success of this new model of U.S.-based African studies in the post–World War II period—that is, the area-studies model that worked in the logic of empire as well as in the silencing of older (Transcontinental) traditions—also depended on the opening provided by sociopolitical events in the country that included, among other things, the fragmentation of the Black radical Left, the emergence of McCarthyism, and the rise of Cold War liberalism.

The fragmentation of the Black radical Left in the postwar period reflects ongoing generational shifts in the political orientation of U.S. Black political leadership. As Penny Von Eschen aptly demonstrates in her study *Race against Empire* (1997), Black scholars and activists in the prewar era sought to create a global movement for Black emancipation by explicitly and continuously linking Jim Crow racism with imperialism. Discussions about U.S. racism occurred alongside those about colonialism and were set within a broader understanding of the "global system of empire and racial capitalism that exploited and appropriated the land, labor, and bodies of black people 'scattered all over the world'" (69). Although it was a movement spearheaded by a small and outnumbered group of Black scholar-activists, this "Black Radical Tradition" (Robinson 2000) nevertheless attained wide popularity among Black populations in the United States and internationally immediately after the war. This powerful moment in Black radicalism did not survive the Cold War, however. In what Von Eschen describes as an abrupt fragmentation in opinion among U.S. Black scholars and activists, the broad support for radical international politics (and organizing) would quickly fade with the varied responses to U.S. foreign policy, particularly the Truman Doctrine and the Marshall Plan.[6] By the early 1950s, in the shadow of Cold War redbaiting and of rising McCarthyism, two prominent camps emerged in U.S. Black scholar-activist and political circles. On the one side were the intellectuals who professed a radical antiracism by continuing the broad critique of colonialism and imperialism and by insisting that diaspora Blacks, Africans, and all colonized people shared a common history of oppression.[7] On the other side were those who, both purposely and unwittingly, embraced the language and framing of Cold War liberalism (what Von Eschen calls "an anti-communist anticolonialism"), including U.S. nationalist and imperialist imaginings, in a seeming effort to improve the specific domestic condition of U.S. Blacks.

These shifts in U.S. Black political rhetoric and strategy were very much aided by the long and powerful reach of the state. In the atmosphere of the Cold War, international political maneuvers among U.S. Blacks still oppressed by Jim Crow were a liability—especially previous and potential alliances with African liberation groups and other anti-imperialist movements. This was especially clear in the ways that the U.S. government persecuted and ultimately forced the disbanding of groups such as the Council on African Affairs (CAA).[8] The CAA was an organization that was known for its "militant diaspora consciousness" and radical anti-imperialism and anticapitalism (Mjagkij 2001, 204). Its activist practices and scholarly enterprise linked the fight for African decolonization to the struggle for civil rights in the United States: "our fight for Negro rights here [in the United States] is inseparably linked with the liberation movements of people of the

Caribbean and Africa and the colonial world in general" (ibid.; see also Campbell 1999, 125; Von Eschen 1997). The demise of such groups as the CAA, as a result of what Horace Campbell (1999) calls "low intensity warfare" in the study of Africa and Africans, meant the end of the broad influence of the long U.S. Black tradition of the Pan-Africanist (and Transcontinental) approach to the study of Africa and the diaspora. The purging of these more radical elements of Pan-African political cooperation also went hand in hand with the rise of the moderate sector of U.S. Black politics and intellectual tradition.

The consequences of these events cannot be overstated. The decidedly political Transcontinental tradition of Black studies was doubly marginalized. By the 1950s U.S. mainstream Black intellectuals adopted, to varying degrees, both the Cold War liberal definitions of race that disaggregated the previous linking of the Black experience to global politics and economy, and particularly to global White supremacy. This move also meant a modification in the understanding of racism: previously, it was seen as constitutive of the shaping of modern society (through the transatlantic slave trade and colonialism); now, it was proclaimed a unique and anomalous feature of U.S. (and South African) democracy. With this, of course, came the acceptance that the U.S. nationalist project was, at its core, free and open—that this "liberal" state was impartial, with fairness and the moral equality of its citizens as its overarching imperatives (Mills 2008). In this context, racism and slavery were but unfortunate appendages to an otherwise sound nationalist program.

The emerging "liberal" idea of race effectively removed attention from global White supremacy. In intellectual practices, the focus shifted from concerns about political economy to interest in isolated notions of "culture." The example in the study of Africa among U.S. Black scholars is instructive; its approach ultimately converged with that of (White) Africanist study of Africa. We need only return to Drake's insistence that pan-Africanism (with a small *p*), the unorganized cultural elements of global Black populations, was the more significant strand of the larger movement.

Von Eschen (1997) demonstrates the many silences about the more radical aspects of transnational Black organizing among the new type of Black scholarship framed by the politics of the Cold War. She singles out Drake—one of the most powerful influences in shaping African diaspora studies from the 1950s to the 1980s—in particular for his general silence on the significant radical *politics* of Black internationalism and for his primary framework being instead "race relations" and his focus on the *cultural expressions* of Black identity. Similar to his other liberally inclined intellectual and political contemporaries in the U.S. Black community, Drake, it seems to me, accepted the role of the United States as world leader against an encroaching communism (ibid.). This was exemplified in the activities of the American Society on African Culture (AMSAC), a group that claimed Drake as an early member. It was later revealed that the AMSAC was organized and funded by the CIA to counter the intellectual and political work of the CAA; its intellectual output would soon replace the popular scholarship on Africa and the diaspora. In its explicitly anticommunist and prodemocracy stance, AMSAC's work demonstrated a shift from concerns with political economy to concerns of "culture." This new organization expressed its main goal as to "defend the great cultural contributions of man against the perversions of political, economic, and natural movements" (Mjagkij 2001, 186). Significantly, the organization understood such "perversions" to be the perceived threat of communism in the former colonies rather than, say, ongoing European imperialism.

More to the point, however, was the clear split between research approaching questions of political economy and studies concerning culture. Whereas the CAA promoted cultural needs and practices and the political economy as integrated (Mjagkij 2001), AMSAC focused primarily on the *cultural* linkages in the relationship between Africa and the diaspora. With this popular shift in focus to culture came a general silence on the racialized inequalities structurally embedded in the global political economy and, eventually, a decidedly nonradical (à la CAA) approach to the study of Africa and the African diaspora. And as the funding of AMSAC rose with the popularity of the group's activities, so too came the marginalization of once prominent leaders of the CAA, including Paul Robeson and W. E. B. DuBois.[9] Drake was ultimately correct, however, in his assessment of the general change in the articulation of Pan-Africanism. But the inward turn of continental and diaspora Blacks toward domestic concerns has to be understood within global dynamics of race, politics, and economics.

In postcolonial Africa, the turn to nation building was also marked by the liberalization of intellectual thought as well as politics. The prominent Pan-Africanist voice of Nkrumah (and a few others) aside, the end of formal colonialism also allowed the silencing of critiques of neoimperialism, neocolonialism, and White supremacy. Although "liberal triumphalism" would not be complete until the late 1980s (Boafo-Arthur 2007), its apparent influence on emerging independent African states would have long-term political and intellectual implications. This signals a major shift. Similar to the ways that conventional views of postcolonial independence equate the transfer of political power from the colonizer with self-determination and national-cultural sovereignty for the previously colonized (Grovogui 1997), emerging African nationalism was articulated in ways that did not allow for direct, local, intellectual analysis of the legacy of White supremacy. In the excitement over "independence," the control over the political kingdom, and belief that decolonization was an end in itself, there was no longer a concern with the relationship of independent African states to global racial politics. I am arguing, in other words, that with the seeming triumph over colonialism, continental African intellectual output left virtually no room for understanding the historical and ongoing "interpellative reach of racialization" (Omi and Winant 2008). Thus, while European colonization was clearly a racializing project—a project that structured not only internal dynamics of ethnicity, culture, and religion, but also the African political and sociocultural marginalization that continues in the postcolonial era— we are hard pressed to find direct analysis of the legacies of this project.[10] Even for radical Continental intellectuals who were influenced by Marxism, Transcontinental research on politics of White supremacy gave way to a priority of class analysis with race/racism understood to be a subset of class relations (Mafeje 2001).

Moreover, and as I argue in the introduction to this book, in this intellectual trend, race is often conceptualized as "racial conflict" or "race relations" and understood to affect primarily multiracial societies in which one dominant racial group exercises power over nondominant ones. Since colonial domination and attendant racism were assumed to be tied to European (White) bodies, independence and the Africanization of political powers, even if rudimentary, seemingly reflected an end to racial discord and conflict in the postcolonies. In this context, the contemporary racial contours of Africa's sociopolitical relations with its former political rulers were muted. The focus, therefore, became primarily the internal impediments to national identity formation—impediments such as tribalism or ethnic conflict, or concerns with modernization and regional and continental integration. Here, we also see the overlapping of the Africanist and African Continentalist specializations. This is not to say, of course, that there were not other points of intellectual inquiry. Christopher Fyfe (1992), for example, admonished his fellow Africanist colonial historians for failing to analyze European colonization of the African continent as a *racial* project. Indeed, while there were certainly Continental scholars who continued to challenge (White) Africanists's exceptionalizing treatment of African societies (Mafeje 1976; Rigby 1996), discussions of the racial undercurrents and current manifestations of imperialism—particularly outside of South Africa—were not common.

Across the Atlantic, the domestic turn for diaspora Blacks was to a cultural nationalism. In the United States as well as in other places on the west Atlantic basin, this emerged primarily within the context of civil rights movements in which the focus was on Black identity formation within hostile nation-states. From the late 1950s, the social movements and antiracist efforts led to various measures of domestic redress for racial terror in the United States, such as the end of legal segregation and the institutionalization of Black studies in predominantly White colleges and universities. Yet, while such domestic racial reforms were real, their incorporation within a liberal paradigm of race and U.S. nation building actually marked a defeat of more radical aspirations. The ironic result was the reinforcement of the underlying system of racialized structural inequality. Significantly, this domestic turn depended on a Black cultural nationalism prominently based on notions of African *cultural* origins and, with it, a necessary relegation of Africa to a (past) history and attendant exclusion—however unwitting—from modern conceptions of Blackness. The turn to domestic concerns on both sides of the Atlantic, therefore, meant, first, a reconceptualization of understandings of race from its global and interconnected structural dimensions to more local concerns with national integration; second, it necessitated the end of the recognition of the coevality of Africa and the diaspora. But we could argue that this was already in the making with the crushing of the radical Black Left, the sedimentation of Cold War politics, and the hegemonic rise of the new liberalism.

It should be remembered, also, that the prominence of the liberal vision of race in the United States in particular signaled a shift in engagements with Africa. No longer prominent were the critical studies of political economy and social structure; instead, the Black press, for example, presented disembodied and random facts about Africa often removed from their broader contexts. This dovetailed with the historical western Africanist representation of the continent. And whereas U.S. Black leaders, intellectuals, and journalists focused earlier on the bonds connecting diaspora and African Blacks, the emphasis at this moment was on *differences* between the two groups (Von Eschen 1997, 145). Moreover, the new exoticization of Africa converged with the politics of the institutional "birth" of African diaspora studies and the ultimate debates over the role of Africa in the cultural practices of African diaspora communities. Nothing encapsulates this more than the manifestation and influence of the Frazier-Herskovits debate that has, arguably, shaped all future framing of scholarship on Black transnational relations. Although there have always been a variety of approaches to the study of Black people internationally, the hegemonic framing of the Frazier-Herskovits debate has helped to all but eclipse other such paradigms. It remains the most influential intellectual legacy for Black diaspora (and perhaps African) studies. For me, what is most significant about this debate is its epistemological force.

The intellectual legacy of the Frazier-Herskovits debate is responsible for a conceptual split between scholarship on Africa and scholarship on the African diaspora. Tellingly, Melville Herskovits is often considered the father of both African studies and African diaspora studies (in the United States), which, for all intents and purposes, signals: the institutionalization and attendant "White" takeover of African studies as well as African diaspora studies; the ironic end of the mutual interrogation of contemporary continental and diasporic phenomena; and the epistemic convergence of mainstream Black and White scholars on Africa as the cultural ancestor rather than coeval coproducer of Black culture and identity (Okpewho 1999, xiv). It was largely the adoption of a liberal sensibility in the institutionalized study of Black and other non-White populations that opened up the space for the Frazier-Herskovits debate in the first place. And through the debate, the exceptionalist construction of continental Africa in intellectual and journalistic circles would be solidified with the epistemological merging of the Africanist tradition of African studies and U.S.-led African diaspora studies, with the attendant marginalization of the Transcontinental tradition and the more radical elements of Black scholarship.

While Martin and West are correct in their conclusion that the Africanist enterprise—particularly the intellectual histories of such an enterprise—has mostly silenced this Transcontinental tradition, we also have to take into account the internal politics of the Black diaspora population (particularly regarding U.S. Black political and intellectual traditions) as members engaged in the ongoing negotiations of identity in the context of global structures that were, and are, inherently anti-Black. Indeed, as Malini Schueller reminds us, "Academic practices within the U.S. university, particularly those of the humanities and social sciences, cannot be understood without their relationship to imperialism, which has structured the production of knowledge through different apparatuses" (2007, 42). The Africanist tradition of African studies emerged directly as a result of interweaving factors of U.S. imperial ascendancy, lasting colonialist structures in a postcolonial world, and the rise of the social sciences with the increasing importance of "narrower scientifically verifiable objects of inquiry" (Von Eschen 1997, 158). This tradition was also, I argue, a beneficiary of the shift in Black African and diaspora internal politics—politics influenced by similar international factors.

Though broad and definitely not exhaustive, this historical background allows us the space to map out and contextualize the rise of certain popular trends in African studies and African diaspora studies. The contemporary study of Africa and Black internationalism is steeped in what many would call nationalist paradigms (Lemelle and Kelley 1994), still subsumed within a liberal framework about race and Africa. This is not to say, of course, that the radical Transcontinental tradition—the tradition that sought to understand the international Black experience as constitutively structured by the history and practice of global White supremacy—no longer exists. It certainly does. Yet it remains on the margins of mainstream (that is, institutionalized) Black studies, overshadowed by debates about whether it is important to, first, link the experiences of Africa, of race and Blackness, and of diaspora; and, second, link them to global processes of racialization and to White supremacy.

To reiterate, some key theoretical and epistemological consequences of this history are as follows: first, there is a shift in the treatment of race in which the analytical lens narrows and moves away from a focus on the interconnected realities of global White supremacy; second, there is a shift in the treatment of Africa in which "culture"—against "structure"—becomes the primary lens through which the continent is apprehended; and, third, there is a clear bifurcation between the scholarship and research on continental Africa and on the African diaspora. An important related consequence of these shifts is, as we have seen throughout the book, the isolated treatment of the transatlantic slave trade and hemispheric colonialism and slavery, on the one hand, and European colonialism of the African continent, on the other. This is a move that not only links issues of race primarily to the experience of enslavement in the New World, but also gives the New World ownership of that history while it simultaneously excludes it from postcolonial Africa. In the rest of the chapter I demonstrate how these consequences play out in prominent trends of contemporary African studies and African diaspora studies, with a primary focus on the discipline of anthropology. I first demonstrate the ways segments of African studies have generally taken race for granted and ignored racialization process. At the same time, their rhetorical and analytical strategies and conceptual assumptions tend, through an acute culturalist exceptionalism, to further racialize continental phenomena. I then shift to African diaspora studies, a field that is consistently radical and rigorous in its analyses of global processes of racialization, but conventional in its treatment of Africa, which converges with the conceptual strategies of African studies.

## Race, Culture, and the Anthropology of Africa

The theoretical discussions anchoring the Frazier-Herskovits debate is a good way to explore the logic underpinning the current treatment of race, culture, and diaspora within prominent circles of African studies. The key point of contention in this well-known intellectual disagreement was over the source of the cultural practices of African diasporic communities. Herskovits argued that Black diasporic cultural practices are "retentions" from an African past, while Frazier located such practices as primarily emerging within the crucible of enslavement in the New World. In making the case for African cultural continuities ("Africanisms") in the Black diaspora, Herskovits was establishing what David Scott would later call diaspora studies' "anthropological problematic" (1991). The "anthropological problematic," Scott posits, is the notion that Black diaspora identity needs to be verified through the determination of an "authentic" past that only anthropology can provide. And anthropology can do so principally through the cultural sites of "Africa" and "slavery." The ideological determinants of this problematic are instructive for our discussion here. Herskovits's "cultural retentions" and his general views on cultural transmission and identity construction came within the context of the rise of anthropology's prominence and, more importantly, the discipline's role in the Western academy and in broader society as *the* "main force in the shift from a racial to a cultural view of human difference" (Malik 1996, 146). It must be remembered that the global proliferation of the racializing of human difference was underwritten by the "science" of early physical anthropology. In that scientific evolutionary worldview, late eighteenth- and early nineteenth-century anthropologists believed that human groups were on a racial path that traversed geographical, spatial, and temporal terrains and that led from social organization founded on peoples, clans, and tribes (that is, savagery and barbarism) to those founded on territory, the state, and the nation (Amselle 1990, 9). Physical anthropology collected physical data—such as meticulous studies of brain size, among other things—which rapidly institutionalized and established it as the discipline supporting the belief in a hierarchical biological human variation and White supremacy.

By the time of these debates and especially by the publication of Herskovits's *The Myth of the Negro Past* (1941), the foundation had been laid for the study of Africa that disarticulated the continent from its diaspora and the modern world. It was also a study of Africa that was shaped by the popularization of anthropology's time-honored particularist constructions of the continent within the context of a world order congealing around a racialized Western universal "ontogology of space and time [established] through scientific and ideological institutions." (Grovogui 2001, 435). Africa's exceptionalism in the racialist demarcation of the world thus came on the heels of the conquest and colonization of the New World and were adopted by the racializing and racialized West and folded into the moral and epistemological universe of Western academia. By the nineteenth century, in addition to physical anthropology, the fields of philology, biology, and history converged in consecrating notions of race, racial superiority, and racial privilege (Grovogui 2001). For Africa, this meant not only the denial of the essential attributes of human civilization, but the assumption of a natural ontology, immutable cultural dispositions, and an essential difference that is irrevocably local and, therefore, not worldly.

But the foundations of the anthropological project also encompassed the twentieth-century antiracist cultural relativism that would, ironically, come to uphold Africa's radical alterity. Herskovits's work pointed to a major theoretical shift within the (liberal) social sciences that would affect the direction of African studies' (and, more generally, society's) deployment of ideas about race and culture in the post–World War II era. At first expressed through the language of race in nineteenth-century physical anthropology in Europe, the particularist conventions of understanding of Africa became articulated, by the early to mid-twentieth century, through a language of culture and cultural difference (Pierre 2006). My interest lies in the contours of this ideological shift from race to culture—particularly in anthropology, but with the knowledge that this shift has reverberations throughout the social sciences and humanities—and what it means for the study of Africa today. I contend that there is a *trained inability* to acknowledge and/or examine the racial underpinnings of postcolonial societies—including Western constructions of Africa and the continent's position on the underside of a global political and economic hierarchy—and that contemporary knowledge production on Africa remains deeply and problematically racialized in very prominent but unacknowledged ways.

Both Herskovits and Frazier promoted radically antiracist agendas in an age when the eugenics movement had a strong foothold, when U.S. Jim Crow laws were entrenched, and when colonialism in Africa was at its height. By the time Herskovits turned to exploring the presence of Africanisms in Black diaspora culture,[11] anthropology's core framing of its subjects had undergone radical ideological and linguistic transformation. This is where we place Herskovits's legacy for African studies and, with the establishment of the first state-sponsored African studies center at North-western University, this is where we credit him with the anthropological, epistemological, and theoretical influence that underwrote research and analysis in the field. A student of Franz Boas, Herskovits was particularly influenced by his teacher's "historical-cultural particularism . . . the emphasis on tracing the geographical distribution of cultural traits, and the interest in cultural areas" (Yelvington 2006, 66). And up until Boas's intervention in establishing a distinction between culture and race, human difference was expressed in racial evolutionary and deterministic terms.[12] Boas's crusade against racial determinism effected a radical break with the assumptions of nineteenth-century racial categorization (and ranking) (Sanjek 1994). His specific impact was in establishing the concept of culture instead of that of race as the key object of anthropological study. However, the shift from race to culture was, significantly, little more than a shift in terms (Amselle 1990; Malik 1996; Pierre 2006; Stocking 1968; Visweswaran 1998). As Michel-Rolph Trouillot (2003) shows us, the culture concept was in effect an "anticoncept": culture was "everything race was not, and race was seen to be what culture was not: given, unchangeable, biology" (Visweswaran 1998, 72). Boasians, despite their liberal politics, actually did not relinquish the value of the scientific study of race. More importantly, they did not define culture (ibid.).

Paradoxically, it was the cultural anthropologists who most strongly affirmed the existence of race in order to clearly distinguish it from culture (Visweswaran 1998). They argued that, unlike the evolutionist conceptions of race, culture was learned, influenced by the environment, and cultures were not amenable to ranking. This was, in effect, cultural relativism, anthropology's main theoretical contribution to the social sciences: "each culture had its own internal dynamics and patterns of being; each resulted from a relation of internal forces, and . . . each had its own self-evident boundary" (Pierre 2006, 46). The growing strength of cultural relativism as the primary way to study and explain difference in human populations, framed by notions of existing bounded cultural groups, fit neatly with the increasingly specialized study of non-White and mostly colonized groups—tribes and ethnics. Studies of human societies (on both sides of the Atlantic)[13] became increasingly specialized and fixated on delineating the internal workings of specific groupings. Ethnographies, in particular, treated communities as cultural isolates, and the goal was to emphasize the "wholeness" of distinct cultures (Trouillot 2003). Against earlier histories of evolutionary progress, the focus on the relative and specific character of individual societies was laudable. At the same time, it led to the "erection of rigid cultural barriers enclosing each group in its singularity" (Amselle 1990, 20). To continually stress a community's singular practices and cultural formations is also to calcify its differences; in the context of ethnographic fieldwork research, this justified such a community's theoretical (as well as temporal) confinement. As Trouillot demonstrates, the concept of culture lost its explanatory power and kernel of relativism and became an object. Thus, the more it explained, the more reified it became: "For Columbus as for Montaigne, savages were those who had no state, no religion, no clothes, and no shame—*because they had nature*. For anthropology, primitives became those who had no complexity, no class, and no history that really mattered—*because they had culture*. Better still, each group had a single culture whose boundaries were thought to be self-evident" (Trouillot 2003, 102; italics added).

Indeed this deployment of culture ironically reconciled the Boasian agenda with the taxonomic schemes of earlier times. In effect, (anthropological) conception on difference based on ideas of culture became racialized: culture became race. The ultimate confluence of the mid-twentieth-century culture concept and the late nineteenth-century race concept is, however, not surprising; it has everything do to with the relationship between the intellectual and political contexts within which early twentieth-century anthropologists and other academics operated. First, as Trouillot (2003) argues, the shift from a focus on race to one on culture was an *intellectual* response to a *political* situation (see also Stocking 1968). In other words, many of the scholars associated with the shift felt compelled to change the *terms* of the debate in the discussion of human difference in order to combat racist thinking and action. At the same time, the institutionalization of the discipline mandated an escape from explicit confrontation from the political world, from the acknowledgment of power and the politics of antiracism. That is, even as the change in terms took place, there was no direct challenge to global racist structures of colonialism and Jim Crow racism. There was, in effect, "the inability to produce a clear theoretical reply to racist practices from the space carved by the Boasians" (Trouillot 2003, 110).

The deployment of culture as a marker of human difference merely masked common racial understandings of human difference. This occurred for two reasons. First, this *theoretical* move within anthropology did not expunge the baggage of racial conceptualization; worse yet, it did not challenge the continued *political* practices of racism—colonial exploitation, Jim Crow racism, and apartheid. Second, by relegating race to the realm of biology, anthropology failed to interrogate both the continued global significance of race and how race actually works to create meaning and structure inequality. Third, because the trajectory of culture is "that of a concept

distancing itself from the context of its practice" (Trouillot 2003), it necessarily cannot erase anthropology's racial, racializing, and racist past. Meanwhile, anthropological and other Africanist research continues on without
missing a beat. But the "fetichization of culture" (ibid.) in both theory and
practice affirms as a priori natural cultural difference and renders the treatment of African phenomena as always already exceptional and (not so implicitly) *racially* distinct.

The point I want to stress here is how, even in embracing a new study
of Africa, the Western scholars that became prominent often were already
constrained by a paradigm (what Grovogui [2001] calls a "hermeneutics of
race") that accepted and promoted cultural-cum-racial difference without
direct attention to a clearly racialized global political hierarchy. This is not
to say that scholars did not, or do not, have knowledge of the global structures of power within which Africa and its peoples are circumscribed. It is to
say, instead, that the specificity of the effects of global White supremacy—
both on local communities and in knowledge production—are usually not
part of the scholarly treatment of Africa. Consequently, with few exceptions
the general trend in the study of Africa is to leave the structures of global
race and power intact, allowing, by implication, the ongoing particulariza-
tion (and negative racialization) of Africans.

The particularist treatment of Africa, without acknowledging that African
distinctiveness is produced within a field of power relations of race, has
much to do with the use, abuse, and the deployment of the culture concept
(in its various forms). We can, following our discussion above, see this in
two specific ways in the anthropological Africanist repertoire.[14] First, there
is a culture-ethnic framework that upholds an essentialist (and racialist)
African difference that is given a definite location in locality (or ethnicity,
as Korang [2003] sees it). Here, we see how current studies of Africa continue to follow the colonialist model of ethnicizing African phenomena.
Second, there is a political-economic framework that frequently depends
on the assumptions of a moral order in which the supposed African failure
at building up states and nations (these entities being already "failed" and
"corrupt") is traceable primarily to its cultural dispositions (or its "agency,"
in the more presumably radical models).

Examples of the first trend abound in the scholarship, and the patterns
are easily traceable with any conscientious analysis of available texts. Indeed,
even a quick glance at the titles of some recent Africanist ethnographies
published by respectable North American and European academic presses,
for example, is revealing: *Between God, the Dead and the Wild: Chamba Interpretations of Ritual and Religion* (Fardon 1991); *Sacred Void: Spatial Images*

*of Work and Ritual among the Giriama of Kenya* (Parkin 1991); *Witchcraft, Violence, and Democracy in South Africa* (Ashforth 2005); *Wombs and Alien Spirits: Women, Men, and the Zār Cult in Northern Sudan* (Boddy 1989); *Under the Kapok Tree: Identity and Difference in Beng Thought* (Gottlieb 1996); *The Modernity of Witchcraft: Politics and the Occult in Postcolonial Africa* (Geschiere 1997); *Guns and Rain: Guerrillas and Spirit Mediums in Zimbabwe* (Lan 1985); *Remotely Global: Village Modernity in West Africa* (Piot 1999); *Prayer Has Spoiled Everything: Possession, Power, and Identity in an Islamic Town of Niger* (Masquelier 2001); *The Possessed and the Dispossessed: Spirits, Identity, and Power in a Madagascar Migrant Town* (Sharp 1996); *In Sorcery's Shadow: A Memoir of Apprenticeship among the Songhay of Niger* (Stoller and Olkes 1987); *Translating the Devil: Religion and Modernity among the Ewe in Ghana* (Meyer 1999); *A Culture of Corruption: Everyday Deception and Popular Discontent in Nigeria* (Smith 2008); *Markets of Dispossession: Ngos, Economic Development, and the State in Cairo* (Elyachar 2005); *Culture and the Senses: Bodily Ways of Knowing in an African Community* (Geurts 2002); and *Over the Lip of the World* (McElroy 2001). What immediately confronts us is the certain unspoken given that not only are these books about Africa, they can *only* be about Africa. (In fact, I challenge readers to find similar tropes in the titles of texts published on the geographical areas of the West.) Here, what makes African phenomena unique, and certain cultural features uniquely African, is revealed. Why are these titles representative only of Africa? The answer, I believe, lies in our sensitization to the embedded assumptions about African matter. In African culture, we see African distinctions—specific practices that denote the ever-present occult ("witchcraft" is the favorite example) and excessively localized events such that the "Kapok tree," for instance, gets exposure (but in a way that diminishes the power of the forest). In this fresco, even "corruption" is described as "cultural."

Over the years of conducting ethnographic research in Ghana, I have often been told by other academics, directly and implicitly, that my subject group was not necessarily the "real" Africa, or that I was not focusing on "the people" since my research focused not only on racialization, but also included data on educated and middle-class professionals.[15] I often jokingly respond that Western academics usually get off the plane in Accra and put on their ethnographic blinders only to take them off when they get to "the bush," the site of "real" Africa. This "real" Africa is a well-known one—it is "ethnic" and "tribal" and the presumed site of contemporary life. In the wealth of research and scholarship on Africa, the culture-ethnic framework is prominent. In addition to various studies on African ethnic identity formation—particularly those about ethnic conflicts—there is the commonplace focus on extremely localized cultural practices that are ostensibly approached from strictly African local terms. The "authentic" African subject in this scenario is the one whose picture we often see in our texts: the village resident, the market woman—in effect, it is the local who struggles to obtain and maintain modernity. In other words, it often seems as if the locus of African authenticity "has to be the pre-colonial cultural elements extant in the contemporary societies of the continent" (Korang 2004, 45).

In his essay "Where Is Africa? When Is the West's Other?" Kwaku Larbi Korang critiques Western liberal Africanists for upholding a "natural African ontology" that allows Africa to reveal "a coherent subjectivity of its own autonomous fashioning" only from within the "ethnic" trope (2004, 45). "For the Westerner to know African alterity properly," he continues, "is for him to identify with Africa through its ethnic realities." Indeed, these "ethnic realities" are often epistemologically taken as authentically African, and these realities exist in a "past continuous" mode in which precolonial cultural elements are extent in contemporary society and can be explained as "a living heritage of actively informing African life" (Korang 2003, 45). As I have argued above (and in chapter 1), it is telling that ethnicity becomes the main site of explanations of African phenomena. Ethnicity seems to be, after all, about *African-African* relations, *not* European-African relations. Within the paradigm of African ethnicization—by which Blacks are ethnicized into cultural (tribal) constellations, while White racial identity remains coherent—it is not surprising that there are few ethnographic studies that address Whites and Whiteness in Africa (outside of southern Africa). Such studies would force engagement with processes of racialization and, ultimately, global racial power.

This is why I insist that the continued deployment of ethnicity to explore African phenomena without recourse to how such ethnic identities are racially structured within a global hierarchy is actually another way to racially mark Africans as radically Other, while ignoring the significance of the force of racial formation. In the previous chapter, I pointed to the ways that anthropologists focusing on heritage tourism often tended to work within a culturalist framework that did not allow room for understanding the racial dynamics of this phenomena (Brunner 1996; Hasty 2002). Consequently, not only is Ghana's own racial formation missing from the analysis, but also the scholars are so determined to establish Ghana's localness that they deny the country and its people worldliness. Whatever arguments are posited to the contrary, the particular culture-ethnicity framework elides the larger relationships that structure local economic and social inequality. In many studies, Africans are understood and deemed to divide naturally into ethnic (or tribal) groups. Moreover, African ethnicity is generally conceptualized as "tribal solidarity," which is also often seen and presented as prone to conflict (Goldberg 1993). In the larger, global context within which Western studies of Africa are situated, the "ethnic" conceptualizations of Africa actually continue to serve specific ends: divide and rule. And, as we saw in chapter 3, issues of privilege, inequality, and power continue to be obfuscated by the singular focus on indigenous "ethnocultural" terms.

This is definitely the case in these culturally drenched discussions of the African "crisis" and the "failure" of the postcolonial African state. Here, the focus on the African state's inability to function properly and its inherently corrupt nature—all under the cloak of African exceptionalism—deserves mention. Even as new ethnographies do not fit the stereotype of traditional ethnographies of African groupings as cultural isolates (see Pierre 2006), there is still a way in which the charge of "failed states," of "corruption," and of the inability of Africans to modernize, as well as the tone in which these critiques are made, works to enforce a certain culturalist-racial interpretation of African experiences. For example, the following could not be about any other place but Africa: "What was once a monument to a booming oil-economy is now crumbling and cracking at the seams, like the *morally* and economically *bankrupt* nation-state so thoroughly plundered by its ruling military clique. . . . Oil, once the demi-god of national rebirth, now stands for national pollution and decay. . . . After years of rapacious looting of oil revenues, today Nigeria is a mess" (Apter 1996, 443; italics added). What allows these types of descriptions of African phenomena to go unchallenged by scholars? Both the author's tone and analysis reflect what Jean-Loup Amselle describes as "a culturalising of corruption of sorts that seem to work to make Nigeria (Africa?) exceptional and to make us forget the universality of corrupt state practices" (Amselle 2003). A quick way to contextualize this is for us to think about how acceptable it would be for a scholar of Andrew Apter's caliber to explain the U.S. role in the conflicts in the Middle East, or the current control of the U.S. government by the major financial institutions, in similar—and particularly culturalist—terms. Such tone and analytical bent in describing the "moral" and "economic" bankruptcy of the U.S. nation-state would be jarring. But this is not the case with Africa because the continent's phenomena, as well as its political and economic predicaments, are presented as particularly and culturally insular. The late Portuguese activist and cultural critic Antonio de Figueriedo described how the culturalist (and ethnic) approach to Africa is framed upon the palimpsest of a racial legacy. He pointed out that, given how late twentieth-century cultural specialists in African politics "focused on corruption as a fundamental cultural characteristic of the African continent," it should cause little surprise when some wonder if "corruption" (linked of course to state and governance failures) is not the "new racial stereotype" for Africans (2005, 54). Indeed, we have to wonder. The point here is not to argue that subjects of state decay or corruption are not permissible academic topics to be explored. There seems to be, however, a way in which scholarly excitement over particular topics—and the terms of engagement with them—"mask the deeper question of Western representations of Africa as a continent of absolute horror, a theatre of primordial savagery only temporarily interrupted by European colonization" (Amselle 2003).

But my discussion here is not so much about representations of Africans as it is about the *racial inflections* that undergird researching, theorizing, and writing about Africa, where our anthropological (and broader social science) enterprise works in a way that demonstrates that the desire to understand other cultures is more about effectively preserving their differences. Africanist engagement with Africa seems to be so inescapably caught within an epistemological tunnel in which continental cultural exceptionalism (even when discussed through the trope of African "agency") makes it impossible for other ways of knowing about Africa; and, as Korang would argue, it shuts Africa out of a worldly temporality. Thus, for example, middle-class or cosmopolitan Africans (such as the groups of young people described in chapter 6) are automatically considered elites and therefore inauthentic Africans. Ultimately, the culturalist engagement with Africa has worked to further mark it as a site of radical racial alterity. I believe that recognizing race and the significance of the process of racialization on the continent has the potential to shift our culturalist lens while allowing us to apprehend the complexities of a modern and active Africa.

One of the few (arguably) Continental scholars that has attracted the attention of Africanist anthropologists even as he directly addresses race is Kwame Anthony Appiah. Not surprisingly, Appiah's primary aim has been to forcefully repudiate the concept of race, especially as an organizing principle for Pan-African identity and politics. He has castigated Pan-Africanism as a misguided tool of those of "partial African ancestry" who, he believes, essentialized racist notions of Blackness (1992). He accuses popular Pan-Africanist figures such as Alexander Crummell and W. E. B. DuBois of intrinsic racism: that is, they espoused Pan-African ideas "that there was a common destiny for the people of Africa—by which we are always to understand black people—not because they shared a common ecology, nor because they had a common historical experience or faced a common threat from imperial Europe, but because they belong to this one race" (1992, 5). At the core of this critique is the assumption that race or Black peoples' claims of racial kinship and solidarity are inherently essentialist and, by extension, racist. Moreover, there is the implication that race and notions of Blackness are only applicable to diaspora—and not African—history and experience. African experiences are deemed, instead, to be directed by "internal moral and cognitive" conceptions (Appiah 1992).

It is indeed significant that Appiah is among the few Continental scholars that have received accolades in the Western academy.[16] I contend that it has to do with the fact that his scholarship maintains the theoretical and epistemological split between, on the one hand, Africa and the diaspora, and, on the other, race and African "cultural" traditions (and alterity). More importantly, Appiah's position not only disarticulates the integrated historical experiences of European empire making so that its legacies are not considered analogous, but he also ascribes pervasive racial thinking solely to diaspora Blacks. I take this up in my discussion of the relationship of diaspora studies to race and the trope of Africa.

## Africa and Black Diaspora Studies

For African-Americans, raised in a segregated American society and exposed to the crudest forms of discrimination, social intercourse with white people was painful and uneasy. Many of the Africans, on the other hand (my father among them) took back to their homes European wives and warm memories of European friends; few of them, even from the "settler" cultures of East and southern Africa, seem to have been committed to ideas of racial separation or to doctrines of racial hatred. Since they came from cultures where black people were in the majority and where lives continued to be largely controlled by indigenous and moral and cognitive conceptions, they had no reason to believe that they were inferior to white people and they had, correspondingly, less reason to resent them (Appiah 1992, 7)

We will leave aside the fact that Appiah's purported *lack* of commitment to ideas of racial separatism or "doctrines of racial hatred" could also be read conversely as a commitment to acquiring status through White association, biological and social. From this description we also get a subtext that points to a Black diaspora (African Americans, specifically) obsessed with race and, at times, feelings of racial hatred. There is also a second subtext, one that is based on the belief that, as Lewis Gordon pointed out, "people of the African continent lived and would continue to live free of racial strife with

Europeans but for the intrusive, racist antics of New World blacks and their cognitively impaired attachments to nineteenth-century racial concepts" (1997, 118). We are then led to believe that the cause of the Black diaspora's obsession with race and Blackness is the historical legacy of racial segregation that, presumably, is a legacy that does not belong to continental Africans. Moreover, Africans, unlike New World Blacks, have cultures that are grounded in traditional mores and values—the so-called indigenous moral and cognitive conceptions. The result is a view of Africa that not only denies its historical legacy of slavery and *racial* colonialism, but that also denies the mutuality of the experiences of this legacy with the Black diaspora. In other words, and similar to other scholars, Appiah segments the overarching colonial order and makes slavery, racialization (and racial antagonism), and Pan-Africanism only significant for diaspora Black populations. This, of course, is both historically incorrect and intellectually disingenuous given Ghana's well-known Pan-African history. And nowhere do we see a critique of the global structures of White privilege that developed out of the colonial order—structures that enable Appiah and his White European friends to have privileged access to Ghana.

Appiah has not been alone in the critique of the presumed racial "pathology" of African Americans. Indeed, Appiah's *In My Father's House: Africa in the Philosophy of Culture* was published in the early 1990s, when there was a concerted attack on Afrocentricism. The most influential of these attackers were Black scholars from the British cultural studies tradition, such as Paul Gilroy, Kobena Mercer, and Stuart Hall. Gilroy, for example, uses "archaic pan-Africanism" and "Afrocentricity" as fodder for his argument that the traditional cannon of Black (American) cultural, intellectual, and political thought represents a type of "ethnic absolutism" (1991). In ways quite similar to Appiah's categorization of Pan-Africanism as "intrinsically" racist, Gilroy claims as comparable "Black nationalism" (which he presumes to be synonymous with Pan-Africanism and Afrocentricity) and British White racism, both of which, he explains, are grounded in overly easy identifications of race and culture with nation. To be sure, Gilroy and these other scholars provided substantial interventions on the theorization of the African diaspora. They attempted to expose the homogenizing tendencies of some conceptualizations of Black diaspora identity as well as demonstrate the limits of closed and totalizing understandings of community. Some of their most serious critiques assail diaspora studies' stagnant view of culture and cultural transformation; its creation of racial/ethnic "authenticity," which is exclusionary and which, in their estimations, reifies Western categories; and its inability to account for the cultural and historical specificity of distinct Black experiences (Gilroy 1991, 1993; Hall 1994, 1995; Mercer 1994). Another crucial contribution was the emphasis on the *construction* of diasporic identity as opposed to one that is believed to "naturally" exist. Without oversimplifying their distinct positions, these scholars attempt to move beyond the focus on "cultural survivals" from Africa and explore how diasporic identities are constituted and reconstituted in opposition to racial terror.

The inordinate attention these scholars have placed on critiquing the idea of African "cultural survivals," however, is significant. It reflects a new trend that forcefully shifted discussion of Blackness from notions of African racial and cultural linkage to its diaspora. The diaspora paradigm, some argued, was often used simply as a "cataloguing of global black experiences" (Vinson 2006, 4) with the related emphasis on shared common (racial) origins. Because Africa—as homeland and racial signifier (Scott 1991)—provided this link, it came to represent, for these scholars, *the* trope of homogenizing and essentialist constructions of Black identity. This takes us back, of course, to the Frazier-Herskovits debate and the resultant "anthropological problematic" by which diaspora identity has to be anthropologically proven to be culturally continuous to an African past. The underlying premise of the debate affirmed culture as a key site of identity formation and Africa as a place of distinct indigenous cultural traditions—a premise assumed by early diaspora scholarship. It is no wonder Herskovits is considered the father of both African studies and African diaspora studies.

The cultural-continuities discussion is important here because it sets the stage for the struggle over the meaning and place of race, identity, and Africa within contemporary theorizations of diaspora. Indeed, it is the foundation upon which much of this theorization has been built. Anthropology was at the forefront of this debate as other scholars (Ortiz 1975, 1986; Bastide 1978) continued with Herskovits's project of delineating aspects of African culture within communities of the diaspora (Patterson and Kelley 2000). Informed also by the Boasian separation of race and culture, the goal of this theorization was to reverse the sustained racism against people of African descent by establishing an autochthonous past beyond slavery and colonialism. Scholars constructed this past through what David Scott determined was a "metonymic narrative that would join Afro-America into a whole differentiated by a measurable proximity to Africa" (1991, 276). This signaled the assumption, as I argued earlier, that for the African diaspora to be fully recognized, its "history and culture has to be argued in terms of a notion of an authentic past" (278). Africa was that authentic past; Africa and its diaspora were seen as linked through the perpetuation of authentically

African cultures. The African diaspora was thus conceptualized as a cultural continuum, uniting Africa and its communities in the diaspora (Gordon and Anderson 1999). Significantly, the "Africa" part of this cultural continuum exists in the (traditional) *past*, rendering continental phenomena static and bounded. It is here, in the conceptualization of Africa, that we can see the convergence of the cultural-continuities approach to diaspora studies and that of U.S.-based African studies.

The Herskovitsian influence in some circles of diaspora studies remains prevalent, underpinning a broad range of scholarship and activism from contemporary Pan-Africanism to Afrocentricism. Scholars such as Joseph Holloway (1990) and Robert Farris-Thompson (1983), for example, called for the recognition of Africanisms in the African diaspora. And in the 1980s, there was a rise in the popularity of the Afrocentric school of thought —associated primarily with the scholarship of Molefe Asante. Indeed, the connection between the Africanisms and the Afrocentric schools of thought is the cultural-continuities thesis about African and diaspora cultural ties. The Afrocentric scholarship, however, would ultimately receive the harshest set of critiques from an emerging cadre of diaspora scholars.

Asante sees Afrocentricity as a "critical corrective to a displaced agency among Africans" and a "recentering" of African minds (1994, 20). He argues that there is a need to challenge and therefore displace the hegemonic centrality of Eurocentrism and place "Africa at the center of analysis of African issues and African people in our own contexts" (22). Although Afrocentricity's premise up to this point recalls the earlier Transcontinental tradition of African studies in that it attempts to actively shift the study of Africa and the diaspora in ways that vindicate and demonstrate Black agency, what seems to attract the ire of critics is the idea that the global Black community is united and culturally connected as "African." According to Asante, "we have one African Cultural System manifested in diversities. . . . We respond to the same rhythms of the universe, the same cosmological sensibilities, the same general historical reality as the African descended people" (1988, 2). In their critiques of the Afrocentric paradigm, scholars argue against the implied belief that the "idea of race is some type of ahistorical phenomenon rooted in a shared genetic heritage" (Ransby 1994, 32). Importantly, because this criticism is based on a reading of Afrocentricism that clearly highlights the cultural-continuities paradigm, it effectively and ironically places contemporary diaspora scholars squarely within the paradigm of the Herskovits-Frazier debate. I would argue, in fact, that most conceptualization of African diaspora identity is structured through this debate.

In what is arguably one of the most definitive historical reviews of diaspora scholarship and theory, Patterson and Kelley assert that "the fundamental and still unresolved question in histories of the African diaspora . . .
is to what degree are New World Black people, 'African'" (2000, 17). But
implicit in this statement is the acceptance of the premise of the cultural-
continuities school in which the goal is to determine the extent to which
diaspora communities are culturally African. A better way for Patterson and
Kelley to have phrased this discussion of diasporic identity formation may
have been to examine how both Africa and the Black diaspora are implicated in the construction of modern Blackness. The question is telling not
only for what it references—the cultural-continuities discussion—but also
for what it reveals about the kinds of anxieties that still occupy diaspora
scholars. Specifically, it points directly to the ambivalence surrounding the
"Africa" part of Black diasporic identity where, as Kadiatu Kanneh argues,
"identification with Africa, or being African, presents itself repeatedly . . . as
a problem of retrospect or distance" (1998, 65). Thus, in current attempts at
conceptualizing the African diaspora, Africa—both as idea and geopolitical
entity—remains central and indispensable. But this indispensability is para-
doxical, not least because claims to the contrary are what frame many of
the contemporary discussions on the African diaspora. In many circles, any
consideration or engagement with Africa automatically signifies a preoccupation with "home" and "origins," and therefore a potent, if not destructive,
deployment of racial essentialism. In this particular advance, strands of diaspora scholarship advocating cultural continuities or establishing connections among dispersed Black populations have become the major culprits,
keeping discussions on diaspora identity locked within an unnecessary
essentialist-constructivist (that is, Herskovits-Frazier) debate (Patterson and
Kelley 2000; Edwards 2001; Vinson 2006).

I believe that the varied critiques of Afrocentrism, Black cultural nationalism, and the idea of cultural retentions within diaspora studies are what
led to more than a decade of scholarship explicitly distancing itself from
continental Africa. This distancing appears to be for the sole purpose of
establishing antiessentialist credentials. Yet, by my reckoning, the critiques
have been excessive in two specific ways. First, they have often overlooked
the important historical precedence of the vindicationist tradition of Afrocentricity. As Patterson and Kelley remind us, "The presumption that black
people worldwide share a common culture was not . . . the result of poor
scholarship. It responded to a political imperative—one that led to the
formation of political and cultural movements premised on international

solidarity" (2000, 19). What appears lost in the critiques of early diaspora scholarship is the recognition that Black peoples (including early scholars) have always been and remain "under a compulsion to affirm a common humanity through a *prior* affirmation of (their) African humanity [especially] insofar as continental peoples and their counterparts in the black diaspora had . . . been denied their share by Westerners in a common fund of humanity and a meaningful place in the human family" (Korang 2003, 278). Second, the critiques of Afrocentricism's claims to racial and cultural unity were often more unforgiving than those against the continuing structures of global White supremacy. There is something deeply problematic about the unequal condemnation levied against Black people's self-affirmation and constructions of identity as compared to anti-Black structures of domination. Yet, while scholars are critical of Afrocentricism's seemingly racial essentialism for claiming African cultural continuity, they remain virtually silent on the construction and representation of Africa as distant and culturally static. Indeed, with very few exceptions (Matory 1999, 2005), these scholars do not take the time to acknowledge, much less engage, a modern Africa. I see three interrelated consequences to this type of diaspora engagement over the past two decades. First, the shift away from engagement with modern Africa without an attendant critique of the alterity inherent in the construction of Africa as cultural ancestor actually marginalizes the continent further, leaving its alterity intact. Second, as a consequence of the sedimentation of African alterity, Africa loses coevality as its cultural practices are not interrogated within a modern context, including prominent discussions of race and Blackness in diaspora studies. Finally, and most importantly, the so-called New World communities remain centered as the primary sites of modern Blackness.

How did we get to a point in diaspora scholarship at which the mere mention of Africa or discussions of African phenomena elicit strong cautions against essentialism?

We can locate clear reasons for this shift in the treatment of Africa and, by extension, of race and modernity in some of the more popular diaspora scholarship. For Gilroy, the African diaspora is a Black Atlantic, a transnational site characterized by "continuously crisscrossed movements of black people" (1993, 16). Effectively decentering Africa as the primary source of diasporic racial and cultural identity, he describes diaspora cultures as "both those residually inherited from Africa and those generated from the special bitterness of new world racial slavery" (1991, 81). Gilroy then uses the concepts of roots and routes to engage the question of unity and identity of transnational Black communities. Although diaspora communities need to affirm cultural integrity in response to racial terror, Gilroy argues, such integrity cannot be found in "shared racial or cultural essences or origins but on similar . . . experiences of racial subordination and struggle" (as quoted in Gordon and Anderson 1999, 10–11). Indeed, routes give meaning to the notion of a Black Atlantic, while roots (African cultural and racial heritage) signify not a globalized Black interaction but a springboard for the creation of hybridized and therefore modern diasporic identities. As such, Gilroy effectively negates the possibility of exploring the mutuality of African and Black diasporic modern identities.

For Stuart Hall, like Gilroy, the diaspora is characterized by its hybridity. Here the Caribbean represents "the original and purest diaspora" with the equal contributions of "Presence Africaine," "Presence Europeene," and "Presence Americaine." The placement of Africa here is instructive: its presence is no more important than a European or American presence, and it is only present in the Caribbean as a "language, the symbolic language for describing what suffering was like . . . a language in which [people] could re-tell and appropriate their stories" (1995, 3). Moreover, in Hall's definition of diaspora, we find the conventional understanding of an Africa that, in turn, deserves dismissal. For Hall, diaspora "does not refer us to those scattered tribes whose identity can only be secured in relation to some sacred homeland to which they must at all costs return. . . . The diaspora . . . is defined not by essence or purity" (1994, 402). If we follow contemporary diaspora scholars, we see how they are informed by this view of Africa in diaspora. It is an Africa primarily of the imagination, but one existing in a long and distant past. As Kanneh rightly observes, "'Africa,' as an original home, exists at the limits of the imagination. It belongs to and is allowed to remain as a point of departure" (1998, 122; see also Matory 1999, 2005). If Africa is indeed contained as past culture and tradition—and its only role is the fulfillment of Black diaspora ideas of cultural origins *away* from such traditions—then the Africa we are left with is one in a "marginalized and troubled space" (Kanneh 1998, 64). It makes sense, then, that diaspora scholars are often quick to present the exploration of Black identity as shifting "the discussion from an African-centered approach" (Patterson and Kelley 2000, 26).

In actuality, however, this move beyond what scholars see as the uncritical and problematic appropriation of Africa is really a move away from theorizing the continent as a living and modern place. As a consequence, the African continent is marginalized. It is stripped of its worldliness, modernity, and hybridity; its history of slavery and colonialism is subsumed under the slavery experience of diaspora populations of the western

Atlantic; and the long history of Afro-Atlantic dialogue and mutual transformation is obscured. Ghanaian scholar Korang reminds us that the "double disposition in consciousness" and the "fracture in Black ontology"—that is, the hybridity that constitutes modern Black experience—are not the property of only the diasporic branch of the Atlantic; they are indeed the fact of Blackness produced by Western imperialism. I would further argue that it is only by denying the interlinked histories of the transatlantic slave trade and colonialism in Africa and the New World that scholars can both keep Africa in a distant past and deny Africa its place in the modern community of Blackness.

In the introduction to this book, I asked, why is it that slavery and colonialism are assumed to have transformed Black identities in the diaspora but not those on the African continent? I contend that it takes a particular kind of blindness to history to not recognize Africa's own transformation in its intimate engagement with imperialism, a transformation that occurred and continues to occur in mutual relation with the Black diaspora. Significantly, diaspora scholars are not unaware of Africa's hyperracialized existence as Black, or of how the continent's history of racial colonialism shaped contemporary identity and community. It is rather that this commonsensical awareness does not usually translate into actual theoretical engagement. Ultimately, what we get is the inevitable and ironic convergence of the strands of diaspora studies with those of African studies whereby African alterity is maintained through the continent's enforced lack of coevality and deracialization while its mutually reinforcing relationship with the diaspora is denied. The result, of course, is the inability to conceive of Black African and diaspora populations as continually and mutually engaged in dialogues and practices that race back and forth across the Atlantic. What also results is the ongoing atomization in the study of these linked populations.

I began this chapter by highlighting the bifurcation in the study of global Black populations that occurs when the historically structured mutuality of Black experiences is not often considered crucial to analyses either in African studies or diaspora studies. This split, I have argued, is a direct result of a confluence of historical events that not only shaped the professional trajectories of the two fields, but also fundamentally impacted theoretical and epistemological developments in each. Key to these events, and consequent developments, is the trope of Africa and the idea of race as well as their relationship to structures of racialization and the power of knowledge production. What I have argued throughout the book, however, is that we must be attentive to the particular set of historical conditions out of which Black communities emerge and through which the particularities of Blackness are such that they render analogous the experiences of diverse communities—on the African continent and in the diaspora. Specifically, the crucial practices of European empire making—practices involving the key events of the transatlantic slave trade and racial colonialism—and the resultant racialization of African peoples into "Blacks" cannot only be assumed, but have to be actively and analytically articulated in our engagement with these populations. My point throughout this chapter, and the book, has been to challenge the systematic isolation of slavery and colonialism and to demonstrate that they are part of a larger historical arc that continues to shape identity and community on both sides of the Atlantic. Without this challenge, we lose the ability to recognize the transnational significance of race and, with that, the ability to understand the interdependent construction of racialized Black African and diasporic identities. Moreover, the bifurcation of African studies and African diaspora studies—along with the theoretical and epistemological divergences—can consequently leave us with a trained inability to explore the active and ongoing "Afro-Atlantic dialogues" (Matory 1999) that make up global Black communities today.

In making the case for a new theoretical imagining of the overlapping Blackness of African and the diaspora, I also want to expose how our current conceptualizations of this integrated history and identity have not only shifted the ideological terrain of Black community formation, but have also eroded the *political* terrain upon which a truly emancipatory struggle can be waged. In other words, the bifurcated approach to Africa and the diaspora is also a political trend, one that diminishes the historical structures informing Black global existence. Yet, the recognition that common historical displacement and attendant racial distinction are constitutive of modern Black experience on *both* sides of the "Black Atlantic"—and therefore also constitutive of the synonymous structures of Black diasporic and African identities—is not novel. It was a conceptual, theoretical, empirical, and political imperative for early scholars of Black African and diaspora communities. This critical scholarly and political tradition established as given the foundational significance of the overarching colonial order (Stam and Shohat 2003) that structured the modern world. Yet, if we explore popular trends in contemporary African diaspora studies, we rarely see traces of this "Black Radical Tradition" (as Cedric Robinson [1983] calls it). I believe that this development is not accidental. In order to understand the trend toward the bifurcation of the study of global Blackness, we have to think historically while bringing together discussions of methodology and epistemology with the relationships of worldwide political imperatives, academic and disciplinary exigencies, and the dynamics of racialized knowledge production. The theoretical reconfiguration of African and diaspora Blackness that I present in this chapter, therefore, is also a way to make the case for the appreciation of a clear *politics* of Black identity and community research.

# Writing Ghana, Imagining Africa, and Interrogating Diaspora

It becomes clear that diaspora represents a global space, a worldwide web, that accounts as much for the mother continent as for wherever in the world her offspring may have been driven by the unkind forces of history.

—Isidor Okpewho, *The African Diaspora*

[Edward] Blyden . . . had reasoned that diaspora time in its blackness overlaps with African time—a time shared by both their common displacement into, and racial disinheritance by, a Western imperial modernity.

—Kwaku Korang, *Writing Ghana, Imagining Africa*

On the evening of March 8, 2007, I accompanied a couple of friends to the Accra International Conference Center to attend the first screening of the documentary film *The Prof: A Man Remembered; The Life, Vision, and Legacy of Dr. K. A. Busia.* I had arrived in Ghana more than a week earlier to attend the many events surrounding the country's Golden Jubilee, marking fifty years of political independence from British colonialism. With our VIP tickets in hand, Kweku, Doran, and I headed straight to the front of the large auditorium and found our seats in the third row.

After a lengthy wait, the auditorium abruptly fell into silence as the hosts of the evening, Dr. Abena Busia and Akosua Busia, daughters of former prime minister of Ghana, appeared on stage to address the crowd. The Busias warmly greeted the audience, thanked everyone for attending, and asked for continued patience. They told us that we would not be disappointed once the special guests arrived. The audience was suddenly buzzing with excitement. Since we had not known much about the event beforehand, my friends and I were especially curious. Two full hours later, as we sat through a number of opening performances, we were still waiting for the guests to arrive and for the screening to begin. As members of the audience grew ever more impatient at the extremely long delay, Akosua Busia briskly walked on stage and quite excitedly introduced her special guest. We all gasped in unison when Stevie Wonder was led out onto the stage. He took the microphone to thunderous applause and a standing ovation. Wonder smiled as he lifted the microphone to his mouth and greeted the audience. He told us that he came directly from the Accra airport, having just arrived from the United States. But he was determined not to miss this important event, he said. He then began to speak about his mother, telling us that her death was the inspiration for his comeback tour in 2007. However, he was abruptly and awkwardly interrupted when Dr. Abena Busia rushed onto the stage and apologetically grabbed the microphone to announce the arrival of the president of Ghana, John Agyekum Kufuor. The audience seemed surprised once again, and we all rose to our feet as the entourage of state dignitaries—including also vice president Aliu Mahama and several ministers of state—made their way to the first and second rows in the auditorium.

Once the dignitaries were seated and the audience settled down, Stevie Wonder continued his monologue. He spoke more about his mother and then moved on to the reason for his visit to Ghana. Wonder's visit was in large part to participate in Ghana's anniversary celebrations. He felt it his duty—"our duty as Black people," he said—to celebrate with Ghana. Wonder spoke of a global Blackness—a Blackness that was as authentic as it was originary. "All people are Africans," he continued, "just different shades of Black." He then affirmed Ghana's significance as the first independent country in Black Africa and as the pride of the Black world. He also heaped praise on Ghana's first president, Kwame Nkrumah, whose Pan-Africanism, Wonder insisted, had to be remembered. (At that moment, I swiftly looked around the auditorium to see if anyone else in the audience noticed the irony of Stevie Wonder extolling the virtues of Kwame Nkrumah at a screening of a documentary about one of his primary political and ideological adversaries, K. A. Busia.) When Wonder finished addressing the audience, he was led to the small keyboard that had been rolled onto the stage earlier in the evening. He sat down and performed a beautiful rendition of his "Love's in Need of Love Today," extending and changing the ending to a medley of songs that culminated with a funky rendition of "Happy Birthday, Ghana," the song he had written to commemorate the birthday of U.S. civil rights leader Martin Luther King Jr. The audience was enthralled by Wonder's surprise visit and rose to its feet in applause as the performance came to an end. Wonder was then led offstage, and soon after the documentary on K. A. Busia finally began.

Over the next two hours of the documentary, I thought about the contradictions of local politics highlighted by the official state endorsement of a celebration of the life of K. A. Busia at the same time that Ghana's fiftieth anniversary focused decided attention on Kwame Nkrumah, the country's founder and Busia's ideological and political rival. I also thought about the interwoven personal and public relationships that marked the production of the event. And I thought of the ways that the articulation of certain global histories within local culture and politics works to delimit—in remarkable ways—the vastly complex landscape that is modern Ghana. Let me demonstrate. Here was a documentary produced by the two daughters of Ghana's former prime minister, K. A. Busia. The two sisters actually have long personal and professional lives in the United States. Akosua Busia is in fact a U.S.-based actress most well known for starring opposite Whoopi Goldberg as Nettie in Steven Spielberg's *The Color Purple*, a popular film about the travails of post-emancipation African American life and culture. She also wrote the screenplay for the cinematic rendition of *Beloved*, Toni Morrison's award-winning novel about slavery in the United States. With a professional and personal life steeped in U.S. Black American culture and politics, many people—particularly those in the United States—may not be familiar with Busia's Ghanaian background. Stevie Wonder's presence at this event is due in part to his long-term friendship with Akosua Busia (who also cowrote one of his songs and has worked with him in other local endeavors). At the same time, Wonder has had a long presence in Ghana. Similar to many Afro-diasporic artists and intellectuals, he took up residence in the country in the mid-1990s, and he often makes appearances at cultural and fundraising events. Wonder's reputation for using his art to make political statements, and his unapologetic Afrocentrism, echoed the legacies of both African American cultural nationalism and continental (political) Pan-Africanism. Nevertheless, his praise of Nkrumah through what might seem a decidedly African diasporic lens in a space where audience members have widely varied histories and ideological commitments could be considered remarkably incongruous. At the same time, audience members included not only state and other officials, but also a number of other prominent individuals, including Nkrumah's own younger son, as well as members of the general population.

My own presence at this significant event was fortuitous. It was the result of my circulation among African-descended communities on both sides of the Atlantic. I am a Haitian-born, U.S.-based anthropologist who travels often to Ghana and in recent years primarily for research purposes. I was in Ghana in February and March 2007 to participate in the fiftieth-anniversary events as well as to conduct follow-up research for my ongoing investigation of the historical and contemporary contours of Ghanaian racial formation. I met Dr. Abena Busia earlier in 2007 at an academic conference in the United States. When she realized that we would both be in Ghana to attend the anniversary celebrations, Dr. Busia made sure to invite me to the premier of the screening of the documentary about her father's life. Because of Dr. Busia's generosity, which allowed me the opportunity to participate in this significant event as an honored guest, I was particularly well placed to witness and participate in this historic moment. The anniversary celebrations brought people from all over the world to Ghana, and some of the audience members whom I knew personally were from places as far flung as Asia and southern Africa, the Caribbean and North America. Indeed, the Busia screening, both in terms of its diverse audience and the intermeshing of African and diaspora personal and professional history and politics that it exhibited, provided a different way to explore modern Ghana.

But what exactly is the story to be told about this event? What makes this event significant?

Of course, there are many ways to read the event. We could, for example, focus on Stevie Wonder's Pan-Africanist message and, perhaps reading it through a conventional African diasporic theoretical lens, consider it both essentialist and an imposition on Ghana's cultural landscape. We could also take a general postcolonial Africanist approach by which Wonder's message is read as a naive misunderstanding of the local politics such that he did not much contemplate the complex position Nkrumah held in Ghanaian political and social history. Yet, Wonder's seemingly intermeshing of Ghana's ideological and political history fits right into the broader contradictions surrounding the modern Ghanaian state and the celebration of fifty years of independence. In light of the global import of this anniversary, the government, headed by the National Patriotic Party (NPP) at the time, had to negotiate its long history as ideological opponents of Nkrumah and his political descendants with Nkrumah's international popularity as the father, simultaneously, of Ghana, Pan-Africanism, African nationalism, and Africa-diasporic relations. State officials had to deal with this contradiction with contradictions of their own—linking J. A. Kufuor to Kwame Nkrumah, for example, and presenting the NPP as extending Nkrumah's Pan-Africanist message of continental and global Black liberation.

Yet, the NPP government was also looking to rehabilitate its party's image as one with a compromising history of complicity with the West against

Nkrumah's more staunchly radical stance. The official support for the Busia event fit perfectly into this often incongruous balancing act. The main storyline could therefore be about conventional renderings of the crisis of the state in postcolonial, neoliberal Africa. At the same time, this could be a story about empire and modern Ghana—indeed, Africa—in which the actions and policies of the state apparatus are apparently very much dictated by the country's marginalized position within the global political economy, and in which the global south in general and African nations in particular continue to exist under the stifling conditions of Western hegemonies. We could also use this framework of empire to explore the transnational power formations that allow for the presence of Lebanese/Europeans in Ghana as well as diaspora Blacks in the same space or, more importantly, that structure ongoing African-diasporic interactions.

My contention is that the various relationships and politics that emerge in the production of the Busia screening are about all of these things and more. What this book argues, however, is that they come together through the history and logic of European empire making and attendant global configurations of race and power. This is especially evident when we link Ghana's independence from British colonial rule to its lengthy history of the slave trade and slavery, to ongoing dialogue and interaction with diaspora Blacks, to the expressly transnational relations and cosmopolitanism structure of its urban centers. Within the local context of the celebration of this important legacy of independence, we can also find global configurations of race and Blackness—direct legacies of the transatlantic slave trade and colonialism—in which Ghana occupies a central role in African and diaspora politics and interaction. And Wonder's presence both at the film screening on Busia and in Ghana for its fiftieth anniversary of independence could not be more symbolic of the history of an active and continuous Afro-Atlantic dialogue. Through the wide-ranging and extremely complex web of relations emerging out of this history of empire and domination, dissemination and interaction, and conflict and dialogue, we see in Ghana—indeed, in Africa—a modern and active cosmopolitanism.

When we think about global processes of racialization, we have to realize that they are significant because they are historically relevant. It is the common race-inflected patterns that bind the flows of Afro-Atlantic movement and relations. The same patterns also shape Ghana's marginalized position in global political relations. In remapping race to reach contemporary continental Africa in order to acknowledge its modernity and coevality, we gain a true sense of postcolonial Ghana's (and Africa's) agency as well as its role as a crucial site, and partner, of diasporic circulation and contact.

And importantly, this question of race and racialization should also frame our understanding of the difficult geopolitical refashioning of Africa at the beginning of the twenty-first century. The "war on terror," the growing influence of BRIC[1] nations in the struggle over the continent's resources, the question of both "African mercenaries" in Libya and the lynching of Black Libyans during the NATO-led war to overthrow Muammar Gaddafi, the U.S. military encroachment through AFRICOM,[2] or the continent's position as the battleground of the Arab Spring—all of these events pivot on the axis and politics of race and power.

My primary goal in this ethnography of processes of racialization in Ghana was twofold: first, it was to (re)insert continental African communities within discussions of race (and racial identity formation) by historically establishing racialization as a global phenomenon that structures the lives of all who are racialized as Black; second, it was to use this sociohistorical reality of African processes of racialization to establish *both* the importance of interrogating race in anthropological studies of Africa *and* the relevance of including the experiences and practices of African communities within our conceptualization of the African diaspora. As I argued in the introduction to the book, this research was motivated in part by the inability of contemporary African diaspora theorization and Africanist anthropology to fully appreciate the sociohistorical reality of Black identity formation on the African continent and its articulations with global notions of Blackness. This limitation, I believe, stemmed from the epistemological failure to recognize the value in mutually interrogating African and diasporic realities. In chapter 7, I attempted to bring together the two major strands of the book's main argument—African diaspora studies' lack of concrete engagement with Africa and (Africanist) anthropology's lack of engagement with race. The effort is to offer a way to rethink Black identity formations and to acknowledge the important role of the legacy of European empire making in the analogous histories and experiences of African and diaspora populations. Consequently, I have argued that the bifurcation in our analysis of these populations—particularly in the ways that, individually, African studies and African diaspora studies often fail to capture their "interconnected particulars"—prevents us from understanding fully the form and content of Black identities, not only in the social and political uses to which such identities are put, but also in the broader global structures of racial formation through which these identities are continually reconstituted. We need to develop new research agendas in African studies, African diaspora studies, and anthropology—on both sides of the Atlantic.

# NOTES

PREFACE

1.  It was after developing and working with the term "racecraft" that I encountered Karen Field's essay: Karen E. Fields, "Witchcraft and Racecraft: Invisible Ontology in Its Sensible Manifestations," in *Witchcraft Dialogues: Anthropological and Philosophical Exchanges*, ed. G. C. Bond (Athens: Ohio University Center for International Studies, 2001), 283–315.

2.  "Black" and "White" are capitalized throughout this book to refer to specifically racialized groupings of people. For example, "Black," in this sense, is more than a simple descriptor (e.g., tall or wealthy): it denotes a set of historical, political, and sociohistorical processes of identity formation. Moreover, the use of the upper- and lowercases in racial terminology has a long history, as when the lowercase *n* was used for "Negro" as part of the construction of a presumably inferior racial being. See Harris 1993.

3.  Some notable exceptions are Holsey 2008; Moore 2005; and Shipley 2003.

INTRODUCTION

1.  The historical exception has been the scholarly debates around the "Blackness" of "classical" civilizations (Ben-Jochannan 1988; Bernal 1987, 1991, 2006; Diop 1974).

2.  This term generally means "stranger" and is usually deployed to describe "White" foreigners. See chapter 2 for a lengthy discussion and analysis.

3.  According to Charles Mills, global White supremacy refers to the "European domination of the planet that has left us with the racialized distributions of economic, political, and cultural power that we have today" (1998, 98). What is significant about this conception is the *racial* dimension of this international system of power, whereby those racialized as White were—and are—structurally advantaged over those racialized as non-White. This is the case whether or not such racialized Whites "are minority or majority, whether it was [in] a country belonging originally to whites or to [nonwhites]" (Walter Rodney quoted in Mills 1998, 99). It is therefore no accident that "third world nations" are "part of a global economy dominated by white capital and white international lending institutions, that the planet as a whole is dominated by cultural products of the white West" (Mills 1998, 102). Indeed, global White supremacy explains to us that racialized power is structurally White power. White

supremacy, at the same time, is not a particular *thing*; rather, it is a system that most often works with other systems of domination. Global White supremacy should also be understood as a "family of forms" with different articulations in different parts of the world, and evolving over time through the arrangement of varying racial projects—of labor, cultural and political representations, legal standings, etc.

4. A good reference for thinking about research in African history and pedagogy is Walter Rodney's "African History in the Service of Black Liberation" (2001).

5. While discussion in the book certainly points to instances of European colonial racism, it is not its focus.

6. Omi and Winant give the U.S. example of the affirmative action debate in which the neoconservatives advanced a "racial project" to interpret race as a morally invalid basis upon which to judge individuals and in which race was considered inconsequential to the working of U.S. identity. A counter "racial project" was advanced by liberals who focused on the ways that the United States historically deployed race in order to establish difference and structure inequality (1994). Though both of these racial projects are discourses vying for political position in the United States, they add to the broader terrain of racial formation, competing with other various projects of race in cultural representation, ideology, practices, interpretations, knowledge, production, etc.

7. David Goldberg has argued that Omi and Winant's formulation of racialization is overly structural and seems to imply that races simply emerge and the various ideologies and practices of racial groups somehow attain significance in political contestation and struggle (1993). He proposes instead that we expand the notion of racialization to consider its "subjective" component. Racialization, in this understanding, has two parts: "race creation" and "racial constitution." Race creation emerges out of the creations of "real" social actors who see and express themselves by means of an established set of discourses. These social "(self-)creations," writes Goldberg, "come as though given, fixed from on high, seemingly natural phenomena imposed almost unchangingly upon an innocent and so nonresponsible social order. . . . Race constitution complements race creation because it is "what gives one racial identity . . . what inscribes one racially in society and in the law and identifiably gives substance to one's social being" (1993, 83). It is a dialectic relationship between these two components of racialization. Race creation occurs through the ways that the individual (the social subject) conceives of herself and others. Yet, this social (self-)conception—that is, this racial self-conception (race creation)—is always mediated, if not quite cemented, by historical reality and the set of practices (and the values embedded in them) already existing in the social order (2). The individual/social understanding of the racial self, then, involves thinking of oneself in terms of the prevailing concepts, ideas, and practices of the sociohistorical order. In this way, there is a sense in which race is arbitrary, where there is a wide range of seemingly straightforward individual dispositions to characterize racially. At the same time, "in the conceptual and historical dialectic between self, other, and social constitution race may be overdetermined both in conception and (often) in application" (82–83). This is because, as Omi and Winant and others recognize, racial identity construction always occurs within a historical order and power—the transatlantic slave trade and colonialism. But to say that race is relatively "overdetermined" is not to deny its fluidity; it is to stress that, in this modern moment, the racial ideologies and significations that structure identities such as "Blackness," "White-

ness," "Asianness," etc., do so within a context whereby the prevailing paradigm (or "common sense" [Gramsci 1971]) of race ensures the continued existence of a racial hierarchy. Here, we see the convergence of Goldberg and Omi and Winant's formulations of racialization with Charles Mills's conception of global White supremacy: to be racialized—to be "Black" or "White" or "Asian"—in a world where White power is naturalized is to always be structured in hierarchical relation to that power.

8. I borrow this from Kwaku Larbi Korang's wonderful tome *Writing Ghana, Imagining Africa: Nation and African Modernity* (2003).

CHAPTER ONE

1. "The Survey of Different Treatment by Race in the Laws of British African Territories," an early 1950 draft of a survey of race relations in the colonies undertaken by the African Studies Branch of the Colonial Office (Ghana National Archives [GNA], Colonial Secretary's Office [CSO] 5/1/1309, August 1950).

2. In Uganda, for example, researchers find that "'native' means any person who is a member of or any one of [*sic*] whose parents is or was a member of an indigenous African tribe or community. The following are excluded: Arab, Abyssinian, Somali, Seychelleois, . . . Malagassy or Comoro Islander." In Kenya, the report continues, "native" is defined along similar lines but includes Swahilis while excluding "a person who is partly non-native descent if he does not conform with the customs and modes of any African tribe." The Kenya situation is further elaborated: in the "townships," a "'Native' means any native of Africa not being of European or Asiatic origin and includes any Swahili or Somali." At the same time, "'African' may be defined . . . as native of Africa not being of European or Asiatic origin . . . or . . . equated with 'Native' and defined positively as a member of the aboriginal tribes or races of Africa including any person having the blood of such tribe or race and living among and after the manner of such tribe or race" (GNA, CSO 5/1/1309, "Survey of Different Treatment by Race in the Laws of British African Territories," Colonial Office African Studies Branch, August 1950).

3. Historian Carina Ray has convincingly argued that no "single definition of 'native' was ever arrived at in the Gold Coast" and that "multiple definitions of 'native' were used in any given moment" (2007, 81). She then points to the evolving definitions, particularly where and when the "mixed-raced" or "mulatto" population was included. While she is correct in this assessment that there was no single definition for "native," what is significant is that "native" was always assumed to be Black and African, subject to "native" rules and tribunals, and variously positioned, racially, against Europeans, Asiatics, and sometimes "mulattos."

4. This shift in colonial policy in Africa was a sharp departure from its practice and experience in India (Lugard 1922; Mamdani 1999).

5. Thus, the definition of "native" in the research report from the Colonial Office was explicit in pointing out that the "normal meaning of 'Native' or 'African' is . . . a member of a . . . tribe or community who lives among and follows the customs of such community" (GNA, CSO 5/1/1309, "Survey of Different Treatment by Race in the Laws of British African Territories," Colonial Office African Studies Branch, August 1950).

6. Early educated Africans attempted to do this, however, in their need to vindicate precolonial African social structures (Casely Hayford 1903; Sarbah 1904; Danquah 1928).

7.   Here the customary power resided in the chiefs, who were often made into the only legitimate and organic group (as opposed to the earlier assimilated African elite). This was a shift from a multiple set of institutions to govern precolonial African societies to one institution of "administratively-appointed chiefs . . . whose interpretation of custom should hold sway over that of every other institution in 'tribal' society." Thus the daily violence of the colonial system was embedded in the "customary" native authority. As Mamdani stresses: "Custom became the language of force" (1999, 871).

8.   See Táíwò 2010 for an extensive philosophical discussion of Lugard's racism and the colonial preemption of African modernity.

9.   Carina Ray details the complex and contradictory processes of racial classification during this period in her dissertation, "Policing Sexual Boundaries: The Politics of Race in Colonial Ghana" (Cornell, 2007). She examines the peculiar case of the racial classification of West Indians in the colonial service at the time of the consolidation of colonial rule and formal Europeanization. The colonial service "organized officers into the category of European or Native, with job postings and attendant salary and benefits determined by this classification" (65). But this rule was never too fixed, as mixed-race colonial workers from the West Indies were often classified in the books as European. This inconsistent position forced the colonial administration to contend with differentiating a Euro-African—who was considered native—from a West Indian of African descent.

10.  The Arab presence is obviously an important aspect of Ghanaian racial formation, but one that I don't cover here (see Akyeampong 2006).

11.  Some scholars have used the reality of this type of rule to argue that "colonial rule was never experienced by the vast majority of the colonized as rule directly by others" (Mamdani 1999, 870; see also Boahen 1987).

12.  Mr. Proven (a pseudonym) is an elderly former civil servant who worked closely with Kwame Nkrumah. He was in his mid-nineties during this interview.

13.  Interview by J. Pierre, September 2005, Accra, Ghana.

14.  J. F. A. Ajayi asserts that the transatlantic slave trade, "with its ramifications in internal slavery and slave trade, provided the basic structure of pre-colonial African economies and thus became key to understanding African history" (Ajayi 2002, 2888).

15.  Kwaku Korang has argued that this "middle stratum of natives" owed its origin historically to "Europe's African civilizing mission as projected in the humanitarian ideology of African reform that followed Britain's early-nineteenth-century abolition of the slave trade" (2003, 36). A result of the ideological forces of this "civilizing mission," along with missionary and Western education, this group emerged, positioned "between the white man on the one side and [their] untutored brethren on the other side" (John Mensah Sarbah quoted in Korang 2003, 37). By the mid-nineteenth century, the missionary impulse had gained momentum: in addition to proselytizing among indigenous communities, and providing the converted with technical skills and education, it also changed the standard of living of such converts. The greatest impact of the missionaries was the further stratification of African societies into a relatively small Christian educated elite and a large group of non-converts (Boahen 1987).

16.  There were also the two waves of Afro-Brazilian emigrants who moved to the town of Accra in the 1830s and were quickly absorbed into the local elite community mainly as merchants (see Gocking 1999).

17. See Carina Ray's fascinating cases of light-skinned West Indians in the British colonial service in West Africa (2007).
18. Cecil Trevor's 1951 report on banking practices in the colony observed that the system favored "European, Levantine and Asiatic communities to the detriment of the African"; available at http://www.ghanadistricts.com/home/?_=49&sa=4768&ssa=809.
19. Memorandum from the director of medical services to the colonial secretary (GNA, CSO 5/1/566, deputy director of health services, "Rules for Residents in Residential Areas of the Gold Coast," April 7, 1937).
20. Ibid. Also, in the 1939 "Rules for Residents in the Residential Areas," the director of medical services supported his claim of the "necessity for the living of Europeans in residential areas" by pointing to the last outbreak of yellow fever in Accra in 1937, when the "total European population was evacuated from the town," and he concluded that "Everything possible should be done to preserve the integrity of the residential areas" (GNA, CSO 11/3/15, deputy director of health services, "Rule No. 1 of the Rules for Residents in Residential Areas," January 30, 1939).
21. This was clearly a seemingly major problem for colonial health officials. In a letter addressed to the deputy director of health services, the director of medical service writes of "nuisances" caused by servants of colonial officials when such officials are on leave. He was expressly concerned by this practice because "Sometimes nuisances arise due to lack of control over these 'masterless' servants. It is not unknown for them to bring in 'brothers' and friends (of both sexes) and sometimes children and give them accommodation when sanitary overcrowding may result. Not infrequently, refuse is promiscuously disposed of particularly as the women tend to set-up small trading concerns for the supply of neighboring house servants; and as is well known, it requires little refuse lying about to increase the fly population in the vicinity of the nuisance" (GNA, CSO 2593/62/1933, Medical Department, "Nuisances Occurring in Compounds of Officials When on Leave Whose Servants Have Been Allowed to Continue Living in the Servants Quarters," August 24, 1936).
22. GNA, CSO 5/1/566, deputy director of health services, "African Children Living in European Bungalows in Residential Areas," October 30, 1933. In the directive, the Gold Coast's deputy director of health services forcefully argued that "such harboring of African children in European bungalows in Residential areas is one fraught with the gravest possibilities. . . . People, wishing to adopt African children, should live outside Residential Areas; and if the practice of accommodating such children is to be permitted the value of the Residential Area ceases."
23. Booker T. Washington, an African American scholar and activist, is known for his advocacy of technical education for Blacks. Because of U.S. racism and segregation, he founded Tuskegee Normal and Industrial Institute; the school supported his philosophy of Black self-help and vocational training. Washington's education philosophy was extremely popular among U.S. and European liberals and conservatives. And the British colonial administration sought to operationalize his philosophy of industrial education for Blacks in their African colonies (see Marable 1974; Lugard 1922, 444–54).
24. For example, in his presidential address to the National Congress of British West Africa delegates, Thomas Hutton-Mills explained: "It is important to note that each one of these Delegates is an *African* belong to a *Distinctive African Family* and thereby commanding the right of property and other interests either in his own right or in the right of the family to which he belongs" (quoted in Crowder 1968, 406).

CHAPTER TWO

1. This is the abbreviated name for the Pan-African Historical Theatre Festival, a state-sponsored biennial celebration. I discuss PANAFEST in great detail in chapter 5.

2. This is perhaps one of Nkrumah's most referenced statements. The full statement reads: "Seek ye first the political kingdom and all other things shall be added unto you" (Nkrumah 1957, 164).

3. Ghana's "Big Six" refer to the six leaders of the United Gold Coast Convention (UGCC), the leading political party in the colony. Colonial authorities detained the Big Six following the 1948 Accra riots (the riots resulted from the colonial government's repressive response to a peaceful march by ex-servicemen to recover compensation for their service to the British army). The colonial government held the UGCC leaders responsible for the riots. The six were: Ebenezer Ako-Adjei, Edward Akufo-Addo, J. B. Danquah, Kwame Nkrumah, Emmanuel Obetsebi-Lamptey, and William Ofori Atta.

4. The NPP is linked to the United Party (UP), which was founded by K. A. Busia in opposition to Nkrumah.

5. DuBois conceived of a twenty-volume inter-African project that would offer Africa the "opportunity to reveal the genius of her people, their history, culture and institutions" (Afari-Gyan 1991, 7). For years he tried to get the project funded in the United States without much success.

6. Afari-Gyan also argues that both Nkrumah and Padmore felt that the civil servants in Ghana's Foreign Affairs Ministry did not have "an adequate sense of urgency" about African emancipation and did not "interpret his [Nkrumah's] African policies with his own vigor and vision" (1991, 4).

7. The name was later changed to the State Shipping Line. I have not been able to find information on the date of or reason for the change.

8. This was converted from Padmore's Office of African Affairs.

9. C. L. R. James argues that Nkrumah (and other anticolonial Africans) had no choice but to enter government and negotiate with the British for independence. One of the main reasons is that, regardless of the power of mass protest, "there remained looking over everything the immense military power of the British government which it would use if it were pushed to desperation" (1977, 152). It was a risk that Nkrumah was not prepared to take.

10. Callaway and Card argue that "Nkrumah's choice was difficult: without the cooperation of the British he could not have come to power unless he was willing to resort to a prolonged armed struggle. . . . From Nkrumah's point of view, the other options were limited. Organizing for revolutionary struggle in the face of British opposition was extremely difficult. If potential support for armed elimination of the British from Ghana existed, the British undercut it through their strategy of supporting the major nationalist demands" (1971, 66).

11. Through the establishment of a state marketing board, the colonial government had extracted surplus reserves from cocoa farmers by paying them less than market value for their product. The logic was that the surplus would be held in reserve for farmers in the Gold Coast in the event of a downturn in the economy.

12. It is important here to point out that both during the formal colonial period and afterward, the Ghanaian cocoa revenue supported the British economy. Callaway and Card argue that while it is "always assumed that Britain played a major role in the economic advancement of Ghana," it is "rather that Ghana has made substantial investment in Britain through the holding there of most of her reserves" (1971, 75).

This continued in the early independence era as well, when "cocoa surplus continued to accumulate in British banks on the advice of colonial officials who argued that it created the stability necessary to woo investors" (Marshall 1976, 51).

13. In fact, the continuous brushes of newly minted African diplomats with U.S. racism were one of the reasons for the federal government's push to dismantle segregation laws (Romano 2000).

14. A good deal of this narrative comes from "Black Power," episode five of the 1992 BBC series *Pandora's Box* (Curtis 1992).

15. By the time the project was completed in February 1966, a drop in worldwide cocoa prices revealed the weakness of Ghana's inherited colonial economy, and the new country's economic dependence was solidified. Kaiser became one of the more profitable aluminum-smelting companies in the world, and Nkrumah's government fell out of power.

16. The full speech can be found at: http://ghana-net.com/Kwame_Nkrumah_speech _at_the_formal_inauguration_of_the_Volta_River_Dam.aspx.

17. In fact, while Handley argues that the initial impulse of the newly independent CPP government was to "squash" local African private business, Akinsanya has a more measured reading. He describes the government's policy on indigenous firms as "passive" because there was no legislation passed either to limit the roles of foreigners in the economic realm or to reserve business for local entrepreneurs (1982, 19).

18. Nkrumah was not shy about articulating his view that the CPP *was* the state. At a rally in 1959, he told his audience: "I want it to be firmly understood that it is the Convention People's Party which makes the Government and not the Government which makes the Convention People's Party and we intend to give public acknowledgement to this fact by raising the prestige of our Party to its proper status in our national structure" (quoted in Austin 1964, 382).

19. This is not to be confused with the later National Patriotic Party.

20. Interview with John Stockwell on "Black Power," episode five of the BBC series *Pandora's Box* (Curtis 1992).

21. To install a ruler (chief or king) onto a throne is to "enstool" him. This is in opposition to "destooling."

22. Judith Marshall demonstrates how in the decade after Nkrumah's fall, "All attempts to decolonize the state came to an abrupt halt. There was a real willingness to construct the steady state desired by the international bourgeoisie, right from the resident Harvard economic advisory team on the Political Committee, made up of old opposition elements like Kofi Busia, who in 1962 had testified before a US Senate subcommittee that Ghana was the centre of subversive Communist activities throughout West Africa. The Economic Committee included technocrats from companies like Mobil, freshly trained at American institutions and ready to do service for international capital" (1976, 55–56).

23. China is now a major presence on the African continent, though its influence is not yet fully measurable.

CHAPTER THREE

1. I say "presumably" here because I am not completely sure of his national background. Accra's population comprises Africans from all over the continent, as well as Black people from the Western Hemisphere. Therefore, a Black person in Accra is not necessarily Ghanaian.

2. This is a pseudonym.

3.  At the same time, a nonrich White can cause shock and disappointment, and her situation *demands* explanation.

4.  Ghanaian immigration officials told me that the government stopped collecting racial and ethnic data a long time ago. One official surmised that this may have been a way to minimize differentiation by what many saw as tribalism. Thus, we can only estimate at the number of White and other groups in Ghana based on the category of "foreign-born." But these include people from other parts of the African continent, Asians, and Indians, as well as Whites.

5.  In a parenthesis within this sentence, the author writes, "let's leave Asians out of this." This is an interesting aside, and it points to the racial and cultural diversity of modern urban centers. As I pointed out in chapter 1, one main consequence of colonialism on the African continent (and throughout the diaspora) was the establishment of a "middle" group made up of Lebanese and Asian populations.

6.  The respondents were from a range of ethnic, religious, educational, professional, and class backgrounds. The survey was conducted randomly by a group of young Ghanaian researchers who occasionally had to use other languages with the respondents. The most prominent languages after English were Twi or Fante and Ga.

7.  This coffee shop has since shut down.

8.  I would also argue that those of us patronizing such "White" spaces become, in a sense, "honorary Whites."

9.  Many interviews and discussions in this section of the chapter were with Ghanaians who had opportunity for direct access to Whites. This is a particular group of students and professionals, many of whom are from the middle class. My argument remains that most people outside of these groups have no direct, individual access to White people.

10. *Tro-tros* are minivans that are used as vehicles for public transportation. They are the cheapest way to travel throughout the country and are mostly used by the working poor.

11. The scholarship on middle-class or wealthy Ghanaians (or other Africans) often works, however unwittingly, from the assumption that Black/African wealth is neither natural nor deserved. Hence all the references to this very heterogeneous class of people as homogeneously "elite." This speaks volumes about the ways that White wealth is considered natural while Black wealth is considered not only suspect, but also unnatural.

12. At the time, in the summer of 2000, Paul said that the official salary for his position as an engineer was US$400 per month. The British electrician earned about US$4,000, in addition to the added benefits, allowances, and payments given to expatriates who agree to work in Ghana.

13. African Americans are often easy to detect in Accra by their physical appearance (manner of dress, usually lighter skin color) and their U.S. accents.

14. This study documents the history of the concert party. What is significant about it is that this party has its origins in the series of minstrelsy shows brought over to West Africa by the colonial government. Thus images of minstrels became a key site of early Ghanaian understanding of African Americans.

CHAPTER FOUR

Sections of this chapter were previously published in Pierre 2008.

1.  Asia experiences an especially virulent skin-bleaching epidemic. Places such as India, Korea, and Malaysia are the highest-grossing sites for pharmaceutical and cosmetic companies selling skin-bleaching creams. L'Oréal's Fair and Lovely cream—which

the company claims drastically whitens skin in a short period—continues to be most popular in that region.

2. Particularly in Akan chieftaincy, "queenmother" denotes a paramount queen, a queen, or a subqueen. This woman is not necessarily the mother of a respective king or chief, but a queenmother sometimes shares equal power with the reigning monarch.

3. Yet, where the intraracial color line was drawn depended on individual social/national contexts (i.e., how light one had to be to be considered white depended on the social norms of a given society affected by slavery-colonialism).

4. Note that very little work on this topic has been done on Africa.

5. Jerry John Rawlings, former dictator and later president of Ghana, who ruled for nearly twenty years, has a Scottish father and a Ghanaian mother. During his first presidential run, he conducted a highly publicized trip to Scotland to search for his unknown father.

CHAPTER FIVE

1. http://www.touringghana.com/emancipation.asp (accessed July 12, 2011).

2. Frederick Worsemao Armah Blay, popularly called Freddie Blay, is a lawyer and politician who served as first deputy speaker in the Fourth Parliament of Ghana representing the Convention People's Party (CPP). He has recently switched his party affiliation to the NPP, a move that raised the ire of CPP members. They have called him a traitor and not a true "Nkrumahist" (http://politics.myjoyonline.com/pages/news/201104/64832.php).

3. From my notes, taken August 22, 2005.

4. Benin, Senegal, and Guinea also remember the slave trade, but only Ghana has an official Emancipation Day celebration in Africa.

5. This chapter is *purposefully* not about the dynamics and politics of heritage tourism as an activity. Much work has been done on this subject—especially since worldwide tourist activity is exploding. There has also been a growth in the scholarship on African American tourists to Ghana. However, this chapter is concerned with the ways that various state-sponsored actions and events (in the broad context of heritage tourism) are structured by, while they also structure, processes of racialization.

6. Here, I understand the "state" to be not an undifferentiated and knowing entity, but a set of projects and practices that, though fractured and contradictory and mediated by various actors and institutions, nevertheless work in more or less a coherent manner to promote official narratives of memory and national identity (Goldberg 2002, 6–8).

7. Rita Marley is the wife of Bob Marley. She has lived in and out of Ghana since the death of her husband. She maintains a residence in Konkonuru, a town located about an hour outside of Accra.

8. This movement was certainly inspired by the earlier arts-centered Pan-African festivals: the World Festival of Black Arts (FESMAN) in 1966 in Senegal, and the second World Black and African Festival of Arts and Culture (FESTAC) in Nigeria in 1977.

9. At the time, Dr. Sutherland was married to an African American activist, William Sutherland, who was living in Ghana in the early 1950s and who established a secondary school in the eastern region of the country. Incidentally, William Sutherland was the secretary for Nkrumah's finance minister, Gbedemah (see chapter 2).

10. http://www.panafestghana.org (accessed July 12, 2002).

11. Jamaica had only just returned to celebrating Emancipation Day (see Thomas 2005 for a full discussion).

12. See Holsey 2008 for a detailed background to this story.

13. Emancipation Day is still an annual holiday, and it is combined with PANAFEST every two years.

14. Of course this strategy has many pitfalls, as many observers have noted. One of the significant critiques of the contemporary heritage-tourism movement argues that "enhanced tourist revenues tend to flow out of African countries because multinational corporations usually own the hotels, airlines, and resorts that generate the most tourist money" (Day 2004, 102).

15. Europeans built some eighty forts in Ghana, including the three largest former slave-trading castle-dungeons—Elmina, Cape Coast, and Christianborg. About thirty of them are still standing.

16. The ministry was renamed Ministry of Tourism in 2009 when a new government was elected.

17. The "Joseph Project" uses the biblical story of Joseph to express the relationship between Africa and its diaspora. According to this story, Joseph, the eleventh son of Jacob, was sold into slavery by his jealous brothers. But he rose to become the most powerful man in Egypt after Pharaoh. He would later use his position to help save his family during a time of extreme famine. In adopting this story as a metaphor, Ghanaian officials problematically accept culpability in the slave trade, painting themselves as the jealous brothers and diaspora Blacks as the favored and redeemed saviors.

18. This is a pseudonym.

19. http://www.panafestghana.org (accessed February 10, 2004).

20. Ghana experienced six changes of government in twelve years.

21. This positioning fluctuates. Most recently, tourism was listed as the fourth-highest foreign-exchange earner for the country.

22. Rawlings's relationship with these advisors was often a contentious one, especially after he decided to fully embrace neoliberal economic policies.

23. This is the way Bridgette Katchu described these early Pan-Africanist leaders during her opening speech at the PANAFEST/Emancipation Day wreath-laying ceremony on July 25, 2005.

24. Out of the many castles in Ghana, the two main castles as those at Elmina and Cape Coast. The various ceremonies alternated between the two.

25. I could not tell if most people (at least local spectators) understood that this was what these men were trying to portray. Moreover, I could not tell whether most of the audience actually saw these young men, since the stage area, like the courtyard, was rather dark except for the various points where the floodlights hit those who were speaking.

26. It was difficult to hear the entire conversation above the various other distractions, such as the continuing arrival of dignitaries and altercations between security detail and local audience members. The four men's conversation was difficult to hear also because they were all sharing one microphone, having to move it around from speaker to speaker.

27. Leonard Jeffries is an African American scholar and activist who is known throughout the world as an advocate of Afrocentricity. He has often had a part in planning the PANAFEST activities.

28. This is an addition to the *akwaaba* (welcome) greeting often heard in Ghana. However, it seems that the officials were concerned particularly by the fact that many diaspora Blacks, particularly African Americans, complained that the locals were also

calling them *obruni* (meaning "White" and/or "foreigner [see chapter 3 for a lengthier discussion]). To change this embarrassing phenomenon, which could also potentially affect tourism, the ministry went on the offensive and began this program of teaching Ghanaians to address this group as "brothers and sisters."

29. The miniseries is based on Alex Haley's *Roots: The Saga of an American Family*. Haley said that the book was based on the history of his family from its capture in Gambia to enslavement in Maryland. *Roots* claimed "the highest ratings record for an entertainment program" in 1977 and has only been surpassed by *M\*A\*S\*H* in 1983 (Holsey 2004). It also won nine Emmy Awards. Some argue that the movie *Roots* brought the history of slavery to the forefront of U.S. national consciousness for the first time.

30. The theme remains the same throughout the years, while the subtheme changes every year.

31. Ferguson was a Ghanaian missionary, surveyor, and cartographer who worked for British colonial powers to establish treaties with various ethnic groups in the northern territories of the Gold Coast. He was purportedly killed by one of those groups, the Samori, in "his endeavor to abolish slavery" (Asomaning 2005), though that remains a point of contention (http://www.ghanaweb.com/GhanaHomePage/ entertainment/artikel.php?ID=86471).

CHAPTER SIX

1. The group's website address is: http://www.aaprp-intl.org/index.html.

2. This 1973 film was based on the novel by the same title written by Sam Greenlee (1969). It is both a satire of the civil rights movement and a serious attempt to focus on Black militancy. The protagonist is a Black man who enlists in the CIA (in its elitist program as its "token Black person"), masters the agency's tactics, and uses them to lead up a group of freedom fighters against the establishment.

3. http://socialjustice.ccnmtl.columbia.edu/index.php/All-African_People's _Revolutionary_Party.

4. The group's literature lists the ideology of Nkrumahism-Touréism as: (1) the primacy of Africa, (2) the integrity of the revolutionary african Personality, (3) humanism, egalitarianism, and collectivism, (4) dialectical and historical materialism, (5) harmony of revolution and religion/spirituality, (6) necessity of mass, permanent political education, organization, and action, and (6) revolutionary ideology as the greatest asset.

5. Both journalistic and scholarly work on this subject singularly focuses on African Americans, as if they are the only group to travel to Ghana. Furthermore, African Americans, as a group, are often undifferentiated in the literature.

6. The experience of this group is often elided because it is seen as less important or "authentic" than others. Yet, it is this very network that also opens up the space for my own movement and engagement with Black communities on both sides of the Atlantic.

7. Ato Ashun, *Elmina: The Castle and the Slave Trade* (Elimina, Ghana: Nyakod Printing Works, 2004).

8. This term is interpreted as "Let it be so." It is usually used in spiritual ceremonies among some people of African descent, and it signals either salutation or agreement with what is being said. According to a number of sources in the United States, the term is Yoruba. I thank Drs. Rheeda Walker and Ezemenari Obasi for the clarification.

9. See http://www.firstfridaysaccra.com (accessed December 10, 2006; site discontinued).
10. Ibid. (accessed July 10, 2008).
11. First Fridays is not a national organization; organizers in each city host individual networking events for local professionals.
12. As I have noted, the foreign-born population in Ghana comprises various groupings and networks. Some of these networks overlap, while others do not. Significantly, the large group of White expatriates in contemporary Ghana (particularly business and aid professionals) seems to be the most distant from local life.
13. First Fridays Accra has also influenced the formation of similar networking events outside of Ghana. There is now, for example, a First Fridays Liberia.

CHAPTER SEVEN

1. Some of the scholars who benefited from this shift were Melville Herskovits, Phillip Curtain, and Jan Vansina (see Martin and West 1999).
2. The most prominent of the foundations supporting African studies is the Ford Foundation.
3. This is not to say, of course, that there wasn't a presence of Continental African scholarship prior to the postcolonial period. It just means that earlier Continental scholars worked within a different tradition—one more aligned with the Transcontinental one because of its overwhelmingly "vindicationist" leanings (see chapters 4 and 5 for this tradition).
4. An example is CODESRIA, which is the Council for the Development of Social Science Research in Africa based in Dakar, Senegal.
5. See especially Drake 1982.
6. Von Eschen 1997 argues that the 1940s were a time when Black scholars and activists attempted to influence U.S. domestic and foreign policy—especially with regard to the colonial question during the formation of the UN.
7. This group epitomized Martin and West's categorization of a Transcontinental tradition: its members were part of a broad international network of likeminded intellectuals and activists concerned with political liberation of Africans and other colonized peoples, and it included key figures such as Paul Robeson and W. E. B. DuBois.
8. Incidentally, members of the Council on African Affairs had reached out to Nkrumah while he was a student in the United States. He became a close associate of Paul Robeson.
9. Von Eschen describes the rightward turn of the CAA's founder, Max Yergan. He purportedly later worked for the FBI against CAA. Yergan's split from the CAA signaled the moderation of Black politics at the time.
10. This was the case even in the socialist shift in many independent African nations.
11. Similar to other North American anthropologists, Herskovits began by studying Native Americans. Only later would he would turn to Africans and diaspora Blacks.
12. See Pierre 2006 for a detailed discussion of this shift and what it means for the status of race, culture, and ethnography in the contemporary anthropological study of Africa.
13. Disciplinary historians usually separate the various Western social science traditions, particularly when it comes to the study of Africans and other non-Whites. I argue that there was symmetry and cooperation among scholars responsible for this split. In terms of thinking through cultural relativism and attendant assumptions of bounded cultures, there existed similar traditions in Europe: the French tradition focused on

culture as a "total social fact," and the British saw it as "social structure" (Amselle 1990).

14. This is not exhaustive.

15. Along with this comes the critique that any focus on literate or even middle-class Africans means that one is only focused on African "elites." The implication, of course, is that "literate Africa is not where Africa is authentically" (Korang 2003, 48).

16. Appiah's book *In My Father's House* (1992) received the Herskovits Award from the African Studies Association.

EPILOGUE

1. BRIC is an acronym for the economies of Brazil, Russia, India, and China. The term was first used in an economic report that speculated that by 2050, these four countries would be wealthier than today's major economic powers. Some analysts expect that China and India will be the dominant suppliers of manufactured goods, while Brazil and Russia will be dominant suppliers of raw materials. As such, these four economies have the potential to form a powerful economic bloc.

2. AFRICOM is an abbreviation for the United States Africa Command. It is responsible for U.S. military operations in Africa and the Middle East, and it began to play an increasingly important role in the militarization of the U.S. "war on terror" campaigns on the African continent.

REFERENCES

Adesamni, Pius. 2008. "Going to Meet Black America." *Zeleza Post*, April 29. http://www
.zeleza.com/blogging/u-s-affairs/going-meet-black-america.
Adi, Hakim. 1998. *West Africans in Britain, 1900–1960: Nationalism, Pan-Africanism, and
Communism.* London: Lawrence & Wishart.
Afari-Gyan, Kwame. 1991. "Kwame Nkrumah, George Padmore and Web DuBois." *Insti-
tute of African Studies Research Review* 7: 1–2.
Aidoo, Ama Ata. 1997. *The Girl Who Can and Other Stories.* Accra: Sub-Saharan Publishers.
Ajayi, J. F. Ade. 2002. *Unfinished Business: Confronting the Legacies of Slavery and Colonialism
in Africa.* Amsterdam: Sephis.
Akinsanya, Adeoye A. 1982. *Economic Independence and Indigenisation of Private Foreign Invest-
ments: The Experiences of Nigeria and Ghana.* Columbia: University of South Carolina.
Akosa, Agyeman. "Skin Bleaching." Accessed September 20, 2011. http://www.ghana
healthservice.org/healthcare.php?nd=11&tt=Skin%20Bleaching.
Akyeampong, Emmanuel K. 2006. "Race, Identity and Citizenship in Black Africa: The
Case of the Lebanese in Ghana." *Africa: Journal of the International African Institute* 76
(3): 297–323.
Alcoff, L. M. 1999. "Towards a phenomenology of racial embodiment." *Radical Philosophy*
95 (May–June): 15–26.
Althusser, Louis. 1971. "Ideology and Ideological State Apparatuses." In *Lenin and Philoso-
phy and Other Essays*, 127–88. New York: Monthly Review Press.
Amory, Deborah. 1997. "African Studies as American Institution." In *Anthropological Lo-
cations: Boundaries and Grounds of a Field Science*, edited by Akhil Gupta and James
Ferguson, 102–16. Berkeley: University of California Press.
Amselle, Jean-Loup. 1990. *Mestizo Logics: Anthropology of Identity in Africa and Elsewhere.*
Stanford, CA: Stanford University Press.
———. 2003. "Africa: A Theme(s) Park." *Anthropoetics* 9 (1).
Angelou, Maya. 1986. *All of God's Children Need Traveling Shoes.* New York: Vintage
Books.
Anin, T. E. 1991. *Essays on the Political Economy of Ghana.* Accra: Selwyn Publishers.
Ankomah, Baffour. 2006. "Nkrumah: 'We Must Unite Now or Perish.'" *New African*,
February.
Appiah, Kwame A. 1992. *In My Father's House: Africa in the Philosophy of Culture.* New York:
Oxford University Press.

Apter, Andrew. 1996. "The Pan-African Nation: Oil-Money and the Spectacle of Culture in Nigeria." *Public Culture* 8 (3): 441–66.

Apter, David E. 1972. *Ghana in Transition, Uniform Title: Gold Coast in Transition.* 2nd rev. ed. Princeton, NJ: Princeton University Press.

Asante, Molefi. 1988. *Afrocentricity.* Trenton, NJ: Africa World Press.

———. 1994. "Afrocentricity, Race, and Reason." *Race and Reason* 1 (1): 20–22.

Ashforth, Adam. 2005. *Witchcraft, Violence, and Democracy in South Africa.* Chicago: University of Chicago Press.

Asomaning, Hannah. 2005. "Understanding Emancipation/PANAFEST." *Ghana Web,* July 23. http://www.ghanaweb.com/GhanaHomePage/entertainment/artikel.php?ID=86471.

Austin, Dennis. 1970. *Politics in Ghana: 1946–1960.* London: Oxford University Press.

Awoonor, Kofi Nyidevu. 1994. *Africa: The Marginalized Continent.* Accra: Woeli Publishing Services.

Baker, Lee D. 1998. *From Savage to Negro: Anthropology and the Construction of Race.* Berkeley: University of California Press.

Barnard, Alan. 2001. "Africa and the Anthropologist." *Africa: Journal of the International African Institute* 71 (1): 162–70.

Bashi, Vilna. 1998. "Racial Categories Matter Because Racial Hierarchies Matter: A Commentary." *Ethnic and Racial Studies* 20 (5): 959–68.

Bastide, Roger. 1978. *The African Religions of Brazil: Toward a Sociology of the Interpenetration of Civilizations.* Baltimore: Johns Hopkins University Press.

BBC News. 2007. "Skin Bleaching Cream Couple Fined." January 4, accessed August 2008. http://news.bbc.co.uk/2/hi/uk_news/england/london/6232343.stm.

Ben-Jochannan, Yosef. 1988. *Africa: Mother of Western Civilization.* Baltimore: Black Classic Press.

Bernal, Martin. 1987. *Black Athena: The Afroasiatic Roots of Classical Civilization.* Volume 1, *The Fabrication of Ancient Greece, 1787–1985.* Newark, NJ: Rutgers University Press.

———. 1991. *Black Athena: The Afroasiatic Roots of Classical Civilization.* Volume 2, *The Archaeology and Documentary Evidence.* Newark, NJ: Rutgers University Press.

———. 2006. *Black Athena: The Afroasiatic Roots of Classical Civilization.* Volume 3, *The Linguistic Evidence.* Newark, NJ: Rutgers University Press.

Bing, Geoffrey. 1968. *Reap the Whirlwind: An Account of Kwame Nkrumah's Ghana from 1950 to 1966.* London: MacGibbon and Kee.

Blyden, Edward W. 1862. *Liberia's Offering.* New York: John Gray.

Boafo-Arthur, Kwame. 1999. "Ghana: Structural Adjustment, Democratization, and the Politics of Continuity." *African Studies Review* 42 (2): 41–72.

———. 2007. "A Decade of Liberalism in Perspective." In *Ghana: One Decade of the Liberal State,* edited by Kwame Boafo-Arthur, 1–20. Dakar: CODESRIA Books.

Boahen, A. A. 1987. *African Perspectives on Colonialism.* Baltimore: Johns Hopkins University Press.

Boateng, Daasebre Oti. 2009. *Barack Obama: Africa's Gift to the World.* Ghana: D. O. Boateng.

Boddy, Janice P. 1989. *Wombs and Alien Spirits: Women, Men, and the Zār Cult in Northern Sudan.* Madison: University of Wisconsin Press.

Bonnett, A. W., and G. L. Watson. 1990. *Emerging Perspectives on the Black Diaspora.* New York: University Press of America.

Bourdieu, Pierre. 1977. *Outline of a Theory of Practice.* Translated by Richard Nice. Cambridge: Cambridge University Press.

Brempong, Nana Arhin. 2006. "Chieftancy: An Overview." In *Chieftaincy in Ghana: Cul-*

*ture, Governance and Development,* edited by Irene K. Odotei and A. K. Awedoba. Accra: Sub-Saharan Publishers.

Brewin, C. R. 1989. "Cognitive Change Processes in Psychotherapy." *Psychological Review* 96 (3): 379.

Brown, Jacqueline Nassy. 1996. "Black Liverpool, Black America, and the Gendering of Diasporic Space." *Cultural Anthropology* 13 (3): 291–325.

Bruner, Edward. 1996. "Tourism in Ghana: The Representation of Slavery and the Return of the Black Diaspora." *American Anthropologist* 98:290–304.

Buah, F. K. 1980. *A History of Ghana.* London: Macmillan.

Burke, Timothy. 1996. *Lifebuoy Men, Lux Women: Commodification, Consumption, and Cleanliness in Modern Zimbabwe.* Durham, NC: Duke University Press.

Bush, Barbara. 1999. *Imperialism, Race and Resistance: Africa and Britain, 1919–1945.* London: Routledge.

Callaway, Barbara, and Emily Card. 1971. "Political Constraints on Economic Development in Ghana." In *The State of the Nations: Constraints on Development in Independent Africa,* edited by Michael F. Lofchie. Berkeley: University of California Press.

Campbell, Horace. 1999. "Low-Intensity Warfare and the Study of Africans at Home and Abroad." In *Out of One, Many Africas: Reconstructing the Study and Meaning of Africa,* edited by William G. Martin and Michael O. West. Champaign: University of Illinois Press.

Carson, Sonny. 1999. "Emancipation Day in Ghana." *New York Daily Challenge,* July 13.

Casely Hayford, John Ephraim, and Fanti Confederation. 1903. *Gold Coast Native Institutions: With Thoughts upon a Healthy Imperial Policy for the Gold Coast and Ashanti.* London: Sweet and Maxwell, Ltd.

Charles, Christopher. 2003. "Skin Bleaching, Self-Hate, and Black Identity in Jamaica." *Journal of Black Studies* 33 (6): 711–28.

Chisholm, Jamiyla. 2002. "Fade to White: Skin Bleaching and the Rejection of Blackness." *Village Voice,* January 22. http://www.villagevoice.com/2002-01-22/news/fade-to-white/.

Chrisman, Laura. 1997. "Journeying to Death: Gilroy's 'Black Atlantic.'" *Race & Class* 39 (2): 51–64.

———. 2003. *Postcolonial Contraventions: Cultural Readings of Race, Imperialism and Transnationalism.* Manchester: Manchester University Press.

Codjoe, Frank K. 1988. *Elites, Ideology, and Development Problems of Ghana.* Ammersbek: Verlag an der Lottbek.

Cole, Catherine. 1996. "Reading Blackface in West Africa: Wonders Taken for Signs." *Critical Inquiry* 23 (1): 183–215.

———. 2001a. *Ghana's Concert Party Theatre.* Bloomington: Indiana University Press.

———. 2001b. Reviews of *Africans on Stage: Studies in Ethnological Show Business,* edited by Bernth Lindfors, and *The Drama of South Africa: Plays, Pageants and Publics since 1910,* by Loren Kruger. *Theatre Journal* 53 (1): 179–81.

Comaroff, John L., and Jean Comaroff. 1992. "Of Totemism and Ethnicity." In *Ethnography and the Historical Imagination,* 49–68. Boulder, CO: Westview Press.

Crewe, Emma, and Priyanthi Fernando. 2006. "The Elephant in the Room: Racism in Representations, Relationships and Rituals." *Progress in Development Studies* 6 (1): 40–54.

Crowder, Michael. 1964. "Indirect Rule: French and British Style." *Africa: Journal of the International African Institute* 34 (3): 197–205.

———. 1968. *West Africa under Colonial Rule.* Evanston, IL: Northwestern University Press.

Curtis, Adam. 1992. "Black Power." Season 1, episode 5 of *Pandora's Box: A Fable from the Age of Science*. Directed by Adam Curtis. London: BBC.

Daabu, Malik Abass. 2010. "People in Oil Producing Towns Expect Mixed Race Babies." *Modern Ghana*, March 10. http://www.modernghana.com/news/267040/1/people-in-oil-producing-towns-expect-mixed-race-ba.html.

*Daily Guide*. 2010. "Hundreds Troop to Ghana to Celebrate Nkrumah!" May 19.

Danquah, Joseph B. 1928. *Gold Coast: Akan Laws and Customs and the Akim Abuakwa Constitution*. London: Routledge.

Davidson, Basil. 1992. *The Black Man's Burden: Africa and the Curse of the Nation-State*. New York: Times Books.

Day, Lynda R. 2004. "What's Tourism Got to Do with It?: The Yaa Asantewa Legacy and Development in Asanteman." *Africa Today* 51 (1): 99–113.

Decker, Stephanie. 2010. "Postcolonial Transitions in Africa: Decolonization in West Africa and Present Day South Africa." *Journal of Management Studies* 47 (5): 791–813.

DeCorse, Christopher R. 2001. *An Archaeology of Elmina: Africans and Europeans on the Gold Coast, 1400–1900*. Washington, DC: Smithsonian Institution Press.

Diop, Cheikh Anta. 1974. *The African Origin of Civilization: Myth or Reality*. Chicago: Lawrence Hill Books.

Drake, St. Clair. 1963. "Representative Government and the Traditional Cultures and Institutions of West African Societies." *Africa: Dynamics of Change*: 9–33.

———. 1975. "The Black Diaspora in Pan-African Perspective." *Black Scholar*, September: 2–13.

———. 1982. "Diaspora Studies and Pan-Africanism." In *Global Dimensions of the African Diaspora*, edited by Joseph Harris, 451–514. Washington, DC: Howard University Press.

DuBois, W. E. B. 1939. *Black Folk, Then and Now: An Essay in the History and Sociology of the Negro Race*. New York: Henry Holt and Company.

———. 1940. *Dusk of Dawn: An Essay toward an Autobiography of a Race Concept*. New York: Harcourt, Brace, and World, Inc.

———. 1970. *The Negro*. London: Oxford University Press.

———. 1971. "The Conservation of Races." In *The Seventh Son*, edited by Julius Lester. New York: Random House.

———. 1999. "The Souls of White Folk." In *Darkwater: Voices from within the Veil*. New York: Dover Publications.

Dunbar, Ernest. 1968. *The Black Expatriates: A Study of American Negroes in Exile*. New York: E. P. Dutton and Co., Inc.

Dyer, Richard. 1997. *White: Essays on Race and Culture*. London: Routledge.

Ebron, Paulla A. 1999. "Tourists as Pilgrims: Commercial Fashioning of Transatlantic Politics." *American Ethnologist* 26 (4): 910–32.

———. 2002. *Performing Africa*. Princeton, NJ: Princeton University Press.

Edwards, Brent Hayes. 2001. "The Uses of Diaspora." *Social Text* 66:45–73.

Ekeh, Peter P. 1990. "Social Anthropology and Two Contrasting Uses of Tribalism in Africa." *Comparative Studies in Society and History* 32 (4): 660–700.

Elyachar, Julia. 2005. *Markets of Dispossession: NGOs, Economic Development, and the State in Cairo*. Durham, NC: Duke University Press.

Esedebe, Olisawuche P. 1982. *Pan-Africanism: The Idea and the Movement, 1776–1963*. Washington, DC: Howard University Press.

Eshun, Ekow. 2006. *Black Gold of the Sun: Searching for Home in England and Africa*. New York: Penguin.

Esseks, John D. 1971. "Political Independence and Economic Decolonization: The Case of Ghana under Nkrumah." *Western Political Quarterly* 24 (1): 59–64.

Fabian, Johannes. 1983. *Time and the Other: How Anthropology Makes Its Object.* New York: Columbia University Press.

Fanon, Franz. 1967. *Black Skin, White Masks.* New York: Grove Press.

———. 1968. *The Wretched of the Earth.* New York: Grove Press.

Fardon, Richard. 1991. *Between God, the Dead and the Wild: Chamba Interpretations of Ritual and Religion.* Edinburgh: Edinburgh University Press.

Ferguson, James. 2005. *Global Shadows: Africa in the Neoliberal World Order.* Durham, NC: Duke University Press.

Figuereido, Antonio de. 2005. "Lest We Forget: Is Corruption a New Racial Stereotype?" *New African* 442:54–55.

Food and Drug Administration. 2006. "Skin Bleaching Drug Products for over-the-Counter Human Use; Proposed Rule." *Federal Register* 71 (August 29): 51146.

Frankenberg, Ruth. 1993. *White Women, Race Matters: The Social Construction of Whiteness.* Minneapolis: University of Minnesota Press.

Frazier, E. Franklin. 1939. *Negro Family in the United States.* Chicago: University of Chicago Press.

Fredrickson, George M. 1982. *White Supremacy: A Comparative Study in American and South African History.* London: Oxford University Press.

Fyfe, Christopher. 1992. "Race, Empire and the Historians." *Race & Class* 33 (4): 15–30.

Gaines, Kevin. 2006. *American Africans in Ghana: Black Expatriates and the Civil Rights Era.* Chapel Hill: University of North Carolina Press.

Geschiere, Peter. 1997. *The Modernity of Witchcraft: Politics and the Occult in Postcolonial Africa.* Translated by Janet Roitman and Peter Geschiere. Charlottesville: University Press of Virginia.

Geurts, Kathryn L. 2002. *Culture and the Senses: Bodily Ways of Knowing in an African Community.* Berkeley: University of California Press.

Ghana Business News. 2010. "Ghana Earns $1.6B from tourism in 2009." July 21, accessed February 2012. http://www.ghanabusinessnews.com/2010/07/21/ghana-earns-1-6b-from-tourism-in-2009/.

Ghana Tourist Board. 2008. "Tourism Statistical Fact Sheet on Ghana." Accessed January 20, 2012. http://www.touringghana.com/documents/Facts_&Figures/Tourism_Statistical _FactSheet_070316.pdf.

Gilroy, Paul. 1991. *'There Ain't No Black in the Union Jack': The Cultural Politics of Race and Nation.* Chicago: University of Chicago Press.

———. 1993. *The Black Atlantic: Modernity and Double Consciousness.* Cambridge, MA: Harvard University Press.

Glenn, Evelyn Nakano. 2009. *Shades of Difference: Why Skin Color Matters.* Stanford, CA: Stanford University Press.

Gocking, Roger. 1999. *Facing Two Ways: Ghana's Coastal Communities under Colonial Rule.* Lanham, MD: University Press of America.

———. 2005. *The History of Ghana.* New York: Greenwood.

Goldberg, David T. 1993. *Racist Culture: Philosophy and the Politics of Meaning.* Oxford: Blackwell.

———. 2002. *The Racial State.* New York: Wiley-Blackwell.

Golden, Marita. 2004. *Don't Play in the Sun: One Woman's Journey through the Color Complex.* New York: Doubleday.

Gomez, Michael A. 1998. *Exchanging Our Country Marks: The Transformation of African*

*Identities in the Colonial and Antebellum South*. Chapel Hill: University of North Carolina Press.

Goody, Jack. 1995. *The Expansive Movement: The Rise of Social Anthropology in Britain and Africa, 1918–1970*. Cambridge: Cambridge University Press.

Gordon, Edmund T., and Mark Anderson. 1999. "The African Diaspora: Toward an Ethnography of Diasporic Identification." *Journal of American Folklore* 112 (445): 282–96.

Gordon, Lewis R. 1997. *Her Majesty's Other Children: Sketches of Racism from a Neocolonial Age*. New York: Rowman and Littlefield.

Gottlieb, Alma. 1996. *Under the Kapok Tree: Identity and Difference in Beng Thought*. Chicago: University of Chicago Press.

Gramsci, Antonio. 1971. *Selections from the Prison Notebooks*. Edited by Quentin Hoare and Geoffre Nowell-Smith. New York: International Publishers.

Green, Reginald H., and Ann W. Seidman. 1968. *Unity or Poverty?: The Economics of Pan-Africanism*. New York: Penguin.

Grovogui, Siba. 1997. *Sovereigns, Quasi-Sovereigns, and Africans: Race and Self-Determination in International Law*. Minneapolis: University of Minnesota Press.

———. 2001. "Come to Africa: A Hermeneutic of Race in International Theory." *Alternatives* 26 (4): 425–48.

Hale, Charles. 2006. *Mas que un Indio (More than an Indian): Racial Ambivalence and the Paradox of Neoliberal Multiculturalism in Guatemala*. Santa Fe: School of American Research Press.

Hall, Ronald. 2005. *An Empirical Analysis of the Impact of Skin Color on African-American Education, Income, and Occupation*. New York: Edwin Mellen Press.

Hall, Stuart. 1980. "Race, Articulation and Societies Structured in Dominance." In *Sociological Theories: Race and Colonialism*, 305–45. London: UNESCO.

———. 1994. "Cultural Identity and Diaspora." In *Colonial Discourse and Post-Colonial Theory: A Reader*, edited by Laura Chrisman and Patricia Williams, 392–403. New York: Columbia University Press.

———. 1995. "Negotiating Caribbean Identities." *New Left Review* 209:3–14.

Hamilton, Darrick, Arthur Goldsmith, and William Darity, Jr. 2009. "Shedding 'Light' on Marriage: The Influence of Skin Shade on Marriage for Black Females." *Journal of Economic Behavior and Organization* 72(1): 30–50.

Handley, Antoinette. 2008. *Business and the State in Africa: Economic Policy-Making in the Neo-Liberal Era*. Cambridge: Cambridge University Press.

Harris, Cheryl. 1993. "Whiteness as Property." *Harvard Law Review* 106 (8): 1710–69.

Harrison, Faye V. 1999. "Introduction: Expanding the Discourse on 'Race.'" *American Anthropologist* 100 (3): 609–31.

Hartman, Saidiya. 2002. "The Time of Slavery." *South Atlantic Quarterly* 101 (4): 757–77.

Hasty, Jennifer. 2002. "Rites of Passage, Routes of Redemption: Emancipation Tourism and the Wealth of Culture." *Africa Today* 49 (3): 47–76.

Heger, Kenneth W. 1999. "Race Relations in the United States and American Cultural and Informational Programs in Ghana, 1957–1966." *Prologue: Quarterly of the National Archives and Records Administration* 31 (Winter): 257–65.

Herskovitz, Melville. 1928. *The American Negro: A Study in Racial Crossing*. New York: A. A. Knopf.

———. 1941. *The Myth of the Negro Past*. Boston: Beacon Press.

Hesse, Barnor. 2007. "Racialized Modernity: An Analytics of White Mythologies." *Ethnic and Racial Studies* 30 (4): 643–63.

Hoetnik, Harry. 1967. *The Two Variants in Caribbean Race Relations: A Contribution to the Sociology of Segmented Societies*. London: Oxford University Press.

Holloway, Joseph. 1990. *Africanisms in American Culture*. Bloomington: Indiana University Press.

Holsey, Bayo. 2004. "Transatlantic Dreaming: Slavery, Tourism, and Diasporic Encounters." In *Homecomings: Unsettling Paths of Return*, edited by Anders Stefanson and Fran Markowitz, 166–82. Lexington, KY: Lexington Books.

———. 2008. *Routes of Remembrance: Refashioning the Slave Trade in Ghana*. Chicago: University of Chicago Press.

*Home Sweet Home*. 2000. "Ghana Goes to the Polls." December.

Howard, Rhoda E. 1978. *Colonialism and Underdevelopment in Ghana*. New York: Africana Publishing Company.

Hunter, Margaret. 2002. "'If You're Light You're Alright': Light Skin Color as Social Capital for Women of Color." *Gender and Society* 19 (2): 175–93.

———. 2007. "The Persistent Problem of Colorism: Skin Tone, Status, and Inequality." *Sociology Compass* 1 (1): 237–54.

Incite! Women of Color Against Violence. 2007. *The Revolution Will Not Be Funded: Beyond the Non-Profit Industrial Complex*. Cambridge, MA: South End Press.

Ingram, Penelope. 2001. "Racializing Babylon: Settler Whiteness and the 'New Racism.'" *New Literary History* 32 (1): 157–76.

James, C. L. R. 1977. *Nkrumah and the Ghana Revolution*. Westport, CT: L. Hill.

Jelks, Randal. 2001. "Far Away from Black Reality." *Detroit Free Press*, October 1.

Kanneh, Kadiatu. 1998. *African Identities: Race, Nation and Culture in Ethnography, Pan-Africanism and Black Literatures*. London: Routledge.

Kay, G., and S. Hymer. 1972. *The Political Economy of Colonialism in Ghana: A Collection of Documents and Statistics, 1900–1960*. Aldershot, England: Gregg Revivals.

Keita, S. O. Y., and Rick A. Kittles. 1997. "The Persistence of Racial Thinking and the Myth of Racial Divergence." *American Anthropologist* 99 (3): 534–44.

Kihss, Peter. 1958. "Harlem Hails Ghanaian Leader as Returning Hero: 10,000 Acclaim Leader of Ghana on Triumphal Return to Harlem." *New York Times*, July 28.

Killingray, David, and Richard Rathbone. 1986. *Africa and the Second World War*. London: Macmillan.

Korang, Kwaku Larbi. 2003. *Writing Ghana, Imagining Africa: Nation and African Modernity*. Rochester, NY: University of Rochester Press.

———. 2004. "Where Is Africa? When Is the West's Other?" *Diacritics* 34 (2): 38–61.

Kothari, Uma. 2006. "Critiquing 'Race' and Racism in Development Discourse and Practice." *Progress in Development Studies* 6 (1): 1–7.

Kovaleski, Serge F. 1999. "In Jamaica: Shades of an Identity Crisis." *Washington Post*, August 5.

Lan, David. 1985. *Guns and Rain: Guerrillas and Spirit Mediums in Zimbabwe*. Berkeley: University of California Press.

Lemelle, Sidney, and Robin G. Kelley, eds. 1994. *Imagining Home: Class, Culture, and Nationalism in the African Diaspora*. London: Verso Press.

Leonard, Pauline. 2010. *Expatriate Identities in Postcolonial Organizations: Working Whiteness*. Burlington, VT: Ashgate.

Lipsitz, George. 1998. *The Possessive Investment in Whiteness: How White People Profit from Identity Politics*. Philadelphia: Temple University Press.

Lofchie, Michael F. 1971. "Political Constraints on African Development." In *The State of the Nations: Constraints on Development in Independent Africa.* Berkeley: University of California Press.

Lovejoy, Paul. 2000. *Transformations in Slavery: A History of Slavery in Africa.* Cambridge: Cambridge University Press.

Lugard, Frederick. 1922. *The Dual Mandate in British Tropical Africa.* London: W. Blackwood and Sons.

Macdonald, George. 1898. *The Gold Coast, Past and Present: A Short Description of the Country and Its People.* New York: Negro Universities Press.

Mafeje, Archie. 1976. "The Problem of Anthropology in Historical Perspective: An Inquiry into the Growth of the Social Sciences." *Canadian Journal of African Studies* 10 (2): 307–33.

———. 2001. "Africanity: A Commentary by Way of Conclusion." *CODESRIA Bulletin* 3-4:14–16.

Mahama, A. A. 2001. "Vice Presidential Address at the Launching of PANAFEST/ Emancipation Day 2001." July 9. http://govt.ghana.gov/story.asp?ID=57 (site discontinued).

Malik, Kenan. 1996. *The Meaning of Race: Race, History and Culture in Western Society.* New York: New York University Press.

Mamdani, Mahmood. 1996. *Citizen and Subject: Contemporary Africa and the Legacy of Late Colonialism.* Princeton, NJ: Princeton University Press.

———. 1999. "Historicizing Power and Responses to Power: Indirect Rule and Its Reform." *Social Research* 66 (3): 859–86.

Marable, Manning. 1974. "Booker T. Washington and African Nationalism." *Phylon* 35 (4): 398–406.

Marshall, Judith. 1976. "The State of Ambivalence: Right and Left Options in Ghana." *Review of African Political Economy* 5 (January–April): 49–62.

Martin, William G., and Michael O. West, eds. 1999. *Out of One, Many Africas: Reconstructing the Study and Meaning of Africa.* Urbana: University of Illinois Press.

Masquelier, Adeline Marie. 2001. *Prayer Has Spoiled Everything: Possession, Power, and Identity in an Islamic Town of Niger.* Durham, NC: Duke University Press.

Matory, J. Lorand. 1999. "Afro-Atlantic Culture: On the Live Dialogue between Africa and the Americas." In *Africana: The Encyclopedia of the African and African American Experience,* edited by Kwame A. Appiah and Henry L. Gates, 36–44. New York: Basic Civitas Books.

———. 2005. *Black Atlantic Religion: Tradition, Transnationalism, and Matriarchy in the Afro-Brazilian Candomblé.* Princeton, NJ: Princeton University Press.

McElroy, Colleen J. 2001. *Over the Lip of the World.* Seattle: University of Washington Press.

Mercer, Kobena. 1994. *Welcome to the Jungle: New Positions in Black Cultural Studies.* New York: Routledge.

Meyer, Birgit. 1999. *Translating the Devil: Religion and Modernity among the Ewe in Ghana.* Edinburgh: Edinburgh University Press for the International African Institute.

Mignolo, Walter. 2000. *Local Histories/Global Designs.* Princeton, NJ: Princeton University Press.

Miller, Laura. 2006. *Beauty Up: Exploring Contemporary Japanese Body Aesthetics.* Berkeley: University of California Press.

Mills, Charles. 1998. *Blackness Visible: Essays on the Philosophy of Race.* Ithaca, NY: Cornell University Press.

———. 2008. "Racial Liberalism." *PMLA* 123 (5): 1380–97.

Mire, Amina. 2005. "Pigmentation and Empire: The Emerging Skin Whitening Industry." *CounterPunch,* July 28. http://www.counterpunch.org/mire07282005.html.

Mjagkij, Nina. 2001. *Organizing Black America: An Encyclopedia of African American Associations*. New York: Taylor and Francis.

Moore, Donald S. 2005. *Suffering for Territory: Race, Place, and Power in Zimbabwe*. Durham, NC: Duke University Press.

Mukhopadhyay, Carol C., and Yolanda T. Moses. 1997. "Reestablishing 'Race' in Anthropological Discourse." *American Anthropologist* 99 (3): 517–33.

*New York Times*. 1958. "Nkrumah Praises Ghana's Ties: Prime Minister Is Guest of City and Cocoa Exchange—Will Leave Tomorrow." July 29.

Nkrumah, K. 1957. *Ghana: The Autobiography of Kwame Nkrumah*. New York: International Publishers.

———. 1963. *Africa Must Unite*. London: Heinemann.

———. 1965. *Neo-colonialism: The Last Stage of Imperialism*. New York: International Publishers.

———. 1973. *Towards Colonial Freedom: Africa in the Struggle against World Imperialism*. London: Panaf.

Obetsebi-Lamptey, Jake. 2005. "Message from the Minister of Tourism and Modernization of the Capital City." PANAFEST souvenir brochure, 5–6.

Okpewho, Isidore. 1999. Introduction to *The African Diaspora: African Origins and New World Identities*, edited by Carole Boyce Davies, Isidore Okpewho, and Ali A. Mazrui. Bloomington: Indiana University Press.

Omi, Michael, and Howard Winant. 1994. *Racial Formation in the United States: From the 1960s to the 1990s*. New York: Routledge.

———. 2008. "Once More, with Feeling: Reflections on Racial Formation." *PMLA* 123 (5): 1565–72.

Ortiz, Fernando. 1975. *Los negros esclavos*. Havana: Editorial de Ciencias Sociales.

———. 1986. *Los negros curros*. Havana: Editorial de Ciencias Sociales.

Owusu, Maxwell. 1970. *Uses and Abuses of Political Power: A Case Study of Continuity and Change in the Politics of Ghana*. Chicago: University of Chicago Press.

Padmore, George. 1969. *How Britain Rules Africa*. New York: Negro Universities Press.

PANAFEST. 2005. "Pan African Historical Theatre Festival: The Re-Emergence of African Civilization" souvenir brochure. Accra: PANAFEST.

Parker, J. 2000. *Making the Town: Ga State and Society in Early Colonial Accra*. London: Heinemann.

Parker, John. 1998. "Mankraloi, Merchants and Mulattos: Carl Reindorf and the Politics of 'Race' in Early Colonial Accra." In *The Recovery of the African Past: African Pastors and African History in the Nineteenth Century*, edited by Paul Jenkins, 31–48. Basel, Switzerland: Basel Mission Archive.

Parkin, David J. 1991. *Sacred Void: Spatial Images of Work and Ritual among the Giriama of Kenya*. Cambridge: Cambridge University Press.

Patterson, Tiffany, and Robin D. G. Kelley. 2000. "Unfinished Migration: Reflection on the African Diaspora and the Making of the Modern World." *African Studies Review* 43 (1): 11–45.

Patton, A., Jr. 1989. "Dr. John Farrell Easmon: Medical Professionalism and Colonial Racism in the Gold Coast, 1856–1900." *International Journal of African Historical Studies* 22 (4): 601–36.

Peiss, Kathy. 1998. *Hope in a Jar: The Making of America's Beauty Culture*. New York: Metropolitan Books.

Perbi, Akosua Adoma. 2004. *A History of Indigenous Slavery in Ghana from the 15th to the 19th Centuries*. Accra: Sub-Saharan Publishers.

Pierre, Jemima. 2006. "Anthropology and the Race for/of Africa." In *The Study of Africa*. Vol. 1, *Disciplinary and Interdisciplinary Encounters*, edited by Paul Zeleza, 39–61. Dakar: Codesria.

———. 2008 "'I like Your Colour': Skin Bleaching and Geographics of Race in Urban Ghana." *Feminist Review* 90: 9–29.

Pierre, Jemima, and Jesse Weaver Shipley. 2003. "African/Diaspora History: W. E. B. Dubois and Pan-Africanism in Ghana." In *Ghana in Africa and the World: Essays in Honor of Adu Boahen*, edited by Toyin Falola, 731–53. Trenton, NJ: Africa World Press.

Piot, Charles. 1999. *Remotely Global: Village Modernity in West Africa*. Chicago: University of Chicago Press.

Ransby, Barbara. 1994. "Afrocentrism, Cultural Nationalism, and the Problem with Essentialist Definitions of Race, Gender, and Sexuality." *Race & Reason* 1 (1): 31–34.

Rathbone, Richard. 2000. *Nkrumah and the Chiefs: The Politics of Chieftaincy in Ghana, 1951–60*. Athens: Ohio State University Press.

Ray, Carina. 2007. "Policing Sexual Boundaries: The Politics of Race in Colonial Ghana." PhD diss., Cornell University. ProQuest (AAT 3246708).

Richards, Sandra. 2003. "Landscapes of Memory: Representing the African Diaspora's Return "Home." Paper presented at the Second Biannual Conference of the Association for the Study of Worldwide African Diasporas (ASWAD), Northwestern University, Evanston, IL, October 2–4.

———. 2005. "What Is to Be Remembered? Tourism to Ghana's Slave Castle-Dungeons." *Theatre Journal* 57 (4): 617–37.

Robinson, C. J. 1983. *Black Marxism: The Making of the Black Radical Tradition*. Chapel Hill: University of North Carolina Press.

Rodney, Walter. 2001. "African History in the Service of the Black Liberation." *Small Axe* 10:66–80.

Romano, Renee. 2000. "No Diplomatic Immunity: African Diplomats, the State Department, and Civil Rights, 1961–1964." *Journal of American History* 87 (2): 546–79.

Rondilla, Joanne, and Paul Spickard. 2007. *Is Lighter Better? Skin-Tone Discrimination among Asian Americans*. Lanham, MD: Rowman and Littlefield.

Sackey, Shiella. "GH¢4million For Nkrumah's Birthday." *Ghana Web*, May 19. http://www.ghanaweb.com/GhanaHomePage/NewsArchive/artikel.php?ID=182395.

Said, Edward. 1993. *Culture and Imperialism*. New York: Vintage.

Sanjek, Roger. 1994. "The Enduring Inequalities of Race." In *Race*, edited by Steven Gregory and Roger Sanjek, 1–17. New Brunswick, NJ: Rutgers University Press.

Sarbah, John Mensah. 1904. *Fanti Customary Laws: A Brief Introduction to the Principles of the Native Laws and Customs of the Fanti and Akan Districts of the Gold Coast*. London: W. Clowes and Sons Ltd.

Schueller, Malini J. 2007. "Area Studies and Multicultural Imperialism." *Social Text* 25 (90): 41–62.

Schuler, C. 1999. "Africans Look for Beauty in Western Mirror: Black Women Turn to Risky Bleaching Creams and Cosmetic Surgery." *Christian Science Monitor*, December 23.

Scott, David. 1991. "That Event, This Memory: Notes on the Anthropology of African Diasporas in the New World." *Diaspora* 1 (3): 261–84.

Seshadri-Crooks, Kalpana. 2000. *Desiring Whiteness: A Lacanian Analysis of Race*. London: Routledge.

Shanklin, Eugenia. 1998. "The Profession of the Color Blind: Sociocultural Anthropology and Racism in the 21st Century." *American Anthropologist* 100 (3): 669–79.

Sharp, Lesley A. 1996. *The Possessed and the Dispossessed: Spirits, Identity, and Power in a Madagascar Migrant Town*. Berkeley: University of California Press.

Shipley, Jesse Weaver. 2003. "National Audiences and Consuming Subjects: A Political Genealogy of Performance in Neoliberal Ghana." PhD diss., University of Chicago. ProQuest (AAT 3108129).

Shipley, Jesse Weaver, and Jemima Pierre. 2007. "The Intellectual and Pragmatic Legacy of DuBois's Pan-Africanism in Contemporary Ghana." In *Re-Cognizing W.E.B. DuBois in the Twenty-First Century: Essays on W.E.B. DuBois*, edited by Mary Keller and Chester J. Fontenot, 61–87. Macon, GA: Mercer University Press.

Shohat, Ella, and Robert Stam. 2003. *Multiculturalism, Postcoloniality, and Transnational Media*. New Brunswick, NJ: Rutgers University Press.

Singleton, Theresa. 1999. *"I, Too, Am America:" Archaeological Studies of African-American Life*. Charlottesville: University of Virginia Press.

Skinner, Elliott P. 1983. "Afro-Americans in Search of Africa: The Scholars' Dilemma." In *Transformation and Resiliency in Africa: As Seen by Afro-American Scholars*, edited by Pearl T. Robinson and Elliott P. Skinner. Washington, DC: Howard University Press.

Smith, Daniel J. 2008. *A Culture of Corruption: Everyday Deception and Popular Discontent in Nigeria*. Princeton, NJ: Princeton University Press.

Stocking, George W. 1968. *Race, Culture, and Evolution: Essays in the History of Anthropology*. Chicago: University of Chicago Press.

———. 1992. *The Ethnographer's Magic and Other Essays in the History of Anthropology*. Madison: University of Wisconsin Press.

———. 1994. "The Turn-of-the-Century Concept of Race." *Modernism/Modernity* 1 (1): 4–16.

Stoller, Paul, and Cheryl Olkes. 1987. *In Sorcery's Shadow: A Memoir of Apprenticeship among the Songhay of Niger*. Chicago: University of Chicago Press.

Táíwò, Olúfémi. 1999. "Reading the Colonizer's Mind: Lord Lugard and the Philosophical Foundations of British Colonialism." In *Racism and Philosophy*, edited by Susan E. Babbitt and Sue Campbell. Ithaca, NY: Cornell University Press.

———. 2010. *How Colonialism Preempted Modernity in Africa*. Bloomington: Indiana University Press.

Teye, Victor B. 1999. "Commentary: Tourism Plans and Planning Challenges in Ghana." *Tourism Geographies* 1 (3): 283–92.

Thomas, Deborah A. 2005. *Modern Blackness: Nationalism, Globalization, and the Politics of Culture in Jamaica*. Durham, NC: Duke University Press.

Thompson, Maxine, and Verna Keith. 2001. "The Blacker the Berry: Gender, Skin Tone, Self Esteem, and Self-Efficacy." *Gender and Society* 15 (3): 336–57.

Trouillot, Michel-Rolph. 1991. "Anthropology and the Savage Slot: The Poetics and Politics of Otherness." In *Recapturing Anthropology: Working in the Present*, edited by Richard Fox, 17–44. Santa Fe: School of American Research Press.

———. 1994. "Culture, Color, and Politics in Haiti." In *Race*, edited by Roger Sanjek and Steven Gregory, 146–74. New Brunswick, NJ: Rutgers University Press.

———. 2003. *Global Transformations: Anthropology and the Modern World*. New York: Palgrave Macmillan.

UNESCO. 2006. "The 2006 Slave Route Brochure" brochure. Paris: UNESCO.

Van Rouveroy van Nieuwaal, E. Adriaan B., and Rijk van Dijk, eds. 1999. *African Chieftaincy in a New Socio-Political Landscape*. London: Lit Verlag.

Vinson, Ben, III. 2006. "Introduction: African (Black) Diaspora History. Latin American History." *Americas* 63 (1): 1–18.

Visweswaran, Kamala. 1998. "Race and the Culture of Anthropology." *American Anthropologist* 100 (1): 70–83.

Von Eschen, Penny. 1997. *Race against Empire: Black Americans and Anticolonialism, 1937–1957.* Ithaca, NY: Cornell University Press.

Wade, Peter. 1997. *Race and Ethnicity in Latin America.* New York: Pluto Press.

Wallerstein, Immanuel. 1971. *Africa, the Politics of Independence: An Interpretation of Modern African History.* New York: Vintage Books.

Walters, Ronald. 1993. *Pan Africanism in the African Diaspora: An Analysis of Modern Afrocentric Political Movements.* Detroit: Wayne State University Press.

White, Sarah. 2002. "Thinking Race, Thinking Development." *Third World Quarterly* 23:407–19.

Williams, Brackette. 1989. "A Class Act: Anthropology and the Race to Nation across Ethnic Terrain." *Annual Review of Anthropology* 18:401–44.

———. 1991. *Stains on My Name, War in My Veins: Guyana and the Politics of Cultural Struggle.* Durham, NC: Duke University Press.

Winant, Howard. 2001. "White Racial Projects." In *The Making and Unmaking of Whiteness*, edited by Birgit Rasmussen, 97–112. Durham, NC: Duke University Press.

Wolton, Suke. 2000. *Lord Hailey, the Colonial Office and the Politics of Race and Empire in the Second World War: The Loss of White Prestige.* Oxford: Macmillan/St. Antony's College.

Yelvington, Kevin A. 2001. "The Anthropology of Afro-Latin America and the Caribbean: Diasporic Dimensions." *Annual Review of Anthropology* 30:227–60.

———. 2006. "The Invention of Africa in Latin America and the Caribbean: Political Discourse and Anthropological Praxis." In *Afro-Atlantic Dialogues: Anthropology in the Diaspora*, edited by Kevin A. Yelvington, 35–82. Santa Fe: School of American Research Press.

Young, Robert. 1995. *Colonial Desire: Hybridity in Theory, Culture, and Race.* London: Routledge.

Zimmerman, Jonathan. 2009. "Ghana's Hype over Obama, Beyond Race." *Christian Science Monitor*, July 9.

Page numbers in italics refer to illustrations.